# The Trial of Julian Assange

# The Trial of Julian Assange

*A Story of Persecution*

Nils Melzer
(with Oliver Kobold)

**VERSO**
London • New York

First published by Verso Books 2022
© Nils Melzer 2022

1 3 5 7 9 10 8 6 4 2

**Verso**
UK: 6 Meard Street, London W1F 0EG
US: 20 Jay Street, Suite 1010, Brooklyn, NY 11201
versobooks.com

Verso is the imprint of New Left Books

ISBN-13: 978-1-83976-622-0
ISBN-13: 978-1-83976-625-1 (US EBK)
ISBN-13: 978-1-83976-624-4 (UK EBK)

**British Library Cataloguing in Publication Data**
A catalogue record for this book is available from the British Library

**Library of Congress Cataloging-in-Publication Data**

Names: Melzer, Nils, author.
Title: The trial of Julian Assange : a story of persecution / Nils Melzer,
  (with Oliver Kobold).
Description: First Edition Hardback. | Brooklyn, NY ; London : Verso Books,
  2022. | Includes bibliographical references and index.
Identifiers: LCCN 2021049427 (print) | LCCN 2021049428 (ebook) | ISBN
  9781839766220 (Hardback) | ISBN 9781839766251 (eBook)
Subjects: LCSH: Political persecution. | Assange, Julian –Trials,
  litigation, etc. | Political corruption. | Asylum, Right of. | Due
  process of law. | Press and politics.
Classification: LCC JC571 .M3985 2022  (print) | LCC JC571  (ebook) | DDC
  323/.044 – dc23/eng/20211109
LC record available at https://lccn.loc.gov/2021049427
LC ebook record available at https://lccn.loc.gov/2021049428

Typeset in Sabon by MJ & N Gavan, Truro, Cornwall
Printed and bound by CPI Group (UK) Ltd, Croydon CRO 4YY

*To all who fearlessly fight for the truth.*

*Those who sleep in a democracy will wake up in a dictatorship.*
—Otto Gritschneder

# Contents

# Introduction

For a special rapporteur of the United Nations, writing a book is not really part of the job description. Especially not a book on an individual case. An explanation is therefore in order. This book is intended to be an urgent appeal. An admonition to the international community of states that the system they have established for the protection of human rights is failing in a very fundamental way. A wake-up call to the general public, because a systemic failure of such magnitude ought to raise alarm bells with any ordinary citizen of a democratic state. A call, therefore, that should also be understood as a personal challenge to each and every one of us: to open our eyes, to face the truth, and to take personal and political responsibility.

As the special rapporteur on torture, I am mandated by the United Nations Human Rights Council to monitor compliance with the prohibition of torture and ill-treatment worldwide, to examine allegations of violations, and to transmit queries and recommendations to the states concerned with a view to clarifying individual cases. I was entrusted with this important mandate because I have been dealing with violations of human rights and humanitarian law for more than twenty years, whether as a senior security policy advisor to my government, as a professor of international law and an expert author, or as a Red Cross delegate and legal advisor in contexts of war and crisis. I have visited thousands of prisoners, refugees and their loved ones on four continents, many of them victims of torture and violence. I have negotiated not only in palaces, ministries and command centres, but also with soldiers and rebels in the no-man's-land between front lines.

Hence, when I investigate allegations of torture and ill-treatment, I know what I am talking about. I am not easily manipulated and don't tend to exaggerate, nor do I seek the limelight. My world is one of diplomatic dialogue and mutual respect – but always also of truth and integrity, because diplomacy must never be allowed to become an end in itself but must always remain a means to a higher end. In my case, this higher end is to achieve compliance with the universal prohibition of torture and ill-treatment, as well as the investigation, punishment and redress of violations. This purpose I must always pursue and may never sacrifice. If it can no longer be achieved through diplomatic channels, then I must choose other means. One of these means, dear reader, is the present book. Thus, to rephrase a martial maxim for my peaceful purposes, this book could be described as the continuation of diplomacy by other means.

I write this book because, when investigating the case of Julian Assange, I came across compelling evidence of political persecution and gross judicial arbitrariness, as well as of deliberate torture and ill-treatment. But the responsible states refused to cooperate with me in clearing up these allegations, and to initiate the investigative measures required by international law. I visited Julian Assange in prison with a team of medical doctors and spoke to the authorities in charge, as well as to lawyers, witnesses and experts. I have repeatedly expressed my concerns to all four states involved – the United Kingdom, Sweden, Ecuador and the United States – through the official channels available to me. I have requested clarifications and recommended specific measures. None of the four governments were willing to engage in a constructive dialogue. Instead, I was confronted with diplomatic platitudes or sweeping rhetorical attacks. When I insisted, the dialogue was terminated by the governments. At the same time, the persecution and mistreatment of Julian Assange intensified, violations of his due process rights became increasingly blatant and my public appeals calling on the authorities to respect human rights were ignored. Even from within the UN system, I received hardly any support, with the notable exception of a few courageous and determined individuals. I expressed my concern about the obstructive stance of the involved states both at the Human Rights Council in Geneva and at the General Assembly in New York – without any substantial reaction. I repeatedly asked the High Commissioner for Human Rights for a personal meeting about the matter, but was fobbed off. I called on other states to exert their influence, but virtually always faced an awkward wall of silence. The institutions and processes I had always believed in were failing before my eyes.

You may wonder why I should speak out so forcefully in this particular case. After all, Julian Assange is hardly the only victim of torture who has not received justice, nor is his abuse the most severe form of torture I have encountered in my work. All of this is correct. The reason for my strong engagement in this case is that its importance extends far beyond Julian Assange as an individual and, indeed, far beyond the states directly involved. It reveals a generalized systemic failure gravely undermining the integrity of our democratic institutions, our fundamental rights, and the rule of law more generally. It is a systemic failure that I routinely encounter in my daily work, but that usually plays out behind the scenes, and therefore remains largely concealed from the broader public.

The Assange case is the story of a man who is being persecuted and abused for exposing the dirty secrets of the powerful, including war crimes, torture and corruption. It is a story of deliberate judicial arbitrariness in Western democracies that are otherwise keen to present themselves as exemplary in the area of human rights. It is a story of wilful collusion by intelligence services behind the backs of national parliaments and the general public. It is a story of manipulated and manipulative reporting in the mainstream media for the purpose of deliberately isolating, demonizing, and destroying a particular individual. It is the story of a man who has been scapegoated by all of us for our own societal failure to address government corruption and state-sanctioned crimes. It is thus also a story about each and every one of us, our lethargy, our self-deception and our co-responsibility for the political, economic and human tragedies of our time.

For two years I have intensively investigated the case of Julian Assange. For two years, I have unsuccessfully tried to get the responsible states to cooperate, and for two years I have publicly communicated my concerns – in official reports, press releases and interviews, before international bodies and parliamentary groups, but also during academic panel discussions and at numerous other events. Now the time has come to publish this book, which summarizes my investigation and conclusions, as well as the available evidence, in an easily accessible form. I decided to take this step because I had run out of viable options within the system, and because my silence or inaction would have been tantamount to complicity in the cover-up of serious crimes, both those exposed by Assange and those committed against him and, thus, against all of us. In exercising my mandate, I do not feel responsible primarily to the serving governments, but to the UN member states themselves and to their people. They have committed to compliance with universal human rights and, therefore, they are also entitled to know what their governments are doing with the power delegated to them. This is especially true when it comes to the practice of torture and abuse, when our fundamental freedoms of expression, of the press, and of information are being deliberately suppressed, and when those in power claim impunity for corruption and the most serious crimes. So, I suppose, in a way, by writing this book, I have become a whistleblower myself.

I have always carried out my investigations objectively and impartially, duly considering all of the available evidence and reaching my conclusions in good faith and to the best of my judgment and conviction. In the case of Julian Assange, this process was rendered particularly difficult by the complete refusal of the involved governments to cooperate with my investigation and to provide the requested evidence and clarifications. Nevertheless, over time, I managed to accumulate around 10,000 pages of reliable procedural files, correspondence and other evidence from a multitude of sources. While for reasons of privacy and source protection names will be used only where necessary for the credibility of my conclusions, I am deeply indebted to countless individuals for valuable information and support of all kinds. All those concerned know who they are and that this book could not have been written without their precious help.

My investigation of the Assange case can be compared to assembling a huge puzzle, piece by piece. Much like a detective, I had to solve an equation with many unknowns in the hope of disentangling the institutional responsibilities for a serious crime. While numerous important puzzle pieces may still be missing, the overall picture is consistent and convincing. That said, as long as the involved states continue to hide behind a convenient veil of secrecy, my conclusions admittedly cannot be regarded as absolute, complete and final. Rather, they should be seen as the result of two years of careful investigation carried out under adverse circumstances. Should the governments in question decide to cease their obstruction and provide contradicting evidence or clarifications, any such input will be gratefully received and taken into account in my future pronouncements in this case. An important purpose of this book – establishing the truth – would then have been achieved.

My most important message is that, ultimately, the trial of Assange is not really about Assange. It is about the integrity of our constitutional institutions and, thus, the essence of the "republic" in the original sense of the word. At stake is nothing less than the future of democracy. I do not intend to leave to our children a world where governments can disregard the rule of law with impunity, and where telling the truth has become a crime. I have always understood my UN mandate as a duty to use my privileged position in order to protect human rights, to expose violations and systemic shortcomings, and to fight for the integrity of our institutions – 'speaking truth to power', as it has been so aptly termed. This I have done since I was first appointed by the Human Rights Council. I have addressed issues as diverse as police brutality, the inhumanity of prevailing migration policies, psychological methods of torture, and the cruelty of domestic violence. I have also highlighted the interrelations between corruption and torture, as well as the collective patterns of self-deception without which torture and ill-treatment could not be practiced with such impunity worldwide.

My work did not make me popular with everyone, because I challenged the impunity of the powerful and the hypocrisy of the self-righteous. In the specific case of Julian Assange, I have been repeatedly accused of betraying my neutrality and impartiality in order to side with Assange. This is not the case. If anything, I was initially biased against Assange and even refused to get involved in his case. Throughout my career, I have attached great importance to the objectivity, neutrality and impartiality of my work. But once my investigation of a case leads to the conclusion that serious human rights violations have indeed been committed, I cannot reasonably be expected to remain neutral between perpetrators and victims. My objectivity as an independent legal expert then requires me to side with the victim of torture, with human rights and with justice. I therefore write this book not as a lawyer for Julian Assange, but as an advocate for humanity, truth, and the rule of law.

# PART I

---

## A GLIMPSE BEHIND THE CURTAIN

# 1

# How to Miss an Elephant

## Out of Sight, Out of Mind!

It was just before Christmas 2018, and I was sitting at my desk working on my annual report for the Human Rights Council in Geneva. This is the UN body that had appointed me and to which I reported, as an independent expert, on the worldwide compliance with the prohibition of torture and ill-treatment. Twice a year I was expected to collectively address the UN member states: in the spring at the Human Rights Council in Geneva, and in the autumn at the General Assembly in New York. These were my opportunities to freely choose an issue relevant to the prohibition of torture and ill-treatment and to put it on the agenda of the world organization. The mandates of UN special rapporteurs are unpaid honorary positions. Like most colleagues, I earn my living as an academic: I am a professor of international law at the University of Glasgow and the Geneva Academy of International Humanitarian Law and Human Rights. The most powerful asset of UN special rapporteurs is their independence. Once elected, mandate holders are to be guided solely by their service to the cause of human rights and may not be influenced by anyone in the performance of their duties. In the exercise of their functions, they enjoy diplomatic immunity and operate largely outside the organization's hierarchies, structures and decision-making processes, which are strongly dominated by political interests.

In an ideal world, with adequate budgets and sufficient staff, dedicated special rapporteurs could achieve a great deal. In the real world, however, states lack not only the financial means but also, and above all, the political will to effectively and comprehensively implement human rights, as this would require them to overcome outdated power structures, privileges and exploitation, which often are deeply intertwined with national politics. A proven means for states to limit the influence of special rapporteurs is the incessant creation of additional mandates and commissions on new human rights topics without increasing the overall budget available for the work of independent experts. In any case, the structural lack of financial and human resources for the special rapporteurs is hardly accidental.

In December 2018, I was busy finalizing my report, this time on the interrelation between corruption and torture (A/HRC/40/59), when suddenly a small window popped up on my screen, indicating the arrival of a new email. 'Julian Assange is seeking your protection', the subject line read. Julian Assange? Was this not the founder of WikiLeaks, the shady hacker with the white hair and the leather jacket who was hiding out in an embassy somewhere because of rape allegations? Out of nowhere, I was overtaken by a host of disparaging thoughts and almost reflexive feelings of rejection. Assange? No, I certainly would not be manipulated by this guy. After all, I had more important things to do: I had to take care of 'real' torture victims! I closed the pop-up window with a single click – out of sight, out of mind! Then I turned back to my report on overcoming prejudice and self-deception in connection with official corruption. Not until a few months later would I realize the striking irony of this situation.

## What's a UN Special Rapporteur?

Anyone can transmit allegations on violations of the prohibition of torture and ill-treatment to the special rapporteur on torture, or, as my full title reads, the 'United Nations Special Rapporteur on torture and other cruel, inhuman or degrading treatment or punishment'. Requests for intervention can be submitted at any time, by standard letter or email, even before any violation has occurred and regardless of whether police reports, court proceedings or other formalities have been initiated.

All special rapporteurs are appointed directly by the forty-seven member states of the UN Human Rights Council in a lengthy selection process and carry out their functions with the strictest independence. We have no hierarchical superiors and may not seek or accept any instruction as to the exercise of our mandates, whether from the United Nations or from individual governments or other actors. My office is located in the Office of the High Commissioner for Human Rights in Geneva, which is the organizational branch of the UN that deals with the protection of human rights. Two staff members are assigned to my mandate there, so-called Human Rights Officers. Every week, we receive about fifty requests for intervention and other enquiries. These can be initiated by torture victims themselves, but also by lawyers, NGO representatives, relatives, witnesses or even by other authorities, states or UN bodies. It is then up to my team to review the requests and, where necessary, obtain additional information in order to assess their credibility. Once consolidated, the case file is passed on to me for consideration and decision on the action to be taken.

Consistent with my mandate, my interventions are generally concerned with the prevention, investigation, prosecution, and redress of torture, corporal punishment and other cruel or degrading treatment, inhumane conditions of detention, and extraditions or deportations to states where people are at risk of being exposed to such abuse. The relevant violations may have been committed by state officials or at their instigation, or merely with their consent or acquiescence. In case of violations,

I can intervene directly with the foreign ministers of all UN member states through the diplomatic missions in Geneva. This means that I transmit allegations I have received of torture and ill-treatment to the state concerned, that I request the government to clarify and comment on these allegations, and that I make recommendations on the measures to be taken. This correspondence and the government's response initially remain confidential but, after sixty days, both are published on the High Commissioner's website. In urgent cases, there is also the possibility of alerting the public through a press release. As special rapporteur, I do not exercise any judicial function, and my conclusions and recommendations are not binding on states.

Of the requests for intervention submitted to my office, we can address one in ten at best. A team of three simply cannot manage more, given that we also have to prepare official country visits, draft official reports and cooperate with other mechanisms for the protection of human rights, first and foremost with the other UN special rapporteurs, Working Groups and relevant committees. Every day we are therefore forced to set priorities and take difficult decisions without the luxury of lengthy reflection. When in doubt, we always prioritize urgent cases where it may still be possible to prevent imminent human rights violations. Depending on the workload, the requests received by my office result in between 100 and 200 official interventions per year. Of these, about a third do not even receive a response. While the remaining two-thirds of our interventions generally do receive responses, these are almost always inadequate in terms of the human rights protection sought. Thus, states often provide lengthy letters replete with diplomatic smooth-talk and assurances but, ultimately, fail to provide the requested information or to initiate the investigations and other measures required under international law. The bottom line is that in the vast majority of cases, documented abuse is neither acknowledged nor punished, corrected or compensated. Unfortunately, this does not apply only to states notorious for their human rights violations. When it comes to protecting their reputation or their economic and security policy interests, even mature democracies priding themselves on longstanding traditions in the rule of law suddenly start compromising on human rights.

As I demonstrated through a comprehensive statistical analysis in my annual report of 2021 (A/HRC/46/26), barely 10 per cent of my interventions receive the 'full cooperation' required by the Human Rights Council and are adequately resolved. It is a deplorable success rate, even if one disregards the countless additional requests that cannot even be acted upon due to the lack of resources. This trend has remained largely unchanged since the creation of my mandate in 1985 and seriously calls into question the credibility of the routinely celebrated commitment of all UN member states to the universal prohibition of torture. On individual allegations of torture, states hardly ever agree to engage in a serious dialogue that goes beyond diplomatic niceties, as this would require genuine changes of behaviour and uncomfortable decisions with which they are generally not prepared to follow through.

Due to our heavy caseload, I refer as many applicants as possible to other institutions and authorities that have greater resources and are better placed to follow individual cases in the long term. For example, it is certainly not the purpose of my mandate to replace the investigative authorities of functioning democracies, so long as the police, prosecutors and courts can actually be relied upon to accomplish their tasks in line with the rule of law. This question must always be weighed very carefully, because even in mature democracies things can go wrong – for example, when suspects are pressured to confess through 'coercive detention'; when police brutality is not prosecuted and punished with sufficient determination; or when persons face extradition or deportation to a state where they would be exposed to a real risk of torture.

An entirely different assessment must be made for requests concerning states in which police and intelligence services are known to routinely kidnap and disappear people in broad daylight. In such cases, family members of the missing often cannot reasonably be expected to trust the local authorities. So I always have to conduct a careful evaluation and be on my guard. Finally,

I must never allow my mandate to be misused for political or other extraneous purposes: beyond the loss of my own credibility, the mandate itself could be irreparably damaged.

## Caught in My Own Prejudice

And now this request for help from Julian Assange's lawyers? At some point during the next few hours, I brought myself to skim the full text of the message. Assange's living conditions in the Ecuadorian embassy in London, where he had been staying since June 2012, were claimed to be incompatible with the prohibition of inhumane treatment and, therefore, to come within the scope of my mandate. I read this but was not convinced, or simply did not take it seriously. The possibility that Assange might truly be ill-treated did not even occur to me. Sure, I could imagine that he was no longer happy staying at the embassy and that he might be suffering a few health issues. Six years can be an eternity for someone confined to the same building. At the same time, I was still affected by all those headlines in the mainstream media which I had almost unconsciously absorbed over recent years: Assange, the cowardly rapist refusing to turn himself in to the Swedish authorities. Assange, the hacker and spy evading justice in the Ecuadorian embassy. Assange, the ruthless narcissist, traitor and bastard. And so forth.

Only later did I realize how much my perception had been distorted by prejudice. Years of exposure to scandalous headlines and biased reporting, though hardly perceived by my conscious mind, had formed an opinion deeply anchored in my emotions – an opinion which I was convinced was based on reliable facts. Thus, even after having read the email, I saw no reason to seriously consider the case of Julian Assange. 'Manufacturing consent' is the term introduced by Edward Herman and Noam Chomsky in the late 1980s to describe the communication model of the American mass media, one that has long since been globalized. They showed how self-censorship, anticipatory obedience and economic constraints lead many media institutions to smoothen their reporting in line with the generally accepted consensus. This is precisely what happened in the Assange case. The official narrative had the desired effect on public opinion – myself included.

The irony was striking. There I was, drafting my report on the links between corruption and torture, and failing to even notice that the intervention request submitted by Assange's lawyers presented me with a prime example of my topic. In reality, the case of Julian Assange is primarily about political corruption, with judicial institutions and processes having been – and still being – abused for political purposes: for suppressing press freedom and freedom of information; for impunity over torture and war crimes; for the political persecution of dissidents, and for the secrecy of machinations incompatible with democracy and the rule of law.

I was not the only UN expert contacted by Assange's lawyers in late 2018. They also wrote to the special rapporteur on the situation of human rights defenders and the UN Working Group on Arbitrary Detention (WGAD). On 21 December 2018, these colleagues issued a joint press release entitled 'UN experts urge UK to honour rights obligations and let Mr. Julian Assange leave Ecuador embassy in London freely.' I had been invited to join but declined. Instead, I shelved the letter from Assange's lawyers without much thought and barely even noticed the press statement. To me, like to most people around the world, Assange was just a rapist, hacker, spy, and narcissist. Like so many, I was convinced that I knew the truth about him, even though I couldn't quite remember where that knowledge had come from. It would be another three months before my opinion fundamentally changed.

# 2

# WikiLeaks' Role
# in Society

## 'Collateral Murder': When War Becomes Real

It was only in 2010 that I took proper notice of WikiLeaks: a disclosure platform that obtains classified information from whistleblowers and other sources and guarantees them anonymity, that is, protection from exposure and prosecution. WikiLeaks makes a point of clarifying that, due to an encrypted data transmission technology preventing their tracing, even the organization itself is unable to identify its sources – fully dedicated to the cypher-punk slogan, 'privacy for the weak, transparency for the powerful.' Thus, starting in 2006, a publicly accessible archive of previously secret documents was created, and its growing contents soon came to be feared by powerful governments, corporations and organizations. Early revelations exposed, for example, the corruption of the Kenyan government, toxic waste dumping by the Trafigura corporation in Ivory Coast, the methods of Scientology, the US Army's guidelines for the treatment of Guantánamo detainees, and the dubious business practices of the Swiss bank Julius Baer. First hits, but nothing compared to the overwhelming power of what was to come.

On 5 April 2010, at Washington's National Press Club, Julian Assange presented 'Collateral Murder' to the world. The eighteen-minute video opened with a quote from George Orwell: 'Political language is designed to make lies sound truthful and murder respectable, and to give an appearance of solidity to pure wind.' After that, nothing but disturbing images in black and white. 'Collateral Murder' places the viewer inside a US combat helicopter circling at low altitude over a residential area of Baghdad. It is 12 July 2007, just another day in a deplorable war of occupation, the news coverage of which has been dominated almost exclusively by the Western military coalition. Now, suddenly, viewers are immersed onboard the helicopter and see everything from the real-time perspective of the gunner. Radio messages go back and forth. Somewhere on the ground, out of sight, American troops are on the move, and the area is being searched from the air for insurgents and other potential threats.

Suddenly, the helicopter crew reports about twenty men standing about on the road in several small groups. Then they appear on the screen. All of them wear civilian clothing, and most are visibly unarmed. Two of the men have something slung across their shoulders which – judging by shape and size – clearly cannot be rifles. It later turns out that they are journalists carrying photo cameras. Another two men appear to be carrying assault rifles or similar long-barrel firearms. All of the men move around unsuspectingly, talk to each other, some cross the open street – it is obvious that they are not about to take cover or prepare an ambush. Other pedestrians also seem to be going about their everyday business. No one seems to notice the two helicopters. The crew reports over the radio: 'Have five to six individuals with AK-47s [Kalashnikov-type assault rifles]. Request permission to engage.' A few seconds later, the permission to open fire arrives, but at the last moment – due to the flight path – a building intrudes between the cannon and the group of people. While the helicopter circles in the distance and moves back into position, a journalist's raised telephoto lens is mistaken for a rocket-propelled grenade (RPG) ready to fire. Shortly thereafter, the line of sight is clear and the gunner opens fire. Ten men are literally mowed down. Some try to escape, but the gunner intercepts them with the next volley. After less than thirty seconds all of them are dead or seriously wounded on the ground. The helicopter continues to circle the attack site, and the troops can be heard commenting: 'Hahaha, I hit them.' – 'Oh yeah, look at those dead bastards.' – 'Nice.' – 'Good shot.' – 'Thank you.'

A few moments later, a seriously wounded man comes into view. He is trying to crawl to safety, but he can hardly move. 'There's one guy moving down there but he's wounded,' the crew reports. 'Roger, we're gonna move down there,' the ground troops reply. 'Roger, we'll cease fire,' the crew assures in response. Apparently, there was initially every intention of rescuing the injured man, as required by the law of war. Shortly thereafter, the crew reports back: 'He's getting up.' – 'Maybe he has a weapon down in his hand?' – 'No, I haven't seen one yet.' The wounded man almost pushes himself up onto his knees, but immediately collapses again. 'Come on, buddy,' the gunner comments, aiming the crosshairs at his helpless target. 'All you gotta do is pick up a weapon.' But the wounded man won't do him the favour. It will emerge that he is a forty-year-old Reuters journalist, Saeed Chmagh. Less than a minute later, a civilian minibus appears on the scene, the driver gets out, and, together with two other men, tries to evacuate the wounded man. All three rescuers wear civilian clothing and are clearly unarmed. Agitated, the helicopter crew reports: 'We have a van approaching ... possibly picking up bodies and weapons. Can I shoot?' A few seconds later comes a clarification request that will be decisive for the legal assessment: 'Picking up the wounded?' – 'Yeah, we're trying to get permission to engage.' – 'Come on, let us shoot!' The wounded man is being carried to the minibus. Then, authorization to open fire is given, and the minibus is literally shot to pieces with the helicopter's 30-mm gun. The driver and the two other rescuers are killed instantly. His five-year-old daughter and ten-year-old son are seriously injured in the back seat of the minibus. They reportedly had been on their way to school with their father. Chmagh himself dies from his injuries shortly afterwards – he, too, a father of four. The soldiers congratulate each other once again on a job well done, as if it were a team sport. When the ground troops arrive on the scene and report that a child has been wounded, the crew only comments, 'Ah, damn. Oh well.' And then, after a pause that must have been weighed down by heavy doubt: 'Well, it's their fault for bringing their kids into a battle.' – 'That's right.' According to US military officials, an AK-47 assault rifle, an RPG rocket launcher with two grenades, and the cameras of the two killed Reuters journalists are later found at the scene.

## 'Collateral Murder' – A War Crime?

Whether the conduct shown in the 'Collateral Murder' video amounts to a war crime, and who bears personal responsibility for it, should be for a court of law to decide. However, given that no such judicial assessment has ever taken place, the question rightly arises as to how this omission by the US authorities should be classified. Was it that lawful acts of war had been taken out of context and unfairly dramatized by WikiLeaks? Or were the US authorities indeed responsible for covering up a murder? When, in the following, I provide my personal views on this question, I am not concerned with determining the criminal culpability or innocence of individual soldiers. Rather, I would like to raise the question of the government's good faith right from the outset and sharpen the reader's eye for it. For the question of the good faith of public authorities runs like a red thread through the entire Assange case, and, even in complex circumstances, always provides external observers with reliable, objective guidance.

When I comment on the 'Collateral Murder' video from the perspective of the law of war, I am not infallible, of course, but I do so nonetheless with a certain amount of expertise and experience. As a former legal advisor and delegate to the International Committee of the Red Cross (ICRC) and as a professor of international law, I have spent more than twenty years intensively studying the practice of the law of war, particularly the rules governing the use of force during military engagements. I have analysed hundreds of operations, both on paper and on the ground in various contexts of war. I have not only written books and academic articles on the subject, I have also seen the destruction and suffering of war with my own eyes and have spoken with the responsible operational forces and politicians as well as with witnesses, survivors, and relatives of victims. And I have led a seven-year international expert process for the ICRC, clarifying the conditions under which civilians lose their protection under the law of war and become legitimate military targets – the key question arising in a legal analysis of 'Collateral Murder'.

The basic rules of the law of war relevant to this case sound simple: Soldiers and other combatants may be attacked, civilians may not. Once combatants have fallen 'out of combat' due to wounds or for other reasons, they may no longer be attacked, but must be collected and cared for regardless of their legal status or affiliation. Civilians may lose their protection only if and for such time as they directly participate in hostilities. Also protected are medical and rescue personnel who are not themselves actively participating in hostilities, whether they are civilians or members of enemy forces. They may even carry pistols, assault rifles and other light weapons for purposes of self-defence and the protection of the wounded. Rescue personnel may also collect and transport the personal weapons of wounded combatants evacuated by them, provided such weapons are no longer used in combat. In all these cases, any person must be presumed to be protected in case of doubt and, therefore, may be attacked only once it is clear that the required legal criteria are fulfilled: either combatant status or direct participation in hostilities – in military parlance, this is called 'positive identification' (PID). Now that we have established the basics of the law of war, let us take another look at 'Collateral Murder'.

The operational context is that two Apache attack helicopters are searching from the air for insurgents that might attack their ground forces. Contrary to what the image resolution might suggest, the helicopters are not circling a mere 300 feet above the scene, but at a distance of approximately one mile, and the screen image is captured through a highly sensitive and automatically controlled telephoto lens. This means that the soldiers cannot just take a quick look through the window to pick up additional details, but must rely on the screen image and, moreover, interpret it in real time. Unlike us, they do not have the luxury of repeatedly reviewing the same scenes, but have to make split-second decisions as to whether they have identified a threat to ground troops that needs to be neutralized. The permissibility of an attack must therefore always be judged by what can and must reasonably be expected of a soldier acting correctly under the prevailing circumstances.

Now, the operation is not taking place above an open battlefield, but above a residential district of Baghdad: a densely populated area where most of the population necessarily consists of protected civilians. As can be seen from the length and contrast of the shadows on the ground, it is broad daylight and visibility is clear. There are no armed confrontations in progress, and no curfew appears to have been imposed. In an environment like this and at this time of day, the soldiers must expect to see civilians out on the street everywhere. Since the US-British invasion, public order in Iraq has largely broken down. Because of the constant threat of looting, the American occupation forces in 2003 explicitly authorized Iraqi civilians to possess assault rifles for crime prevention purposes. By 2007, Kalashnikovs were so widespread in Iraqi private households that even the public carrying of a few isolated weapons, without more, could not be interpreted as an expression of 'hostile intent'. While this admittedly does not apply to RPG rocket launchers, in the present case, the 'permission to engage' clearly had been given already on the basis of the – rather casual – suspicion of 'five to six persons with AK-47s'. Only the confusion of a camera with a rocket launcher, which occurred after the authorization to open fire, could potentially be interpreted as an honest – albeit mistaken – identification of a 'hostile intent'. But even this alleged rocket launcher is nowhere in sight at the moment of the attack, and neither is the assault rifle. In the given circumstances there is obviously no risk of an imminent attack on the helicopter or the ground troops, and the status of the targeted men is doubtful at best. Consequently, there is no basis for claiming the positive identification of a legitimate target or imminent threat as required for a lawful attack. In this situation, any law-abiding shooter would have to at least pause and try to get a clearer picture. The fact that, instead, ten evidently unarmed men are massacred can at best be considered a reckless, unprofessional and irresponsible mistake – true to the slogan 'shoot first, ask questions later'. At worst, this stage of the attack already amounts to the deliberate killing of presumably protected persons and, thus, already constitutes a war crime.

If the first attack was reckless at best, the second is criminal without question. As the radio transmissions show, the soldiers are fully aware that they cannot lawfully attack the wounded Chmagh. But they are clearly looking for a pretext, almost begging him to reach for a weapon, that would allow them to shoot him. As soldiers deployed in a war context, they must know that medical personnel and other non-combatant rescuers are protected under the law of war, regardless of any official identification or affiliation with a medical service. In the present case, it is obvious that Chmagh's unarmed rescuers are only concerned with life-saving measures. Under the law of war, the rescue of the wounded cannot be considered a 'hostile act' even when – unlike here – their personal weapons are also collected in the process. In any case, American ground forces would arrive on the scene moments later and could easily have brought the situation under control. Against this undisputed factual background, the attack on the wounded Chmagh and his rescuers cannot be qualified as a negligent error but amounts to a deliberate war crime.

The soldiers knew it, their commanders knew it, and so did the US Department of Defense. The fact that the internal investigation conducted by US Army command nonetheless concluded that the soldiers had acted in compliance with the laws of war and declared case closed without any criminal prosecution of the perpetrators, let alone any compensation payments to the surviving relatives, is deeply disturbing. By taking this path, the superiors in charge not only became personally complicit in a war crime; they also betrayed the law of their own country, the reputation of their own armed forces, and the trust and security of their own people. Had the US government had its way, the American public would never have known about this murder, because the video was destined to vanish forever into the black hole of state secrets. Just like the 'Pentagon Papers' that exposed the government's deliberate deception of the American public during the Vietnam War. Just like the torture videos that CIA director Gina Haspel ordered to be destroyed while she was still commanding an American 'black site' in Thailand. Just like the unpublished photos from Abu Ghraib prison, which reportedly show the sadistic torture, rape and humiliation of defenceless prisoners in repulsive detail. Just like the full US Senate committee report, which over 7,000 pages exposes the personal and institutional responsibilities for the CIA's systematic torture practices.

None of this may lawfully be disclosed to the American public, and certainly not to the entire world. For the chain of criminal responsibility for these offences does not end with the lower ranks of those doing the dirty work, but leads to finely furnished offices with thick carpets. So the public is shamelessly lied to. Officially, this secrecy aims to protect 'national security' and 'decent men and women in uniform', not to ensure the impunity of murderers, torturers, rapists and – above all – their superiors. Officially, it is the whistleblowers exposing war crimes who are called 'traitors to the country', not the war criminals and their superiors. Officially, it is the journalists publishing evidence for war crimes who are accused of acting 'irresponsibly', not the secretive authorities suppressing such evidence. Officially, any proven perpetrators are described as isolated 'bad apples', not as scapegoats for systemic shortcomings. The public at large happily swallows the official narrative, because acknowledging the reality of a broader systemic failure would be too threatening, too unsettling, too much work. It is this tendency towards lethargy, conformity, and self-deception which is responsible for the failure of what arguably is the most famous WikiLeaks slogan: 'If wars can be started by lies, they can be ended by the truth.' Unfortunately, as a general rule, the problem is not that we do not know the truth, but that we do not want to know it.

## On the Difference between Confidentiality and Secrecy

'Collateral Murder' shook up world public opinion. The video gives but a glimpse of the daily slaughter in the Iraq War, yet makes it almost unbearably real. Every second of the clip virtually screams at us: Look, this is the real face of war. From now on, you can't say you didn't know. From now on you are informed and, therefore, also responsible for what your government does with your tax money. Gone are the days when you were still able to blindly believe the official narratives disseminated at press conferences, on government websites, and in Sunday speeches.

But 'Collateral Murder' was just the beginning of a veritable flood of WikiLeaks revelations still to be published in 2010. In accomplishing the task, Assange cooperated with prestigious daily and weekly newspapers, most notably the *New York Times*, the *Guardian*, *Der Spiegel*, *Le Monde* and *El País*. The sheer volume of the material to be processed required the support of professional journalistic organizations: 90,000 documents with field reports from the Afghanistan War, several hundred thousand from the Iraq War and, starting from November, a quarter of a million diplomatic cables sent by US embassy employees in just about every country in the world. Importantly, on Assange's instructions, all these publications were preceded by a rigorous 'harm reduction' process in which names of potentially endangered persons were individually censored. Thus, when the 'Afghan War Diary' was published in July 2010, Assange withheld some 15,000 documents in order to give the US government and the NATO-led International Security Assistance Force (ISAF) time to identify sensitive data that needed to be redacted. It was only one year later, after the publication by two *Guardian* journalists of the password to original unredacted documents, encrypted by WikiLeaks, that Assange decided to also publish the relevant documents in unredacted form himself. We will discuss this in more detail at a later stage.

Personally, I took note of the WikiLeaks publications at the time, of course. But I was not as shocked by their contents as the general public was, because much of it – and then some – I already knew. For more than a decade, I had been dealing with the reality of war day in, day out at the ICRC and had also experienced it in my own flesh and soul in the Balkans, the Middle East, and Afghanistan. When WikiLeaks broke the silence, I felt a sense of relief. Finally, I thought, something would change, and the world would no longer be able to look the other way.

At the ICRC, we always treated the information we collected with strict confidentiality. This was a matter of life and death – both for the war victims and for us. In a war context, there is little protection. There are no police enforcing law and order, and witnesses to war crimes are a nuisance that can be easily eliminated. So, unless all warring parties can be certain that the ICRC will not go public with its information, it would simply be impossible for the organization to carry out its humanitarian mission deep inside zones of conflict. That is why ICRC staff are explicitly exempted from testifying before the International Criminal Court in The Hague. There is no viable alternative to this exemption because, once an ICRC delegate testifies in a war crimes trial, warring parties worldwide would immediately question whether they could continue to grant the organization access to prisoners of war and civilian war victims, and whether delegates who already 'know too much' should perhaps be made to suffer some 'tragic accident' rather than allowing them to escape with their knowledge. Beyond strict respect for confidentiality, constant communication also had to be maintained with all parties to the conflict. Thus, in Afghanistan, the address books of our phones not only listed the mobile numbers of ISAF commanders, but also those of Taliban leaders. Every movement outside the capital had to be coordinated with all concerned parties, every change in the situation had to be detected, reported and assessed. After all, too many colleagues had already paid the ultimate price for their humanitarian mission – whether in the Hindu Kush, the Congo or Chechnya. The resulting golden rule for our public communication was: 'We say what we do, but not what we see.'

This is not to say that, in our confidential dialogue with the warring parties, we limited ourselves to diplomatic niceties. On the contrary, thanks to the confidentiality of our exchange, we could communicate openly and clearly and, if necessary, could even play hardball at times. We always had to strike a delicate balance between uncompromising toughness and pragmatic realism. Whenever we noticed that the authorities exploited our commitment to confidentiality as cover for their own inaction, we would very quickly move the dialogue on to the next hierarchical level, all the way up to the state leadership. If that also failed, we began to involve friendly third countries – still on a confidential basis. Our last resort, the public press release, was used extremely rarely, usually after years of unsuccessful work behind the scenes.

What, then, is the difference between confidentiality and secrecy? To put it simply, secrecy not only withholds certain facts from public knowledge, but also removes those facts from judicial oversight and potential sanctions. It creates a legal vacuum. I have worked for well over two decades inside the international system, and I have come to the conclusion that this type of secrecy, which shields entire areas of state activity from the purview of the public, is neither necessary nor acceptable. There can be no justification ever for exempting any sphere of governance from public knowledge and oversight. Doing so always opens the door to abuse and inevitably leads to cover-ups for crimes, exploitation and corruption.

What we do need, however, is confidentiality, both in a diplomatic and in an individual sense. Diplomatic confidentiality creates a protected framework for negotiations, inspections and other confidence-building measures aimed at de-escalating tensions and maintaining or restoring a lawful situation. If this goal cannot be achieved within a reasonable time frame, then diplomatic confidentiality loses its justification and can easily turn into secrecy and complicity. We also need individual confidentiality, such as privacy, source protection, and personality rights – all of which have nothing to do with secrecy and do not exempt the protected individual from oversight and accountability under the law.

I believe we are generally too optimistic about our own ability to behave lawfully without oversight in the long term. As human beings, we are all primarily driven by perceived short-term self-interest. This is an expression of our neurobiological and psychosocial nature and manifests regardless of status and education, over and above cultural, religious, or ideological factors. It is therefore not a moral question, but a scientific fact that must be duly taken into account when shaping our legal, political and economic governance systems. Basic constitutional principles such as democracy, the separation of powers and the rule of law, for example, reflect a realistic assessment of our inherently limited ability to faithfully exercise governmental power entrusted to us without effective constraints and oversight.

But the constitutional codification and institutional implementation of such basic principles is not sufficient to mitigate the weaknesses of human nature. Even if we are fortunate enough to live in a democracy, our electoral and legislative processes are already so distorted by campaign financing and lobbying schemes that the legitimate interests of the voting population hardly ever find genuine representation. The rule of law, in turn, can only be effective if the executive branch is properly subject to independent and impartial judicial oversight. In reality, however, the rifts separating the three branches of government are always far shallower than those separating the authorities of all three branches from the general population. Officials know each other personally, have lunch together, value good relations, share information, consult informally, and avoid stabbing one another in the back – in other words, they behave exactly as decent people are expected to behave. In practice, though, their mutual impartiality has already been largely undermined. In the context of daily administrative routine, this phenomenon tends to be harmless and can even help to avoid bureaucratic inefficiencies. However, as soon as the reputation and essential interests of influential stakeholders are concerned, it almost always causes collusion, corruption, and system failure, up to and including the worst of crimes – the 'banality of evil', as Hannah Arendt so aptly put it.

As a result of the failure or deliberate obstruction of the US military's oversight mechanisms, the war crime documented in 'Collateral Murder' was never prosecuted or compensated. Several US Iraq veterans subsequently confirmed that the operation in question was not a singular exception and that such massacres were commonplace at the time, without anyone ever being held to account. The resulting impunity has consolidated a culture of tolerance towards violent crime that has become almost impossible to correct. The appalling sense of entitlement with which the defenceless African American George Floyd was publicly choked to death by police officers in Minneapolis on 25 May 2020 is the direct consequence of decades of American leniency towards its own criminals in uniform. The same misguided policy is also reflected in the aggressive stance of the US towards the International Criminal Court and its employees – as if war crimes could ever be undone by the suppression of evidence and the intimidation of judges. As I have stressed in my annual report to the General Assembly in 2021 (A/76/168), the only way to end collusion and impunity is through strict transparency and systematic enforcement of personal and institutional accountability. This, of course, is precisely the political agenda of WikiLeaks.

## WikiLeaks as a Safety Valve

In my view, WikiLeaks can be described as a societal safety valve. When an employee working for a government or corporation witnesses wrongdoing, they may initially look the other way. If the misconduct is serious enough, their silence will eventually give rise to an unbearable moral dilemma, until they conclude: I can't take it anymore, I can't keep my knowledge to myself, I need to find a way to free myself of this moral burden. If the government or corporation fail to offer internal structures and procedures through which such legal and moral grievances can be adequately remedied, then eventually the pressure grows too great and blows the alarm whistle on the safety valve: the employee literally becomes a 'whistleblower'. WikiLeaks provides a mechanism that guarantees such whistleblowers absolute anonymity.

Thus, through the safety valve of WikiLeaks, information finds its way to the public. Unlike traditional journalism, such information is minimally edited. Contrary to what is often claimed, information that could expose individuals to danger, and which is not otherwise publicly available, is redacted by WikiLeaks. Everything else is generally made available in the form of unredacted originals. In 2010, the media partners associated with WikiLeaks provided valuable support in separating public interest information from trivialities. At the same time, it also became apparent that traditional journalism no longer fulfilled the indispensable societal functions of the 'Fourth Estate': monitoring the checks and balances between the branches of government, informing the public about systemic shortcomings and their implications for the average citizen and, thus, enabling the latter to take the necessary remedial action through the democratic process.

Even an organization committed to full transparency must, of course, act responsibly. It must be emphasized, however, that the US government has never offered any evidence for its claim that people have been endangered by the WikiLeaks disclosures. In fact, in 2010, then US vice-president Joe Biden even acknowledged during a session of the UN Security Council that WikiLeaks' publications had caused 'no substantive damage' other than being 'embarrassing' for the US government. In reality, of course, these leaks were far beyond embarrassing – they endangered the impunity of officials at all levels of the chain of command for war crimes, torture and corruption.

Like any safety valve, WikiLeaks is not the problem, but merely a visible symptom of more deep-rooted shortcomings.

The real problem is always the crimes – not the fact that they are being revealed. And yet precisely the contrary is being communicated to the public. By its very existence, WikiLeaks calls into question an entire governance system based on secrecy, a way of doing business that has become deeply entrenched: secret diplomatic notes, blurred lines between private and public interests, routine corruption, cronyism and abuse of power.

Had the crimes revealed by WikiLeaks been prosecuted and redressed in good faith, it might then have been possible and appropriate to initiate a balanced discussion about the accountability of whistleblowers and journalists. But when murderers, torturers and their superiors go unpunished, whereas non-violent truth-tellers like Chelsea Manning, Julian Assange and Edward Snowden are prosecuted and threatened with sanctions normally reserved for perpetrators of the most serious crimes, then any presumption of good faith on the part of the authorities has been effectively disproved.

Democratically elected governments unwilling to be held accountable for crimes and misconduct fear nothing more than the unrestrained transparency promoted by WikiLeaks. Hence their excessively aggressive reaction and the ferocity with which people like Manning, Assange and Snowden are being persecuted. None of this is happening because of any real-world harm caused by these dissidents. After all, no one was seriously endangered, no government went bankrupt, and no war was lost. The only real threat posed by WikiLeaks is that it challenges the impunity of the powerful. In order to prevent this idea from spreading through the establishment of a second, third, or hundredth WikiLeaks, potential emulators must be intimidated worldwide. This is why the methodology of WikiLeaks is persecuted and punished in the person of Assange. The spotlight no longer illuminates the official misconduct revealed by WikiLeaks but is pointed exclusively at the messenger. He is declared a rapist, a hacker, a spy and a narcissist who is trying to evade justice and is not entitled to the protections of press freedom. Obediently, public opinion follows the guiding spotlight and discusses avidly and freely – about Julian Assange, his cat and his skateboard. To some he is a hero, to others a villain. But to the powerful, this question is irrelevant. To them, only one thing matters: that the real elephant in the room, their own dirty secrets, has been successfully blanked out and vanished back into the darkness of our collective amnesia.

# 3

# Initial Contradictions Come to Light

## The Fog Begins to Clear

When Julian Assange's lawyers contacted me again, in late March 2019, their tone had become significantly more urgent. There were reasons to suspect that Assange's expulsion from the Ecuadorian embassy, and consequently his arrest by British police, might be imminent. In recent weeks, Ecuadorian President Lenín Moreno had made statements leaving little doubt that he wanted to get rid of his embassy guest sooner rather than later. The British tabloid press had eagerly picked up the topic and gossiped about the increasingly strained relationship between embassy staff and Assange, and about the latter's allegedly erratic and unpleasant behaviour. It did not take more than a cursory glance at the headlines to put two and two together. In May 2017, US-friendly Moreno had replaced US-sceptic Rafael Correa as president of Ecuador, a change which appeared to have sealed Assange's fate. It was entirely clear to me that, if Assange were to be expelled from the embassy, the risk of his extradition to the United States would increase massively, and with it the risk of serious violations of his human rights.

A question started forming in my mind. Had I overlooked something when I dismissed this case the last time around? I decided to look into the matter a bit more closely and began to open the attached documents that had been forwarded to me. Among them I found a summary of events since the WikiLeaks publications of 2010. The case was more complex than I had thought. Already the case history of the Swedish rape investigation, which had been discontinued without any results in 2017, raised many questions. Next, I read a medical report written by Dr Sondra Crosby just a month earlier, after visiting Assange at the Ecuadorian embassy in February 2019. Crosby was not just anyone. A medical doctor and professor of medicine at Boston University, she was specialized in the examination of refugees and victims of torture and had been one of the first physicians to independently examine detainees in Guantánamo. She had an excellent reputation and her voice carried weight. Most importantly to me, she was not associated with the Assange activist camp and was therefore unlikely to take a one-sided position.

Crosby's report, which has since been leaked on the internet, described a cornered man whose strength was dwindling after seven years of confinement. Ill-equipped for long-term accommodation to begin with, the embassy had now become an increasingly hostile and intimidating environment for Assange, with serious effects on his mental and physical health. According to Crosby, Assange was suffering from increasingly severe chronic stress caused by an accumulation of factors including cramped quarters, lack of sunlight and exercise, sensory deprivation, social isolation, and punitive suspension of his access to visitors, phone calls and the internet. In conjunction with the indefinite and uncertain nature of his confinement and the lack of adequate medical care, these factors were conducive to serious physical and psychological risks, including suicide.

In addition, Crosby expressed grave concern at the 'persistent and personal attacks on Mr. Assange's dignity, and acts meant to degrade and humiliate him', including increasingly intrusive surveillance. Crosby's medical examination of Assange had been monitored by surveillance cameras, and they were forced to speak over the noise of a radio to avoid being overheard. During Crosby's brief absence from the interview room, her confidential medical notes were removed and later found in an office used by the embassy's security staff, where they evidently had been leafed through and read, in blatant violation of doctor–patient confidentiality. Crosby's conclusion was unequivocal: 'It is my professional opinion that the synergistic and cumulative effect of the pain and suffering inflicted on Mr. Assange – both physical and psychological – is in violation of the 1984 Convention Against Torture, Article 1 and Article 16. I believe the psychological, physical, and social sequelae will be long-lasting and severe.'

Another attachment included a report by the UN Working Group on Arbitrary Detention (WGAD), the body that had issued that press release on the Assange case, and which I had declined to join three months earlier. Although the WGAD's report No. 54/2015 dated from 4 December 2015, it was only now, in March 2019, that I actually took the time to read it. The opinion had been written at a time when the Swedish case was still open but had been pending at the very initial stage of a 'preliminary investigation' for more than five years. Throughout this time, the Swedish prosecutor had apparently never even brought formal charges against Assange. The UN experts rightly observed that prolonged confinement without charge was incompatible with the presumption of innocence. It seemed that the perpetuation of this procedural stalemate and, in particular, Assange's fear of extradition to the United States, were what prevented him from leaving the embassy. Given that both Sweden and the United Kingdom refused to offer any assurances against Assange's onward extradition to the United States, the status quo of his embassy asylum was likely to continue indefinitely.

Did this mean that Assange's confinement at the embassy amounted to arbitrary deprivation of liberty? The WGAD answered in the affirmative, thus implicitly accepting the argument that Assange's embassy asylum was his only option to avoid extradition to the United States and the related risk of political persecution and inhumane conditions of detention. Like any other human being, Assange could not reasonably be expected to give up his safety and expose himself to the risk of serious human rights violations. Consequently, if Assange's fear of persecution was taken seriously, his continued stay in the embassy could not be described as voluntary. By providing guarantees against his onward extradition to the United States, Sweden and the United Kingdom could easily have ended the stalemate and enabled Assange to participate in the Swedish investigation. In view of their refusal to provide such guarantees, the only logical conclusion for the Working Group was that Assange was being arbitrarily deprived of his liberty by both countries.

Their governments disagreed, of course. First, they demanded that the WGAD reconsider. When the Working Group confirmed its conclusions, they declared that they disagreed with the UN body's opinion and therefore would simply ignore it. It is downright absurd, of course, for states claiming to be governed by the rule of law to first engage in legal proceedings before a mandated UN body, and then to accept its conclusions only if they go in their favour. But this did not seem to bother either government. Instead, and rather ironically, they continued to accuse Assange of evading justice and downplayed their own responsibility for the situation: 'Mr Assange is free to leave the embassy at any time, and the [Swedish / British] authorities have no control over his decision to remain in the embassy.'

To me, the Working Group's assessment seemed plausible. I could only agree with its rationale. A year earlier, in March 2018, my report to the Human Rights Council had focused on migration-related torture (A/HRC/37/50). In all regions of the world, countless asylum seekers reach the border of their destination state only to be stopped there and held in closed camps. Here too, the authorities claim that asylum seekers are not being deprived of their liberty, that they are not being arbitrarily detained, but are completely free to leave at any time. Indeed, 'free to leave' they are, but only in one direction – back to where they came from, back to the risks of war, violence and abuse. So let us be clear: whenever we give a person no other choice but to remain locked up or else expose themselves to serious danger, then we are effectively depriving them of their liberty. Anything else is delusional.

Hence the WGAD's finding that Assange's confinement at the embassy amounted to arbitrary deprivation of liberty. The clarity with which the Working Group analysed Assange's situation was remarkable. Usually, a single special rapporteur is more likely to take a courageous and outspoken position than a collective body of five independent UN experts, which tends to settle for the lowest common denominator. In the Assange case, there was only one dissenting opinion within the Working Group, making the unanimity of the majority of members all the more significant.

Another document I consulted was an interview with James Goodale, former general counsel of the *New York Times*. What would be the impact of US prosecution of Assange on press freedom as guaranteed under the First Amendment of the US Constitution? Goodale knew what he was talking about. Already in 1971, when the *New York Times* published the so-called Pentagon Papers about the Vietnam War, he had forcefully and successfully fought against the attempted criminalization of journalism under the US Espionage Act. Goodale made clear that whatever Assange may have published via WikiLeaks and whoever may have provided him with the material, he was the publisher, not the source. Moreover, Assange had not stolen the published material, but had obtained it freely from a whistleblower. His actions were therefore protected under the First Amendment of the Constitution. If Assange were to be prosecuted nonetheless, it would set a terrible precedent for investigative journalism. It would mean that, from then on, any publication based on leaked material would become a crime. The resulting danger for press freedom could not be overstated.

I had been reading for a long time. For a moment, I looked through my window across the lowlands that separated the Jura from the Alps. The air had cleared, and the snow-covered triple peaks of the Eiger, Mönch and Jungfrau rose into the bright blue sky like giants from the fog dissolving beneath them. Crosby's medical report, the Working Group's conclusions, and Goodale's assessment had made me think. I slowly began to wake up to my own prejudice, which had clouded my judgment and led me to summarily dismiss Assange's initial appeal three months earlier. What troubled me most was the self-righteous ease and unshakeable certainty with which I had accepted a largely unsubstantiated narrative as unquestionable fact. Now that I had scratched the thin veneer of this narrative and caught a first glimpse behind the curtain, I could no longer close my eyes to the enormous political dimensions of this case. It had become clear to me that, at the very least, I owed it to my personal and professional integrity to take a closer look and form my own opinion – based not on hearsay, but on verified fact.

## Preliminary Protective Measures

At this early stage, my main concern was to prevent Assange's fast-track extradition to the United States, whether directly by the Ecuadorians or, after his expulsion from the embassy, by the British. The CIA's extraordinary renditions, which involved kidnappings without any legal process, followed by torture and arbitrary detention in secret 'black sites' around the globe, had set a disturbing precedent. Although the US indictment against Assange had not yet been unsealed, its existence had been an open secret for a long time. While one could only speculate on the precise charges, I was seriously concerned that, in the United States, Assange would be exposed to an unfair, politically motivated trial and a draconian punishment. Moreover, the conditions of detention in US Supermax prisons and other high-security facilities, where Assange would most likely be held, had long been regarded as cruel, inhuman and degrading both by my predecessors and by various relevant human rights organizations.

These were the thoughts that guided my next steps. I would send two official letters to Ecuador and the United Kingdom, reminding them of the universal principle of 'non-refoulement', which establishes an absolute prohibition against returning or deporting people to countries where they risk being tortured, executed or subjected to other serious violations of their human rights. At the same time, I would announce my intention to visit Assange at the Ecuadorian embassy and to meet with the Ecuadorian ambassador and senior British government officials. Most importantly, however, I would formally appeal to the Ecuadorian government to refrain from expelling Assange until the protection of his human rights could be guaranteed and, in the meantime, to do everything possible to prevent a deterioration in his health.

The deeper I looked into this case, the more apparent it became that much more was at stake here than Assange's personal fate. It was hard to deny that, with the criminalization of Assange's publications, a dangerous precedent would be set for investigative journalism as a whole. If indeed this was the real motivation behind prosecuting Assange, then my diplomatic letters alone would not be sufficient to resolve the matter, and could even be counterproductive. To forestall unpredictable knee-jerk reactions on the part of the involved states, it would be important to generate public attention before I transmitted my official letters to the United Kingdom and Ecuador. In a first step, I therefore issued a press statement entitled: 'UN expert on torture alarmed by reports Assange could soon be expelled from Ecuadorian embassy'. It announced my intention to personally investigate the case and summarized my human-rights concerns. It further urged Ecuador and the United Kingdom not to revoke Assange's asylum and not to take any steps towards his extradition to the United States. The primary purpose of the statement was to alert the public and the media, and to send an unequivocal message to the two governments: whatever may have happened so far, from now on, the UN special rapporteur is watching you closely and soon will be coming to London to investigate this case.

The press statement was issued on the evening of Friday, 5 April, and immediately on the following Monday morning my two official letters were sent to the Permanent Missions of the United Kingdom and Ecuador. They announced my intention to visit the embassy on 25 April and requested face-to-face meetings with Julian Assange and the Ecuadorian ambassador in London. This was to be followed by meetings with British government officials, particularly those who would be responsible for the decision-making process in the event of Assange's expulsion from the embassy and a US extradition request. The declared purpose of my visit was to find a long-term solution to Assange's situation in compliance with human rights requirements.

## 'Operation Pelican': Assange's Arrest

The British ambassador to the United Nations in Geneva replied two days later with a short and rather tight-lipped letter. Apparently, my decision to inform the public before reaching out to the government had caused a degree of irritation. The British government agreed to my proposed visit to Assange at the Ecuadorian embassy on 25 April, but declined my request to meet with British authorities: 'You will appreciate that it would not be appropriate for officials to speculate on hypothetical scenarios.' Instead, I was directed to a government website where I could find general information about the British asylum procedures. 'Speculate on hypothetical scenarios': this referred to my concern that Assange might be arrested and extradited by the United Kingdom to the United States. Hypothetical. Pure speculation. These were the words used by the British ambassador on 10 April 2019.

Less than twenty-four hours later, on the morning of 11 April, the Ecuadorian embassy in London opened its doors to officers of the Metropolitan Police, and Julian Assange was arrested, dragged out of the embassy and pushed into a police van. On that very same day he was brought before Westminster Magistrates' Court for adjudication. The judge did not appear to require the luxury of a fully-fledged criminal trial to make up his mind; after a fifteen-minute hearing, he swiftly convicted Assange of a bail violation committed seven years earlier. Then he sent him to Britain's toughest high-security prison to await sentencing. Assange now faced up to one year in prison.

In its official press statement, the Ecuadorian government tried to justify Assange's expulsion from the embassy based on claims that he had repeatedly violated Inter-American treaties on diplomatic asylum, as well as a 'Special Protocol of Coexistence' that had been drafted specifically for the purpose of regulating his everyday life at the embassy. Whatever the factual accuracy of these accusations, as a matter of law, neither of them was capable of overriding the absolute prohibition of 'refoulement'. Assange clearly had not been offered any form of due process, as would be imperatively required prior to any revocation of asylum. He had not been informed of the government's intention in advance and had not been given the opportunity to consult with a lawyer, nor to comment on, object to or appeal the decision – he was simply expelled by a unilateral 'order' of the Ecuadorian president. Moreover, Assange had been granted Ecuadorian citizenship in 2017, and that country's constitution categorically prohibits the extradition of nationals. Therefore, one hour before Assange's expulsion, Ecuador not only revoked his asylum but also 'suspended' his citizenship, allegedly due to 'irregularities' in his papers and, again, without any form of due process. One wonders what kind of 'irregularities' could possibly have existed in the papers of a national who had lived inside the Ecuadorian embassy for the entire duration of his citizenship with no opportunity to travel, change his residence or even leave it. Tellingly, President Moreno described all of this as a 'sovereign act of state', a perspective reminiscent of the infamous words attributed to Louis XIV, the absolutist Sun King of the seventeenth century: '*L'État, c'est moi*' – the antithesis of the rule of law. In his press statement of 11 April, Moreno expressly assured the world that he had received guarantees from the United Kingdom that Assange would not be extradited to a country where he could face the death penalty, torture or ill-treatment – precisely those guarantees that both the United Kingdom and Sweden had always insisted could not be given to Assange.

Assange had always predicted that were he ever to set foot outside the embassy he would immediately be arrested on a US extradition request. On 11 April 2019, all those who had ridiculed his fears as narcissistic paranoia were proved wrong. Within an hour of his expulsion and arrest, the United States handed over their extradition request to the British authorities and unsealed their secret indictment against Assange. To the surprise of most observers, the indictment turned out to be much less severe than anticipated. Assange was not, as some expected, charged with espionage, but only with a single count of 'conspiracy to commit computer intrusion'. More precisely, he was accused of having conspired with his source, Chelsea Manning – then still known as US Army Private First-Class Bradley Manning – to help decrypt a password hash for the US Department of Defense computer system. Importantly, Manning already had full 'top secret' access privileges to the system and all the documents she leaked to Assange. So, even according to the US government, the point of the alleged attempt to decode the password hash was not to gain unauthorized access to classified information ('hacking'), but to help Manning to cover her tracks inside the system by logging in with a different identity ('source protection'). In any case, the alleged attempt undisputedly remained unsuccessful and did not result in any harm whatsoever.

If Assange were to be convicted on this charge, he would face a prison sentence of up to five years. Given that this is the maximum sentence, applicable only to the most serious and harmful cases of computer intrusion, the sanction for Assange's alleged unsuccessful attempt would probably have to be reduced to a suspended prison sentence of a few weeks or even just a moderate fine. But I was under no illusion that the United States could have pursued Assange for almost a decade, across several jurisdictions, just to let him get away with a minor sanction for an unsuccessful attempt at computer intrusion – a petty offence that is committed literally millions of times every single day. No, I was certain that this was only the beginning, and that the US would significantly expand their indictment at some convenient point down the line.

It was obvious that the events of 11 April 2019 had been planned and coordinated well in advance between Ecuador, the United Kingdom, and the United States. Anyone acquainted with the cumbersome communication and decision-making processes of political hierarchies, bureaucracies and diplomatic services knows that achieving such a tight sequencing of highly complex events and having them unfold within a few hours with the involvement of officials from various branches of government and three jurisdictions on three different continents takes weeks, if not months, to prepare. When less than twenty-four hours before Assange's expulsion and arrest the British ambassador in his letter to me formally dismissed my concerns as groundless 'speculation' about a 'hypothetical scenario', he must have known that he was deliberately misleading an officially mandated special rapporteur of the United Nations. The ambassador may not have been notified of the precise date of Assange's expulsion but, in a politicized case like this, it is completely out of the question that he would have approved my visit request to the UK for 25 April without prior consultation with the political leadership in London, themselves closely involved in the planning of 'Operation Pelican' – the code name for Assange's forcible removal from the Ecuadorian embassy.

Indeed, as we now know from the memoirs of Alan Duncan, the then British minister of state for Europe and the Americas, direct negotiations started around the time of the secret US indictment in March 2018. In October of that year, Duncan notes: 'The Assange issue is progressing. Our channels into Ecuador are paving the way to a solution.' It seems Assange's expulsion had originally been planned for 9 January 2019. However, on 8 January, the minister notes in his diary, 'Annoyingly Assange's forcible exit from the Ecuadorian embassy has been delayed.' The following months see regular diary entries by the minister recounting a slow but steady progress in the negotiations between British and Ecuadorian officials. By 28 March, Duncan is confident. 'I think I am nearly there with Ecuador to get Julian Assange out of their London embassy. It's taken months of delicate negotiations, but nearly, nearly ...' Then, on 11 April: 'Suddenly it's game on: I'm told that Assange will be sprung from the embassy today. So I drop everything and head to the Operations Room at the top of the Foreign Office.'

With hindsight, and without overestimating the influence of my mandate, I believe that my initiative may inadvertently have accelerated the course of events. My public appeal, together with the announcement of an official on-site investigation, appear to have touched a sensitive nerve. For this human rights–based appeal contradicted the carefully constructed narrative of Assange as the spoiled coward, traitor, rapist and hacker who finally needed to be dragged out of his luxurious hiding place and brought to justice. In the eyes of the governments involved, my investigation would – at best – mean an unwelcome delay in Assange's long-decided expulsion, arrest, and extradition. At worst, it could cause considerable disruption and embarrassment, expose the authorities to public scrutiny and require them to justify their actions.

Be that as it may, a new fait accompli had now been established, in a manner that set all alarm bells ringing in my mind. Why now, suddenly, after almost seven years of lethargic stagnation, this hasty expulsion, arrest and conviction in such obvious violation of due process and the rule of law? Why this suspiciously mild US indictment, which virtually screamed for worse? And why had the British ambassador lied to me? Why such contempt for my mandate? After all, I was no enemy, political activist, or dissident. I had been appointed and mandated by states to exercise my function in partnership and constructive cooperation with them. What was going on here? Something was obviously wrong – and now I began to seriously doubt the good faith of the governments involved.

## Judicial Bias

Does an arrest warrant for a bail violation remain formally valid, even when the underlying extradition request has been withdrawn? If so, is there still a public interest in prosecuting such a bail violation, especially if it was committed exclusively to avoid serious human rights violations and, thus, without any criminal intent? In February 2018, just over a year before

Assange's expulsion from the embassy, his lawyers had raised these questions in court and filed an application to cancel the original British arrest warrant for bail violation, which had been issued in 2012. The Swedish extradition request, in relation to which Assange had been arrested and subsequently released on bail in December 2010, had been formally withdrawn in May 2017, after the Swedish prosecution had closed its preliminary investigation into allegations of rape for the second time in almost seven years. Further, the UN Working Group on Arbitrary Detention had found that Assange's prolonged confinement at the embassy amounted to arbitrary deprivation of liberty. In the view of his lawyers, the difficult conditions of Assange's confinement at the embassy since 2012, as well as its justification as diplomatic asylum from political persecution, rendered the continued prosecution and punishment for that offence disproportionate and outside the realm of public interest.

In her ruling of 13 February 2018, Emma Arbuthnot, senior district judge at Westminster Magistrates' Court, dismissed all of these arguments: 'He [Assange] appears to consider himself above the normal rules of law and wants justice only if it goes in his favour.' Earlier, she had painted a distorted, almost trivializing picture of Assange's living conditions in the Ecuadorian embassy and seemed to mock its equation by the UN Working Group with arbitrary deprivation of liberty. According to Arbuthnot, Assange could sit in the sunlight on the balcony of the embassy at any time; his internet access was permanently guaranteed; his meetings with visitors were unlimited and not supervised, and he could choose what he wanted to eat. Of course, she did not miss the opportunity to point out that Assange 'could leave the embassy whenever he wishes', adding that the inmates of Wandsworth Prison would be likely to dispute the assertion that such living conditions were akin to a remand in custody. Having dismissed the WGAD's assessment as wrong and inaccurate, Judge Arbuthnot accorded it 'little weight' in her decision. In so doing she echoed the self-righteous attitude of the British government which, after two years of active participation in the proceedings, refused to respect and implement the WGAD's conclusions, simply because they had not turned out in favour of the United Kingdom. The judge seemed completely oblivious to the striking irony of dismissing the Working Group's official conclusions and, in the same breath, accusing Assange of accepting justice only when it was in his favour.

What Assange's lawyers could not know is that none of the legal arguments they raised during this hearing ever mattered. The real plot being played out was an entirely different one. Exactly three weeks later, on 6 March 2018, a US Grand Jury would issue its secret indictment against Assange. Judge Arbuthnot, no doubt, was well informed. Already two months earlier, on 22 December 2017, the United States had transmitted a diplomatic note to the British government requesting Assange's provisional arrest in preparation for his impending indictment. On the very same day, Judge Snow at Westminster Magistrates' Court – the judge who would summarily convict Assange of bail violation on 11 April 2019 – hastened to comply and issued a second arrest warrant for Assange. Had Arbuthnot cancelled the first arrest warrant as requested by Assange, the second warrant requested by the United States would have been difficult to conceal. So, in February 2018, it was absolutely crucial to uphold the first arrest warrant, relating to the alleged bail violation, as a smokescreen for the second. Accordingly, until the very moment of Assange's expulsion and arrest, the impending US indictment and extradition request had to be treated as a 'hypothetical scenario' which 'it would not be appropriate for officials to speculate on'.

But there was an even more serious catch to Judge Arbuthnot's ruling. Her husband, Lord James Arbuthnot, not only sits as a Tory in the House of Lords. He has also held high positions in the British defence industry for decades, and, until 2014, was chairman of the Defence Select Committee, whose tasks include overseeing the British military. The crux of the matter: WikiLeaks had reportedly published numerous documents relating to activities by organizations and individuals with close professional and political connections to Lord Arbuthnot. Judge Arbuthnot herself is said to have received gifts from a security company exposed by WikiLeaks. Nonetheless, Judge Arbuthnot not only ruled to uphold Assange's arrest warrant in 2018, she also personally presided over the US extradition proceedings against Assange until the summer of 2019. After that, District Judge Vanessa Baraitser, a colleague subordinate to her at the same court, took over the case.

Irrespective of their veracity, these alleged conflicts of interest create a reasonable perception of bias. Due process requires that any judge must recuse themselves as soon as the facts of the case suggest a real possibility of judicial prejudice. It is not only the right of the defendant to a fair trial which is at stake, but also the public interest in due process. Therefore, in clear cases like this one, there can be no discretion on the part of either the judge or even the defendant himself in this matter. Based on evidence of possible conflicts of interest, Assange's lawyers filed an application for recusal on 8 April 2019. Of course, a formal recusal of Judge Arbuthnot would not only have prevented her future involvement in the case, it would also have challenged the validity of any decision against Assange in which she had been previously involved, including her confirmation of the current arrest warrant. Without a valid arrest warrant, however, the British police would have been unable to arrest Assange in the event of his expulsion from the Ecuadorian embassy. Sweden had withdrawn its own arrest warrant and extradition request two years earlier, and the United States had not yet unsealed their indictment and filed their extradition request. In the absence of an arrest warrant, Assange would have been free to leave not only the Ecuadorian embassy but also the United Kingdom for any destination of his choice. It is therefore reasonable to assume that, in addition to my press release of 5 April and my two letters to the British and Ecuadorian governments of 8 April, Assange's application for recusal put the authorities under considerable time pressure. Suddenly, everything had to happen very fast. Assange had to be expelled, arrested and – above all – convicted by a different judge without delay, to ensure a formally unassailable legal basis for his arrest.

Not surprisingly, therefore, things speeded up. Only three

days later, on 11 April, Assange had lost both his Ecuadorian citizenship and his diplomatic asylum and was standing before Judge Michael Snow at Westminster Magistrates' Court. During the hearing, defence counsel Liam Walker argued that, in 2012, Assange had a reasonable justification for seeking diplomatic asylum in the Ecuadorian embassy rather than surrendering to British custody for extradition to Sweden. Most notably, Assange feared that, once in Swedish custody, he would not receive adequate judicial protection against onward extradition to the United States – a fear which had been officially recognized as reasonable by the government of Ecuador. Walker also reiterated Assange's formal objection in relation to Judge Arbuthnot's possible conflicts of interest.

In normal circumstances, any such objection would have required Judge Snow to suspend the hearing in order to formally address the question of recusal – particularly since a well-documented application to that effect had already been submitted to the same court three days earlier. But Judge Snow reportedly found it 'unacceptable', 'grossly unfair' and 'improper' for Assange to raise the due process objection of judicial bias against Judge Arbuthnot, 'just to ruin the reputation of a senior and able judge in front of the press'. Speaking in front of the same press gallery, however, the honourable Judge Snow saw nothing unacceptable, grossly unfair or improper in describing Assange's legitimate concerns as 'laughable' and his behaviour as that of 'a narcissist who cannot get beyond his own selfish interests', even though, during the entire hearing, Assange had said nothing except 'I plead not guilty.'

The ease with which Judge Snow ridiculed and insulted Assange in open court was astonishing. A year earlier, Judge Arbuthnot also openly trivialized Assange's arbitrary confinement in the embassy and simply dismissed the opinion of the United Nations' WGAD in the matter. Both judges must have been rather confident that their attitude expressed a consensus on Julian Assange that was shared not only within the British judiciary, but also within the other branches of government and the mainstream media.

Of course, Assange's criminal trial should never have been scheduled for the day of his arrest in the first place – a day which would foreseeably have generated high levels of stress and anxiety in a defendant who had just spent close to seven years in a confined and increasingly claustrophobic and hostile space. In the morning, at around 9:15 a.m., officers of the London Metropolitan Police entered the Ecuadorian embassy. Within the following hour, the Ecuadorian ambassador informed Assange of the termination of his diplomatic asylum and the 'suspension' of his Ecuadorian citizenship and asked him to leave the premises. When Assange refused, protesting the blatant illegality of expulsion without due process, the ambassador had him handcuffed and forcibly dragged out of the embassy by the British police. It was about 10:15 a.m. when he was carried into a waiting police van, forced to leave all his personal belongings, computers and documents behind.

At the police station, Assange was promptly served with the second arrest warrant in connection with the US extradition request, which had been transmitted to the British government immediately upon his expulsion. It goes without saying that, under due process requirements, no defendant can reasonably be expected to prepare his defence and stand trial within a few hours of undergoing the sudden and cumulative trauma of unlawful expulsion, violent arrest, criminal charges and an extradition request. But due process manifestly was not part of the plan. Instead, a court hearing had already been pre-arranged for the same afternoon, quite evidently with the sole purpose of finding Assange guilty of an offence alleged to have been committed almost seven years earlier. Since the judge did not appear to find any added value in considering the legal arguments brought by the defendant, he allowed Assange no more than fifteen minutes of preparation time together with his lawyer, and then pushed through the entire hearing in less than half an hour. This is what summary trials look like everywhere in the world.

On 1 May, a third judge, Deborah Taylor, handed down the sentence: fifty weeks in prison – just two weeks shy of the maximum sentence of one year. According to Taylor, it was 'difficult to imagine a more serious example of a bail violation'. After all, she explained, Assange's surveillance during his years at the embassy had cost the British taxpayer £16 million. The absurdity of her reasoning is obvious. The gravity of an offence does not increase with the costs for the surveillance of the suspect. Involuntary manslaughter does not become first degree murder just because it took ten years to track down the perpetrator. A theft of £100 remains a comparatively minor offence, even if the authorities choose to spend £100,000 on its investigation. Clearly, it was not Assange, but the British authorities alone, who had decided not to recognize the diplomatic asylum lawfully granted by Ecuador and to have the embassy besieged around the clock for seven years. By British standards, fifty weeks in prison for a bail violation is a completely disproportionate sanction. The vast majority of bail violations that do not involve the perpetration of additional serious offences are punished with fines or disciplinary sanctions. Even if a bail violation were to result in a short custodial sentence, that sentence would certainly not be served in a high-security setting amounting to solitary confinement. Except in the case of Julian Assange. He was immediately returned to Belmarsh prison in London – infamous as 'Britain's Guantánamo Bay'.

## Now More Than Ever!

From my perspective, the circumstances had now changed entirely. My visit to the Ecuadorian embassy had become obsolete, of course, but I had not abandoned my plan to visit Assange. On the contrary, my initial reluctance had given way to an ever-strengthening determination to get to the bottom of this matter. On 18 April 2019, I sent a follow-up letter to the government of Ecuador expressing strong criticism of Assange's expulsion without advance notice, legal remedy, or any other form of due process. I further requested answers to several pressing questions. Why had the Ecuadorian government completely ignored my appeal to suspend Assange's expulsion at least for the duration of my official investigation? How was the termination of Assange's citizenship and diplomatic asylum compatible with international human rights standards and the rule of law more generally? How was it compatible with Ecuador's longstanding position that Assange needed diplomatic protection against the danger of extradition to the United States – a danger which had now materialized precisely as a consequence of Assange's expulsion from the Ecuadorian embassy? What measures had been taken by Ecuador with a view to preventing violations of Assange's human rights, whether by the United Kingdom or by any other state? I concluded by expressing my expectation that the alleged violations would be investigated and those responsible held accountable. This was all I could do. Media attention had already moved on to the new scenario, and the wider public appeared unconcerned with my uncomfortable questions. By expelling Assange, Ecuador had relieved itself of a problem which its leadership no longer had any interest in resolving constructively. From their perspective, the ball was now back in Britain's court.

On the same day, therefore, I also sent a follow-up letter to the British government, requesting permission to visit Assange in prison within a month of his arrest, no later than 10 May. In line with the UN standard terms of reference for detention visits, I explained that I intended to conduct a confidential interview with Assange, to evaluate his conditions of detention, and to carry out a thorough medical examination with the help of specialized doctors. I also reiterated my request for meetings with relevant British authorities and urged the British government to refrain from extraditing or otherwise surrendering Assange to the United States or any other country, until his entitlement to international protection had been determined in a transparent and impartial proceeding granting all due process and fair trial guarantees. On the face of it, my two letters to the British government of 8 and 18 April 2019 were not that different. And yet, within the intervening ten days, my perspective on the case had changed quite fundamentally.

# 4

# My Investigation Begins

## Visit to HMP Belmarsh

By the time I began my investigation, I was keenly aware of the enormous political dimension of this case. There was a real danger that people would try to manipulate me and abuse my mandate. I therefore had to remain cautious and wary of any attempts to influence me, no matter where they came from. In order to avoid any suspicion of a conflict of interest, I had to keep my distance, both from the authorities involved and from Julian Assange's supporters. I needed to collect as many reliable facts as possible and to triangulate my own observations with the assessments made by other experts, lawyers and witnesses, as well as with the positions taken by the authorities.

My visit to Julian Assange in London's Belmarsh high-security prison had been approved by the British Ministry of Justice for 9 May 2019. I wanted to personally examine Assange's health, prison conditions, and treatment so that I could draw clear conclusions based on reliable information. What impact, if any, had almost seven years of confinement in the Ecuadorian embassy had on Assange's physical health? What had been the psychological effects of being trapped for so long and exposed to a progressively hostile environment of isolation, reprisals and the constant danger of extradition? From the perspective of my mandate, everything ultimately boiled down to a single question: was there credible evidence that Julian Assange was, had been or might be exposed to an act or risk of torture or ill-treatment, whether currently in British custody, previously at the Ecuadorian embassy, or in the event of his extradition to the United States?

Whatever my findings, at least one party in this strongly politicized case would probably try to question my motives and undermine my credibility. It was therefore particularly important for me to be able to rely not only on my personal judgment and experience but also on the expertise of independent medical professionals. I therefore asked two medical doctors specialized in the examination of torture victims to accompany me on my visit. I had worked with both of them before, including during numerous prison visits, and was confident that I could rely on their professional and personal integrity. Professor Duarte Nuno Vieira was dean and professor for forensic medicine at the Faculty of Medicine of the University of Coimbra in Portugal, chairman of numerous professional associations and, until a few years ago, president of the International Association of Forensic Sciences. A world-class forensic expert who had seen it all – from the mass graves of the Yugoslav War to the bodies recovered from the wreck of MH17, the Malaysian airliner shot down by a Russian-built missile over eastern Ukraine in 2014.

Dr Pau Pérez-Sales was a psychiatrist at La Paz University Hospital in Madrid, an internationally recognized specialist and author in the field of psychological torture and former director of a rehabilitation centre for torture victims, at the Mental Health and Human Rights Resource Centre in Madrid. Both Professor Vieira and Dr Pérez-Sales were world-renowned experts in identifying, examining, and documenting possible traces of physical and psychological torture or other ill-treatment, and were regularly called upon as expert witnesses by national and international courts and institutions. Neither of them would ever think of using the Assange case for their own profiling, and both would strictly adhere to medical confidentiality and leave any public statements following the prison visit to me as the mandate holder. This was important, because the purpose of my mandate was not, of course, to disclose confidential medical information to the public, but to use our medical diagnosis as a basis for my legal assessment as to whether the prohibition of torture and ill-treatment had been violated.

In line with customary practice, the medical report would not be made available to the authorities, nor to Assange or his legal team, but would be kept under lock and key at the Office of the High Commissioner for Human Rights and used exclusively as the medical basis for my official findings. On the one hand, Assange needed to be sure that the medical information he entrusted us with would not be used against him. On the other, the confidentiality of our diagnosis also had to apply to Assange himself, as it would not have been acceptable to give him preferential treatment in this investigation. Given that my official conclusions would not be legally binding for either party or for the United Nations, but that they had the evidentiary strength of an expert opinion, the non-disclosure of the underlying medical diagnosis remained compatible with the principles of due process. In order to ensure maximum objectivity and credibility, I had instructed both doctors to conduct their medical examination in line with the 'Istanbul Protocol' – a UN document enshrining the internationally recognized legal standards and medical guidelines on how to effectively investigate and document allegations of torture and ill-treatment.

On the morning of 9 May, we took a black cab from our hotel in central London to Thamesmead, about ten miles east of Tower Bridge and Big Ben. Her Majesty's Prison Belmarsh is a thirty-year-old, high-security prison with a capacity of about 900 inmates. In the media, Belmarsh is frequently referred to as Britain's Guantánamo Bay. Not only because it houses quite a few terrorism suspects, but also because of the strict security regime. Assange was brought to Belmarsh on 11 April 2019, immediately after his arrest and conviction by the British authorities. At the time of our visit, that was barely a month ago.

We stepped out of the cab. I had already seen photographs of the place, but its dimensions remained imposing. It was a rectangular compound enclosed by high walls, which looked a bit like a medieval fortress. The prison reception was located behind the main portal built of clinker bricks. I reported to the receptionist presenting my official UN identification and the credentials provided by the Ministry of Justice. Everywhere in the world, whenever I conduct an official prison visit in my capacity as a UN special rapporteur, my team and I are immediately welcomed by the governor and their key staff. We are smoothly escorted through the security barriers, usually without any search, and we are not asked to hand over our documents, or cell phones, as we may need the latter to photographically register physical traces of torture and evidence of inadequate material conditions of detention. Also, in cases of emergency, we have to be able to communicate with the outside world. From the provincial prisons in the Ukraine to the gigantic Silivri complex in Turkey and the closed psychiatric ward in Argentina: with a few regrettable exceptions, prison managements tend to go out of their way to demonstrate their respect for the United Nations.

Not so in Belmarsh. The reception staff had obviously not received any particular instructions with a view to the appropriate handling of an official visit from the United Nations. After a remarkably unhurried verification of our papers, we were first sent back to the visitor centre, a few minutes' walk away, where we were asked to deposit our bags, computers, phones, keys and valuables in lockers. Once back at the reception desk, we were asked to move to the opposite corner of the entrance hall, where other visitors – presumably family members and lawyers – were already queuing to get through the first of several security gates. We got in line. My two doctors were growing visibly impatient, but I urged them to remain calm: 'Don't be provoked, my friends – I am sure there is more to come.'

Given the well-known British predilection for formal etiquette, diplomatic protocol and indirect messaging, this kind of lukewarm welcome clearly was not an accidental oversight on the part of the authorities. From the first moment, I was made to understand that, in the United Kingdom, special rapporteurs cannot expect special treatment. We were not treated as an institutional partner, but as a potential security risk. I took this for what it was: a form of communication, but also a demonstration of power. My visit was being tolerated, nothing more.

Not that this upset me. Particularly during my field deployments with the Red Cross, I had developed a thick skin playing the waiting game at barriers, fences, gates and checkpoints. So many times, and in so many places, I had been blocked for endless hours in dusty heat, pouring rain and freezing cold, waiting to finally get through to the other side, where our humanitarian action was needed. Whether I was facing indifferent soldiers, nervous rebels or frustrated border guards, never did I allow myself to react emotionally, for the goodwill of my interlocutors was fragile, short-lived and sometimes quite literally a question of life or death. Against this background, the unenthusiastic reception at Belmarsh could not deter me, but it certainly contributed to my rapidly declining perception of Britain as a reliable partner in the area of human rights. In the war zones of Kosovo and Afghanistan, my dialogue with British operational forces had always been constructive, efficient and marked by mutual respect. Here in London, the United Kingdom showed me a very different face – an attitude of demonstrative indifference, with a hint of royal condescension. The motivation for all of this was not personal, of course, but purely political. The interests pursued by governments are always political, and their priority is never the promotion of human rights. If and when human rights are put on the political agenda, it almost always serves ulterior motives such as enhancing national reputation, denigrating other states, obtaining financial aid packages, or justifying military interventions.

So, I was not disconcerted when the security check at Belmarsh dragged on. The security officers went about their business with painstaking meticulousness and did everything in their power to ensure that the UN special rapporteur and his medical team would not be smuggling drugs, weapons or other prohibited items into the prison. Together with the other visitors we inched forward. From the queue at reception, we squeezed into a densely packed first lock and then, a few eternal minutes later, through metal detectors into the inner area. Here, the actual security check took place. Removal of shoes, jackets and watches; then an individual parade, in our socks, through even more powerful metal detectors and, after a thorough inspection of the doctor's clinical thermometer, stethoscope and ballpoint pen, and a tick-off on our list of pre-authorized items, a second passage through the X-ray machine for us and all of our shoes. Only then were we admitted. The security officers themselves had no bad intentions, for sure, they had simply not been given any special instructions. As a result, they did their job with the usual thoroughness, and any protest or lack of cooperation on our part would have immediately triggered a forceful response. And, probably, would have meant the end of my visit. This is how 'soft harassment' works. We endured the procedure stoically – which seemed to be slightly more taxing for my Iberian colleagues than for my Swiss-Swedish temperament.

Behind the security check we were welcomed by a female officer, whose open and friendly demeanour made a pleasant contrast with the government's demonstrative indifference. She explained that she had been tasked with accompanying us throughout the visit and escorted us to Belmarsh's health care unit. This had been one of my requests. I did not want to meet Assange in the usual visitors' quarters. A conversation or a medical examination, with other prisoners and their relatives present, was out of the question. Moreover, such rooms are almost always covered by CCTV and offer no confidentiality whatsoever.

We passed through corridors and barred doors that were immediately locked behind us. The room we were finally assigned to was not very different from the examination room in an ordinary doctor's surgery. White walls, a desk with a computer and a few chairs, an examination couch, and a door with a window made of thick glass and covered with adjustable blinds. As a matter of routine, I quickly checked the room for visible cameras and microphones, including under the desk and chairs. I did not find anything, of course, but I was not reassured. I knew that modern surveillance technology had lately reached a level of sophistication that made its detection virtually impossible.

Above the door, a clock marked every second with an audible click. The minutes passed. We waited. A total of four hours had been agreed for our personal meetings with Assange, from 10:00 a.m. to 12:00 and from 2:00 to 4:00 p.m. But it was already well past 10:30 a.m. when the door finally opened and Assange was brought in. I immediately knew that this was the moment to put my foot down. As long as our exposure to 'soft harassment' did not interfere with the agreed purpose and modalities of my visit, the only reaction I would show was unshakeable patience. But the duration of our confidential meetings with Assange was non-negotiable. I formally protested with our liaison officer and insisted that the session would have to be extended to compensate for our waiting time. While my demand was being processed and, ultimately, approved through the institutional hierarchy, the clock kept ticking. Next, I had to insist that our liaison officer leave the room so that we could interview Assange in confidence.

Although interviews without witnesses had long been part of the standard modalities applicable to all detention visits carried out by UN experts worldwide, and despite express prior notification, this had not, it seemed, been contemplated, so that permission had once more to be obtained through the institutional hierarchy. As we waited, the clock kept ticking louder and louder. Finally, and for good measure, the special permission procedure had to be repeated a third time because, although authorized to leave the examination room, our liaison officer had been instructed to visually monitor our meeting with Assange through the window in the door. On this point, resistance got more tenacious, but I categorically insisted on medical confidentiality and finally achieved agreement that the blinds would remain closed for the entire duration of our meetings, and that our liaison officer could not enter the room without first knocking on the door. Then, at last, we were alone.

## First Impressions

When Assange entered, he immediately sought eye contact. He looked tense and nervous, as if he were unsure what to expect from his external visitors. But I soon realized that I didn't need to explain my function to him. He was well aware of the UN's human rights mechanisms – at least since the WGAD had concluded, in December 2015, that his continued confinement at the embassy amounted to a form of arbitrary deprivation of liberty.

Assange wore a blue sweatshirt, grey track pants and sneakers. Clean-shaven, his white hair neatly trimmed, he bore no resemblance to the man who had been dragged out of the Ecuadorian embassy a few weeks earlier. Then Assange had looked unkempt, pale and much older, with long, matted hair and a messy beard. The pictures had gone around the world. What the public had not been told, however, was that Assange's squalid appearance had been deliberately staged by the Ecuadorian authorities to make him look repulsive and bizarre in the media. According to Assange, three months before his arrest, his shaving kit had been taken away by the embassy's security personnel – one of countless small reprisals with which they obstructed his daily struggle for a dignified existence.

Seemingly a minor detail, it fit perfectly with the narrative assiduously spread by the Ecuadorian government about Assange being an ungrateful, self-indulgent parasite who skateboarded and played soccer inside the embassy, mistreated his cat, and smeared faeces on the walls. But the images and video clips released to the public told a different story. They mainly showed Assange's meetings with medical doctors, lawyers and other visitors, as well as completely innocuous scenes from his private life – all recorded in secret and published without his authorization. The few visitors Assange was still allowed to receive during his last year at the embassy also reported systematic surveillance, abusive restrictions and harassment, and even tampering with their cell phones and devices which had been deposited with security personnel. Assange's expulsion without any form of due process had been planned well in advance, and it was clear that the general public was more likely to accept this step without sympathy or protest if during his arrest Assange looked as filthy and dehumanized as he had been portrayed in the media.

I intended to use the first hour for my bilateral conversation with Assange, and then hand over to Professor Vieira for the forensic examination. As always in my interviews with individual prisoners, the purpose of the first few minutes was to build trust and ask standard questions about well-being, conditions of detention, contacts with family and lawyers, and any other primary concerns. This normally allows me to quickly get a reliable overview of the situation and its potential challenges. Depending on the complexity of an individual case, working through a list of basic questions usually takes around ten to twenty minutes. It takes incomparably longer, however, when the prisoner tries to take the lead himself and asks completely different questions. Assange pulled a piece of paper out of his pocket on which he had scribbled several names. Suddenly I was being interviewed. Had I been in contact with this lawyer yet? Had I met that UN official? Every time I tried to steer the conversation back on course, Assange's mind was already elsewhere, and he asked the next question. It seemed as if he couldn't really process what I was saying. Again he interrupted, this time to engage me in a weighty discussion about what he saw as the waning influence of human rights mechanisms. His statements were clear and convincing, but at the same time seemed erratic and almost rushed. As soon as he had expressed a thought, he instantly opened a new drawer in his mind, as it were, and pulled out another topic.

I have been visiting prisoners for twenty years in a wide variety of contexts. Prisons are a difficult environment for open conversations, and many inmates are intimidated, distrustful, and traumatized. Over time, I've learned to also pay attention to non-verbal signals: body language, mood shifts, everything that is perceptible without being explicitly articulated. When talking to Julian Assange, I was immediately reminded of conversations with other political prisoners who had been isolated for a long time. All of them had thought about their own situation for many, many hours – often too many. But because of their isolation they were unable to process and express more than a fraction of their thoughts and emotions with other people. As a result, they lived in an increasingly self-contained, overstimulated inner world with thoughts and emotions slowly spinning out of control. It is a well-known phenomenon of prolonged solitary confinement. At some point, this leads to a permanent state of stress and apprehension. The accumulated tension can no longer be relieved, and a vicious cycle of insomnia, anxiety and depression begins, often to the point of total exhaustion and with potentially severe neurological and cardiovascular consequences. The corrosive effect of isolation can also be seen in a prisoner's posture, facial expressions and gestures. They appear fragile, overwhelmed and rushed. Their ability to absorb and process information is diminished. They seem to have lost their grip internally because they have been deliberately deprived of all certainties. The psychological destabilization caused by isolation and arbitrariness is routinely employed by torturers in order to break the victim's resistance.

My impression of Assange was that of a highly intelligent, mentally extremely resilient man who was desperately trying to retain some measure of control over his own fate, even though it was obvious that he was no longer in charge. This, too, is a typical reaction of people exposed to a hostile and arbitrary environment for a prolonged period. In reality, they are completely defenceless, and they know it. Nevertheless, somehow, they still cling to the idea of having that last ace up their sleeve which would turn the tide in their favour. But during my conversation with Assange, I also perceived a trait of his that had been mentioned by many others before, in more or less flattering terms depending on their perspective. While some had praised him for his extreme ability to concentrate, others had complained of his indifference towards the legitimate concerns of others. My own impression is that this divergence of views reflects two slightly distorted sides of the same coin. Although I had explained the purpose of our interview to Assange, it was difficult to keep the conversation on track, and I repeatedly had to perform rhetorical U-turns to make sure I obtained the information I needed.

However, I did not experience Assange as self-indulgent or arrogant at all. He was simply too focused on his own thoughts to pay attention to what I had in mind unless and until I clearly verbalized it – a symptom congruent with his medical diagnosis of Asperger's, a mild form of autism. Had Assange been a ruthless narcissist, as some insist, he would hardly have been prepared to endure so much personal humiliation, isolation and suffering for the sake of truth and justice for others. Had his quest been his own self-aggrandizement, then his continued confrontation with the world's most powerful governments certainly had not produced the desired results. Assange was too intelligent not to understand the risks to his own reputation and well-being when he decided to expose the dirty secrets of the most powerful. He knew the price for his actions, and he decided to pay it – not for personal benefit, but because he believed it needed to be done.

The two doctors had followed our conversation from the background, so they could get a first impression and avoid repeating the same basic questions during their examination. After one hour, I thanked Assange, explained the rest of my visit and handed over to Professor Vieira for the first part of the medical examination. Together with Dr Pérez-Sales, I went to the chief nurse's office to have a copy of Assange's medical records printed out, with Assange's consent, and to get the prison doctors' opinion on various aspects of his health. However, not a single prison doctor was said to be present all day. In a high-security prison with almost 1,000 inmates. At the time of an officially announced visit by a UN expert and his medical team. This no longer seemed like a mere coincidence; more like another variation of 'soft harassment'.

After some unexpected technical difficulties with the printer, which we met with our default attitude of unshakeable patience, we at least received a copy of Assange's medical records – another non-negotiable element of my visit. According to these, the prison doctors had already taken the most urgent dental and other measures to treat the most pressing physical ailments that had arisen during Assange's asylum at the Ecuadorian embassy. Nevertheless, he was not in good health. As our physical examination showed, he had lost weight since his arrest and the constant anxiety and stress of the past months and years had caused neurological and cognitive impairments that were already objectively measurable.

In the run-up to my visit, I had announced that I would be available to respond to questions from the press during the lunch break. But when I arrived at the designated meeting place in front of the prison, only one journalist was waiting. He worked for Ruptly, a news agency affiliated with Russia's state-run RT television network. I delivered a short statement into his video camera, thanking the British Ministry of Justice for its cooperation and explaining the procedure and purpose of my stay in London. It would include not only today's prison visit to Assange, but also a meeting the following day with representatives of the British authorities and other interlocutors. As expressly agreed with the British government, I announced that the results of my investigation would first be transmitted to the British authorities and then also shared with the public.

Given the prominence of the Assange case and the public announcement of my visit, I had expected strong interest from the British mainstream media, including the BBC, Sky News, the *Guardian* and the *Times*. Instead, there was only a lone reporter from Ruptly.

I was more surprised than disappointed. On the one hand, the low turnout was not inconvenient, as I was keen to avoid burdening my investigation and mediation efforts with sensational headlines. On the other hand, I had certainly not expected total radio silence from the mainstream media. I later learned that, on the same day, the Swedish Prosecution Authority had publicly announced that in four days' time it would publicly announce whether the criminal investigation against Assange for rape, that had been closed two years earlier, was to be reopened. An announcement of an announcement, so to speak. Was its temporal concurrence with my visit to Assange a coincidence, or a well-planned device to tie up media attention? Or were there perhaps entirely different reasons for the lack of media interest in my visit? I was still far from understanding the true dimensions of this case. For the moment, I was just relieved that public attention to my investigation of this highly politicized case had been postponed.

A few minutes' walk from Belmarsh, on Battery Road, we found a Domino's Pizza. We placed our orders and sat down on the only two benches that could fit in the small storefront. Outside, people went about their business under a grey drizzly sky, for most of them no doubt just an ordinary day of British spring weather. It felt strange to be waiting for food, Coke in hand, discussing impressions and next steps in whispered innuendos. There were only a few hundred yards between Belmarsh and Domino's, and yet the prison walls separated two fundamentally different worlds.

## 'Please, save my life!'

In the afternoon, we returned to the prison reception early, well aware that we would have to go through the entire security procedure all over again. While Dr Pérez-Sales conducted the psychiatric examination, Professor Vieira and I, with Assange's consent, visited his cell and other relevant parts of the prison. The same officer who had been assigned to us in the morning led us through the corridors and willingly answered all our questions. At no point did we experience or observe any cynicism or hostility on the part of the prison staff, whether towards us or towards Assange or the other inmates. They had the challenging task of managing the security and daily routine of nearly 1,000 inmates and, as far as we could tell, they were all doing their jobs with a calm, friendly and professional attitude. As I knew too well, this could not be taken for granted. In many places around the world, prison staff had made no secret of what they thought of us visiting the 'enemy', the 'traitors', the 'terrorists', or whatever unflattering term they had reserved for the people in their custody, and the relationship between guards and inmates was often marked by a palpable atmosphere of fear and violence. Not so here. Assange may have been considered a public enemy by the governments of many countries, but not by the guards in Belmarsh. If anything, I had the impression that the prison staff were anxious to protect him from the 'bad influence' of other prisoners, some of whom had committed very serious crimes. As a non-violent political prisoner, Assange should never have been brought to Belmarsh.

We visited the library, the gym, the shower rooms, and the courtyard for outdoor walks. Like in most high-security prisons, the individual cell wings at Belmarsh each spread over two floors, but were strictly separated from the other wings, so as to facilitate de-escalation and restoration of control in the event of a riot. For individual inmates, the daily routine depends largely on their assigned security regime. In the United Kingdom, the spectrum ranges from Category A (maximum security) to Category D (open prison). At the time of our visit, Assange was assigned to Category B (high security). We learned about the daily routine there from the guards on duty and were able to cross-check the information with other sources: The inmates on Assange's wing worked for three to four hours per day, one group in the morning and the other group in the afternoon. In the other half of the day, the cell doors were left open for three to four hours of socialization time, during which inmates could move freely around the corridors of their wing but were not allowed to enter other cells. Yard time depended on the weather, but was usually forty-five to sixty minutes per day. Cell doors remained closed for the rest of the day and during the night. All meals were taken inside the cells, mostly single cells and a few double cells.

Assange's single cell was number 37 in Wing II. When the heavy steel door was opened, I immediately saw that the cell had been designed and equipped in conformity with the United Nations Standard Minimum Rules for the Treatment of Prisoners, or the 'Nelson Mandela Rules', as they have been called since their revision in 2015. Nothing fancy, of course: about six square metres of floor space, well over two metres high, and a reasonably sized window. A plastic chair, a sink, a toilet, a closet, a simple bed and bedding. From the smell and the look, it was clear that the cell had just been freshly painted, possibly in anticipation of my visit, with water-resistant 'laundry room' eggshell. There is a short video clip circulating on the internet, which must have been secretly recorded a few days before my visit, and which shows Assange and another inmate preparing his cell for the paint job. On the lino floor, under the bed, and on every conceivable shelf lay books, handwritten notes, and countless letters from supporters around the world that evidently had been delivered to Assange by the prison authorities. Well, I thought, given that the internal mail distribution system seemed to work quite efficiently, there really was no excuse for Assange not receiving his legal correspondence and case documents, as he had complained.

Our liaison officer explained that Assange had not yet been integrated into the usual prison routine. One month after his arrest, he was still in the induction phase, which served to gradually integrate inmates into the system. Initially, detainees typically spent about twenty-two hours alone in their cells, interrupted only by meals, showers, and yard time, as well as any visits, medical appointments, or court hearings. Daily time for work and social interaction with other inmates, as well as access to the library and gym, would be added only later. In the case of Assange, she said, the prison management had to be particularly careful because Sweden had publicly portrayed him as a rape suspect for years. This image had become deeply entrenched in the minds of the prisoners, including a number of violent criminals whose behaviour was difficult to predict.

During the preparation for my visit, I had formally requested that a meeting with the prison governor be scheduled for the end of the day. It emerged, however, that he had 'exceptionally' gone home already at 4 p.m. that day, and so I ended up with his deputy. Yet another opportunity for the government to officially demonstrate how little importance it attached to my visit although, paradoxically, quite the opposite was really the case. In Britain, only a government feeling extremely uncomfortable about its role in this case would go out of its way to disregard just about every convention of diplomatic protocol and mutual respect, simply to downplay the political weight of my official visit. The deputy director himself, of course, behaved impeccably, provided me with all requested information and duly took note of my concerns. I cautioned that after a full month, it was time to end the restrictions of the induction period and to allow Assange access to the library, gym, and daily work. Most importantly, I made it clear that Assange urgently needed access to an independent psychiatrist he could trust, and that under the current security regime he was unable to adequately prepare for the upcoming court hearings. Unlike the vast majority of other inmates, he was simultaneously involved in complex legal proceedings in multiple jurisdictions. To prepare his defence, Assange clearly needed to be able to review and write documents on a computer, even without internet access, and to hold regular and intensive exchanges with his legal teams in the respective countries. Under the current detention regime in Belmarsh, this requirement simply could not be guaranteed in a manner consistent with human rights law. The deputy director took note, but then explained that it was the judge who had ordered Assange's detention in Belmarsh and that the prison administration could not influence this decision in any way. The judge, of course, would subsequently argue that the responsibility for Assange's well-being falls on the prison administration alone, and that the judiciary has no authority whatsoever to interfere with its decisions. Bureaucratic evasion of responsibility, if applied by the executive and the judiciary in mutual buck-passing, can be an effective method of undermining the rule of law.

Thus this important day came to an end. Not many words were exchanged in our black cab back to central London. I sat in the back of the car and stared through the raindrops on the right rear window into the void. In my mind, I kept replaying the moment of saying goodbye to Assange at the end of the afternoon. We had shaken hands, I wished him well and was about to leave, with the doctors already at the door. Then suddenly Assange's grip on my hand tightened and he held me back. What he wanted to say was visibly difficult for him. 'I hate to say this,' he began. Then he hesitated for an eternal instant until the words finally spilled out: 'Please, save my life!' During our conversation, he had made it absolutely clear that he would not be extradited to the United States alive. In view of what awaited him there, this was a rational decision, he had said. During a cell search two days before our visit, prison staff had confiscated a razor blade hidden by Assange just in case. I knew he was serious, and he knew, of course, that his fate was not in my hands. As so often at the end of intense visits, I did the only humanely possible thing I could do in this situation – I gave him a silent hug, from one person to another. Then I heard myself reply, as if from afar: 'I'll do my best!'

## Officials, Lawyers and Witnesses

In the afternoon of the following day, I met with the British authorities. Professor Vieira was due to testify in court elsewhere and had already left London, but Dr Pérez-Sales accompanied me to the headquarters of the Home Office in Marsham Street. During official visits by UN special rapporteurs, opening meetings with the authorities of the host state normally take place at the ministerial level, while the discussion of technical issues is subsequently delegated to the 'working level' – the people actually running the administration.

Not so in London, at least not in the Assange case. From the outset, I was confronted with administrative officials who could brief me on the applicable domestic normative, institutional and procedural framework, but – even with the best of intentions – were not in a position to discuss the political decisions that would have been necessary to resolve the Assange case. Again, I was being signalled that the British government tolerated my investigation as a matter of window-dressing but was not willing to seriously question its own approach.

With a minister, I could have addressed completely different questions. Home Secretary Sajid Javid, for instance, would personally sign off on the US extradition request for Assange only a few weeks later, and Foreign Secretary Jeremy Hunt was responsible for British relations with the United States, Ecuador, and Sweden, but also with the United Nations. With them, I could have discussed the political and human rights implications of the Assange case and explored face-saving compromise solutions that would have been acceptable to all parties. But that was obviously not what the British government had in mind. Instead, they preferred to keep our dialogue locked into a mirror maze of bureaucratic technicalities – a proven diplomatic tactic for feigning a solutions-oriented attitude while preventing any meaningful progress. So, I ended up having a technical discussion with administrative officials from the Home Office and the Ministry of Justice on how best to ensure the most expedient transition for Assange to an acceptable prison routine that would allow him regular social contact and, most importantly, adequate access to his lawyers and case documents. I also emphasized that, based on our medical examinations, I was seriously concerned about Assange's health and was of the opinion that he urgently needed access to an independent psychiatrist he could trust.

But my primary concern was the American extradition request. For almost a decade, the US Department of Justice had been preparing its case against Assange behind closed doors. Since 2010, there had been reports about secret hearings of a 'Grand Jury', a longstanding US judicial procedure extremely vulnerable to prosecutorial manipulation, in which a group of laypersons decides on whether to bring charges against an individual – without judicial guidance, based solely on evidence provided by the prosecutor, and under complete exclusion of both the public and the suspect himself. With more than 95 per cent of prosecutions in the US never being tried in court but 'resolved' through plea bargaining, the Grand Jury's original purpose of protecting the public from governmental overreach has unfortunately been increasingly corrupted, transforming this once honourable institution into a convenient tool for shielding abuse of executive and prosecutorial power from judicial or public oversight.

In the case of Assange, the Grand Jury finally issued its first indictment on 6 March 2018, but it was kept secret – 'sealed' –

until his arrest on 11 April 2019. Already the optics of that indictment were not credible. How likely was it, really, that the US Department of Justice would investigate against Assange for nine long years, only to come up with a single charge of 'conspiracy to commit computer intrusion' – an offence for which the maximum sentence was a paltry five years? A maximum sentence, moreover, which could only be applied in particularly serious cases, and would have to be significantly reduced in the case of Assange, as he was accused of a mere unsuccessful attempt causing no damage whatsoever. To any objective observer it was obvious that the US authorities had not investigated and surveilled Assange for almost a decade, and certainly would not conduct a full-blown extradition trial in the United Kingdom, simply to convict him of a petty offence punishable with a prison sentence of a few weeks at best.

A much more convincing explanation for this stunted indictment was that the US wanted to avoid officially charging Assange with espionage, at least for the time being. Espionage being the classic example of a political offence, any such charge would have blocked Assange's extradition under Article 4 of the Anglo-American extradition treaty of 2003, which expressly prohibits extraditions for political offences. The computer intrusion charge was sufficient to satisfy the requirement of 'dual criminality', according to which no person can be extradited unless the alleged offence constitutes a crime in both countries. Furthermore, by restricting the charges to computer crimes, the US aimed to avoid a discussion about the implications of Assange's indictment for press freedom. The official narrative being pushed here was that attempting to decode the password hash of a government computer, even if unsuccessful, was not a journalistic activity protected by the US Constitution, thus deflecting public attention from the dirty state secrets exposed by WikiLeaks. These were, of course, the real reason for Assange's aggressive persecution.

There was one provision of the extradition treaty which I was particularly concerned about. According to the so-called 'specialty principle', the United States would only be able to prosecute Assange for offences for which his extradition had been requested and granted. On the face of it, this principle appeared to suggest that, once extradited, Assange could only be prosecuted for that single charge of 'computer intrusion', as set out in the indictment underlying the US-extradition request. But, as virtually always in law, there is a loophole. Thus, Article 18 provides that the extradited person may also be detained, tried or punished for 'a differently denominated offence', so long as it is based on the same facts as the offence on which extradition was granted. As I pointed out to my British interlocutors, the practical relevance of this provision could hardly be overstated. On this basis, even after Assange's extradition from the United Kingdom, the United States could freely add new and different charges to its indictment against him, so long as they were supported by the facts described in the extradition request. This also explained why the description of facts in the extradition request was unusually broad and clearly exceeded what was required for a single count of computer intrusion. Of course, the addition of new charges would also open the door to more severe sanctions, possibly even the death penalty or a life sentence without parole. Neither would be compatible with British human rights obligations.

My interlocutors were visibly taken aback. They had not expected me to ask for their assessment of the human rights risks arising from the fine print of the Anglo-American extradition treaty. In a moment of carelessness, the official in charge of extradition policy exchanged a meaningful glance with his colleague responsible for international legal assistance. Then he cleared his throat and responded, his eyes firmly locked on the documents in front of him: 'Well, yes ... I suppose that is something we will have to look at if and when such a situation should arise.' Sensing that I was going to insist on the point, his colleague quickly intervened: 'I think we should now let the British judiciary do their work!' Her decisive tone and facial expression made clear that this was the – non-negotiable – British proposal for a shared public position and that this was the end of our conversation.

In the morning of that same day, I had visited the offices of Doughty Street Chambers, a renowned law firm specializing in human rights, to meet with some of Assange's lawyers, leading representatives of WikiLeaks, and a whole range of other witnesses. Among them was Stella Moris, who was introduced to me as a member of Assange's legal team. At the time, the world was still unaware that she and Assange were secretly engaged and had even become parents, twice, during his stay at the embassy. I also met with Fidel Narváez, the former consul-general of the Ecuadorian embassy in London, and Guillaume Long, who had been Ecuador's foreign minister until the election of President Lenín Moreno in 2017.

My two doctors had not yet finalized their medical report, and I knew that I would need time to triangulate and incorporate their findings with the evidence obtained from these witnesses, from the authorities, and from other sources into consolidated conclusions that I felt comfortable presenting both to the government and to the public. Nevertheless, we had of course already exchanged views and formed a preliminary opinion, which allowed us to compile a list of open questions to be further investigated. We all agreed that the physical and psychological symptoms shown by Assange constituted a normal response to prolonged isolation, stress, and anxiety. These symptoms included, most notably, early manifestations of neurological and cognitive impairment; restlessness and volatility; desperate attempts to suppress feelings of powerlessness; severe depression; and, underlying the rest, a permanent fear of being extradited to the United States and exposed to lifelong dehumanization in a Supermax prison. Assange suffered from severe post-traumatic stress disorder (PTSD), and the continuation and escalation of his cumulative stressors would very likely trigger a rapid deterioration of his health, and, in the worst case, a nervous breakdown, cardiac arrest, or even suicide. Without any doubt, Assange needed access to a trusted psychiatrist who was independent from the authorities. Ultimately, however, my task as the special rapporteur on torture was not to provide the authorities with a medical diagnosis, but to determine whether the diagnosed medical symptoms had been caused by torture or other cruel, inhuman, or degrading treatment, or whether other causes remained conceivable, such as pre-existing medical conditions or traumatic experiences not amounting to human rights violations.

## Psychological Torture

My conclusion that Assange has been exposed to psychological torture has been repeatedly criticized, albeit not yet by anyone possessing the expertise and experience required to do so with a certain level of credibility. As far as I am aware, of all these critics, not one has personally examined Assange; none has any practical experience in identifying and documenting the traces of torture, or juridical expertise regarding contemporary forms of torture; and next to no one has bothered to actually read the official UN documents detailing my findings. Nevertheless, all kinds of self-appointed experts – from journalists to politicians and from functionaries to seasoned law professors – feel called upon to publicly attack my official conclusions as 'absurd', 'nonsense', and 'wrong', or as a 'trivialization' of the concept of torture. In the absence of the necessary professional competence, trumpeting such harsh criticism appears to be rather bold and, in many cases, outright embarrassing. While it says very little about the objectivity of my findings, it speaks volumes to the largely unconscious emotional strongholds of the predominant mindset against Assange.

I say this without assigning blame or ridicule. After all, in December 2018, I had reacted just as hastily and judgmentally to Assange's first request for intervention. I had been deceived by the same relentless and perfidious smear campaign against him, which is still ongoing today and aims to deflect public attention away from what this case is really about. At the time, I would have fiercely rejected any suggestion that I had been deceived. But that is of course the whole point of deception – for once the deceived become aware of their deception, they are no longer deceived. So, in fact, my own cavalier attitude towards Assange was living proof that the deception was working. Even I, in my role as the officially appointed UN expert on the prohibition of torture, somehow 'knew' immediately that his case did not involve any real form of ill-treatment – at least as long as I managed to avoid looking at the facts. In order to bring some objectivity back into this discussion, we shall therefore take a quick look at the basic legal reasoning underlying my finding of psychological torture. The related factual evidence will only be summarized here, as it will be discussed at length in the following chapters.

The term 'torture' as defined in the UN Convention against Torture essentially refers to the intentional infliction of severe physical or mental pain or suffering in order to achieve a specific purpose. It is most commonly associated with the extraction or suppression of testimony or confessions, but can also involve other forms of coercion, intimidation, punishment or discrimination. Ultimately, torture always intends to break the will of the targeted person and to subjugate them to the will of the torturer. Importantly, the targeted persons – whose will the torturer intends to break – need not be only the immediate victims themselves, but can also be their husbands, wives, parents or children, their friends or associates, or even the general public. Also, torture is always directed against powerless individuals, who in the circumstances cannot do anything to resist or escape the infliction of pain or suffering.

The alternative term 'other cruel, inhuman or degrading treatment or punishment' – 'ill-treatment' for short – is used when the infliction of pain or suffering does not pursue a lawful purpose, or is unnecessary or disproportionate for the achievement of such a purpose, but lacks at least one of the characteristics of torture, namely intentionality, purposefulness, the intensity of the resulting suffering or the powerlessness of the victim. Examples of ill-treatment would include the negligent exposure of prisoners to inhumane conditions of detention without purposefully exploiting the resulting suffering; the disproportionate use of tear gas or physical violence against peaceful protesters;

and humiliating, intimidating, or discriminatory statements or acts that cannot be justified but, in the circumstances, do not cause pain or suffering of sufficient intensity to achieve the purposes of torture.

From the perspective of international law, both torture and ill-treatment are subject to a universal, absolute prohibition and cannot therefore be justified under any circumstances. For torture, moreover, there is a worldwide treaty obligation to criminalize and prosecute, which reflects the special stigma attached to the cold-blooded instrumentalization of pain and suffering.

As I have pointed out in a dedicated report to the Human Rights Council in March 2020 (A/HRC/43/49), psychological torture differs from physical torture not in its purposes but in its methods. Whereas physical torture seeks to achieve its ends primarily through physical pain, psychological torture does so through the direct infliction of mental suffering; that is, without using the conduit of the physical body. In both cases, however, the ultimate goal is not the body, but the mind and emotions of the victim or the intimidated third party, which are to be broken and subjected to the torturer. In the long run, psychological torture causes not only mental pain or suffering, but also measurable physical harm, primarily through relentless over-stimulation and destabilization of the victim's psycho-emotional balance. Strictly speaking, there really is no such thing as purely physical or purely psychological torture, and in most cases both forms of abuse are quite deliberately combined. Nevertheless, this distinction is useful in practice because physical and psychological torture methods cause different primary symptoms, the identification and documentation of which in turn requires different forensic examination methods.

In most cases, psychological torture focuses on the coordinated interaction of four elements: intimidation, isolation, arbitrariness, and humiliation. First, the torture victim's need for security and protection is undermined by creating and sustaining a constant threat scenario, generating a profound sense of fear and intimidation. Second, the resulting anxiety is intensified by isolating the victim from their normal environment

74

and social world and making them totally dependent on their torturers, even for the simplest and most intimate aspects of their daily life. Third, in order to further destabilize the victim, normal rules of social interaction are replaced by a deliberately arbitrary and confusing regime of 'do's' and 'don'ts'. Decisions are no longer made on the basis of clear and coherent criteria, but become increasingly erratic and unpredictable, exposing the victim to a growing sense of insecurity and helplessness. Finally, the torture victim's sense of dignity and self-esteem is eroded through humiliation, shaming, and defamation. In the case of political dissidents especially, this also aims to destroy the victim's public reputation and credibility, to make their persecution appear justified, and to render their return to their community difficult, if not impossible.

There could be no doubt that, during our visit to Belmarsh, Assange exhibited the medical symptoms typical of prolonged exposure to psychological torture. Several other medical doctors had earlier come to the same conclusion, when Assange was still confined at the Ecuadorian embassy. Given that a pre-existing mental condition could be ruled out as the cause of these symptoms, they had to be the result of external factors having impacted him over an extended period of time. In Assange's case, these factors could be identified with a high degree of certainty and, cumulatively, created dynamics that can only be described as a concerted and sustained campaign of public mobbing.

As will be shown, Assange was deliberately demonized, humiliated and socially isolated shortly after the groundbreaking publication of the Afghan War Diary by WikiLeaks in July 2010. This was achieved primarily through the aggressive use by Swedish authorities of the mass media to disseminate rape allegations against Assange, in conjunction with extreme prosecutorial procrastination purposely perpetuating and instrumentalizing these allegations for almost a decade without any prospect of judicial resolution. Assange's resulting vilification made it easy to pile on additional slander defaming him as a ruthless hacker, spy, and narcissist with blood on his hands. Meanwhile, in the background, the US government used their shadowy Grand Jury system to build up the threat scenario of a political trial followed by Assange's burial alive in US solitary confinement – alarming enough for Assange to feel constantly threatened, yet secretive enough for his fears to be widely ridiculed as paranoia. In the following weeks and months, Assange gradually went from being hailed as a hero of press freedom to being despised as a tragicomic outcast, whose human rights and dignity no longer appeared to be a factor to be considered. Accordingly, his legitimate interests could now be openly trampled on without risking a public outcry or any form of accountability. With a predictability reminiscent of the witch trials of the seventeenth century, each official act or omission on the part of the public authorities made unmistakably clear that Assange could not rely on due process and would not be treated in accordance with the law in any of the involved jurisdictions. Thus, the basic elements of psychological torture were already in place: intimidation, isolation, arbitrariness and humiliation. But Assange was not yet completely defenceless. He still had an – albeit dwindling – circle of friends and supporters, he could still pursue his work and, crucially, at a time when all other doors had already closed against him, he still enjoyed the diplomatic protection of Ecuador – the one country that dared to step out of line.

Nonetheless, Assange's situation became much more precarious when he fled to the Ecuadorian embassy in June 2012. Although he was temporarily protected from extradition to the United States, his freedom of movement was now limited to a few square metres. Then, five years later, the change of government in Ecuador abruptly turned Assange's last refuge into an inescapable trap. The embassy turned into a hostile environment marked by overregulation, increasing isolation and constant surveillance. Visits from friends and supporters were made increasingly difficult, and his ability to communicate with the outside world was progressively restricted, culminating in the complete suppression of his internet access and phone communications shortly after the secret US indictment in March 2018. As will be shown, Assange's isolation was deliberate, purposeful, and coordinated. His world became more and more confined until he was left with virtually no protected space and was rendered completely powerless against his continued mistreatment. Most importantly, however, with the change of government in Quito, the threat scenario of a potential extradition to the US had suddenly become very real again. This greatly increased the psychological pressure on Assange and generated a constant state of extreme anxiety and stress.

As if that were not enough, the public humiliation of Assange also intensified during that last phase at the embassy. From the dawn of history to contemporary 'cancel culture', public mobbing has been very effective at destroying people's reputation, depriving them of their human dignity and excluding them from the group, often permanently. However, the methods have changed. Today, tarring and feathering has become superfluous; the exclusion and demonization is done by tweet, blog entry or scandalous headlines on the front pages. Over the years, Assange has been subjected to an unprecedented campaign of vilification, intimidation, humiliation and, ultimately, dehumanization. This has involved not only journalists, but also current and former politicians, and even officials directly occupied with processing and adjudicating his case. The spectrum of such statements ranges from ridicule and defamation all the way to open threats and calls for his murder.

For example, on 16 August 2012, the day Ecuador formally approved Assange's asylum request, BBC reporter Thom Phipps recommended via Twitter that the Metropolitan Police 'drag Assange out the embassy and shoot him in the back of the head in the middle of Trafalgar Square'. And Hillary Clinton, then US secretary of state, reportedly asked during a team meeting, 'Can't we just drone this guy?' Significantly, when asked about the reported incident at a subsequent press conference, Clinton did not deny the alleged statement with the appropriate clarity, but merely claimed that she did not recall making such a 'joke'. The casual attitude with which such disgraceful statements were shrugged off was not uncommon at the time. We shall return to this in more detail later. In any case, no government or media organization seemed to find it necessary to intervene and stop such incendiary pronouncements. Assange had become an outlaw.

It should come as no surprise that Assange's prolonged exposure to such levels of intimidation, isolation, arbitrariness and humiliation has caused him to experience a progressively intensifying state of mental and emotional distress, anxiety and depression, which ended up exceeding the threshold of 'severe pain or suffering' associated with torture. For it to amount to psychological torture, such suffering must furthermore be inflicted intentionally and purposefully. While it is clear that isolated procedural mistakes or questionable judicial decisions generally cannot be equated with torture or ill-treatment, the following chapters will make just as clear that the gross arbitrariness and denial of justice experienced by Assange in all involved jurisdictions far exceed the imperfections which may occasionally arise in any due process proceeding. When a person's fundamental rights are being systematically violated at every stage of every proceeding in every jurisdiction, and when such arbitrariness fails to trigger any effective corrective action for more than a decade, then the presumption of good faith on the part of the authorities simply cannot be upheld. In democracies governed by the rule of law, denial of justice on this scale cannot happen by accident or negligence, but only with intent. In international law, intent on the part of state officials exists regardless of criminal culpability, whenever it is reasonably foreseeable that their acts or omissions will, in fact, contribute to a human rights violation.

In terms of purpose, the public mistreatment of Assange is not about forcing a confession or otherwise coercing him to cooperate, but primarily serves to intimidate and deter other publishers, journalists, and whistleblowers who might be tempted to follow his example. In the absence of any evidence for a prosecutable crime, Assange's persecution also aims to punish him arbitrarily – through intimidation, isolation, humiliation and endless proceedings – for having publicized the dirty secrets of the powerful. The public mobbing of defenceless individuals is one of the most primitive forms of social communication. Deeply rooted in the human subconscious since the dawn of history, it is a demonstration of power that requires no explanation and generally triggers instinctive behavioural patterns of self-protection, conformity and complicity. From the popular condemnation of Jesus Christ to the European witch trials of the seventeenth century and the political show trials of all dictatorships and sham democracies in human history, state-sanctioned mobbing has been one of the most effective methods of controlling public opinion and silencing inconvenient dissent.

When I informed Assange's legal team that, in my official statements, I would be likely to speak not only of cruel, inhuman, and degrading treatment, but even of psychological torture, they were initially surprised. Not that they disagreed with my assessment, but they had not expected me to be willing to expose myself with such an unpopular view, in light of the overwhelming hostility of public opinion. They also seemed to be worried about my reputation and reminded me that, so far, no one in a position of influence who dared to speak up for Assange had escaped unharmed. Of course, they looked at the matter primarily from the perspective of their client's interests. If I were to be 'shot down', Assange would lose an important advocate in his fight against extradition to the United States. Thus, they suggested that it might be preferable not to speak of 'torture' but only of 'cruel, inhuman and degrading treatment'. Based on years of frustrating experience, they feared that allegations of torture would not be taken seriously and that a terminological compromise solution might be more promising than calling things by their name. It was then that I realized how fighting an uphill battle for years had worn down not only Assange, but even his lawyers. Systematic arbitrariness, rejection and 'soft harassment' on the part of the authorities, added to constant hostility on the part of the public, the press and even personal friends and acquaintances, had all contributed to what could be described as 'vicarious trauma'.

But I was under no illusions that, after ten years of arbitrariness and persecution, the involved governments would be so swayed by terminological nuances as to suddenly comply with their human rights obligations towards Assange. If I was to retain my integrity and credibility, my reasoning had to be objective, coherent and convincing. Therefore, should my investigation lead to the conclusion that Assange had been exposed to psychological torture, then it was my duty to say so.

## Reopening of the Swedish Investigation

Three days after my visit to London, on 13 May 2019, the Swedish Prosecution Authority announced the reopening of their preliminary investigation against Assange – for the third time since 2010. The official narrative had remained the same: Assange was suspected of rape. In all those years, however, the Swedish authorities had never been able to produce sufficient evidence to formally charge him of any criminal offence. Now, it seemed the prosecutor wanted to make a third attempt to finally get beyond the initial stage of a 'preliminary investigation'. It had become somewhat of a race against time because, under Swedish law, the rape allegation would become time-barred in August 2020 – fifteen months later. A second allegation, regarding the sexual harassment of another woman, had already quietly expired in August 2015, also without sufficient evidence for a formal indictment.

At a press conference, the prosecutor explained her decision saying that Assange's expulsion from the embassy had brought him once more within the reach of the Swedish authorities, and that his renewed interrogation was indispensable for a formal indictment for the alleged rape. Therefore, a new European Arrest Warrant would be requested for Assange, aiming to ensure his extradition to Sweden as soon as possible after completing his current prison sentence for bail violation in London.

During my conversation with Assange, I had hardly spoken about the Swedish investigation, as my focus had been on his current conditions of detention and the risks associated with his potential extradition to the United States. It was only the reopening of the preliminary investigation on 13 May that prompted me to look into the Swedish dimension of the case in more detail. My main concern was that the 'rape suspect' narrative could be used to facilitate his transfer to the United States via Sweden without the benefit of fair proceedings meeting the standards of due process. This scenario was by no means exaggerated. Already the ease with which the Swedish judiciary had upheld the previous arrest warrant against Assange did not bode well for a fair trial. For more than six years, the courts had consistently confirmed that Assange was suspected on 'probable cause' of rape, despite an obvious lack of prosecutable evidence as well as persistent procrastination and obstruction of the part of the prosecution. In conjunction with the customary secrecy with which criminal proceedings for sexual offences are conducted in Sweden, there really was no objectively verifiable safeguard against an arbitrary conviction based on flimsy evidence provided by a biased prosecutor behind closed doors.

In a next step, Assange would be sent to the United States, most likely through the mechanism of 'temporary surrender', a loophole in the US-Swedish extradition treaty permitting the United States to 'borrow' a suspect from Sweden for the purposes of criminal prosecution without full extradition proceedings. While such surrender must remain 'temporary', its duration is to be agreed by the two governments on a case-by-case basis – enough room for a tailor-made arrangement ensuring Assange's permanent disappearance into the black hole of a US Supermax prison. The British, of course, would hasten to give their consent, never mind human rights and due process. For a convicted rapist, there would be no public outcry. Not in Britain, and certainly not in Sweden. Even influential human rights organizations would be wary of finding themselves on the wrong side of political correctness, especially in the eyes of their funders. It is not a coincidence, for example, that Amnesty International could not bring itself to recognize Assange as a 'prisoner of conscience' for more than a decade, in spite of the facts that he clearly fits the criteria for such designation, is persecuted for large-scale exposure of war crimes, torture and corruption, has previously received the Amnesty International Media Award, and risks spending the rest of his life in conditions of detention that can only be described as cruel, inhuman and degrading.

Assange was intelligent and realistic enough to know what awaited him in Sweden. He certainly did not choose to spend eighteen months in British house arrest followed by almost seven years inside the Ecuadorian embassy just to avoid a Swedish criminal trial which – in the worst of all cases – might entail a maximum sentence of four years in prison. He simply knew too much about the reality of international politics to believe that Swedish constitutional safeguards would be strong enough to protect him against the only serious danger to his life and dignity – his onward extradition to the United States.

That this danger was very real, despite Swedish claims to the contrary, is perhaps most poignantly illustrated by the shocking cases of Ahmed Agiza and Muhammad Al Zery, two Egyptian asylum seekers who had been officially registered in Sweden. On 18 December 2001, Agiza and Al Zery were arrested in Stockholm by the Swedish security police (Säpo) and handed over to CIA agents at Bromma Airport. From there, they were abducted to Egypt without any form of due process and tortured as suspected terrorists in the notorious Tora Prison. The Swedish authorities were later condemned in two separate proceedings, by the UN Human Rights Committee and the UN Committee against Torture, for a clear violation of the 'non-refoulement' principle derived from the prohibition of torture, and Sweden was ordered to pay damages of $500,000 to each of the victims. Despite obvious misconduct on the part of the Swedish authorities, the government refused to fully cooperate with the UN investigation as legally required and had to be explicitly reprimanded in this respect. The Swedish Parliament's ombudsman for the judiciary subsequently criticized the responsible authorities 'very seriously' but, once more, the responsible authorities declined to initiate any criminal or disciplinary sanctions – in renewed violation of the Convention against Torture.

As evidenced by a long trail of internal correspondence and legal analyses of the Australian government, in the year 2011, even the foreign minister and other senior members of that government were seriously concerned that Sweden would use the mechanism of 'temporary surrender' to hand over Assange to the United States, in circumvention of regular extradition proceedings. Contrary to popular perception, therefore, the scenario most feared by Assange was not paranoid at all but – at least behind closed doors – perceived as a thoroughly realistic assessment, even in diplomatic circles of close US allies such as Australia.

## US Indictment for Espionage

In 2019, however, the United States seemed to have changed their mind and decided to pursue Assange's direct extradition from the United Kingdom. Since President Trump's election, a different wind had been blowing across the Atlantic. Gone was the diplomatic façade of his predecessor, along with any more pretence of multilateral equality and cooperation. American foreign policy had become blunt, crude and erratic, while the British government had settled for an increasingly uncritical position of servility – the only part left for it to play in its 'special relationship' with the United States.

By reopening their investigation on 13 May 2019, Sweden now inadvertently challenged the United States. Suddenly, there could be two competing extradition requests. Which one would have priority? According to the Anglo-American extradition treaty, priority among competing requests would depend, among other things, on the seriousness of the alleged crime and on the temporal order in which the requests had been made. On both counts, a Swedish request would probably have to be prioritized. Sweden's first extradition request in the same matter dated back to November 2010 and, by June 2012, it had been successfully litigated all the way through to the British Supreme Court. Moreover, the 'less serious' form of rape Assange was suspected of in Sweden carried a maximum sentence of four years in prison. While this was less than the maximum of five years applicable to the single count of conspiracy to commit computer intrusion of the US indictment, the probable sanction for the alleged unsuccessful attempt to commit such intrusion was significantly lower than that likely to be imposed in the case of a rape conviction in Sweden.

It took the United States just ten days to put their heavy foot down. On 23 May 2019, still within the sixty-five-day deadline for completing their extradition request, the US Department of Justice transmitted its first 'superseding indictment', extending their list of charges by seventeen additional counts under the Espionage Act of 1917. From now on, the US case against Assange was no longer about some failed attempt to decode a password hash, but plainly and blatantly about espionage – the classic textbook example of a political offence. Moreover, since all seventeen new charges accused Assange of obtaining, receiving or disclosing national defence information, it was also clear that the indictment constituted a frontal attack on press freedom as guaranteed in the US Constitution. For each count, Assange now faced an additional sentence of up to ten years in prison, resulting in a possible prison sentence of up to 175 years. The disparity with the Swedish maximum sentence of four years was now so great, and the US claim to priority had been so unequivocally stated, that a possible Swedish extradition request would necessarily have to come second. It little mattered that 175 years in prison would be a grotesque sanction for alleged offences involving neither death nor violence, injury or material harm. By way of comparison, in 2010 the UN Criminal Tribunal for the former Yugoslavia sentenced two former Serbian military officers to life in prison for their role in the 1995 genocide of 7,000 Bosnian Muslims in Srebrenica. Still, after thirty years, both would be eligible for early release. Conversely, once in a US Supermax prison, Assange would almost certainly die there with no opportunity for early release.

Moreover, the now eighteen charges might not be the last word, as the expanded description of facts could serve as a basis for adding further, even more serious charges. All that needed to happen in order for this scenario to materialize was that the competent US court – the notorious 'Espionage Court' in Alexandria, Virginia – should come to a different conclusion than the US Department of Justice as to which crimes may have been committed in the present case. Depending on which offence was added, even the death penalty would become conceivable, although it could not be lawfully carried out due to restrictions imposed by the Anglo-American extradition treaty. In the worst case, therefore, Assange would spend the rest of his life on death row, either in complete isolation or surrounded by other death row inmates and without any hope of release.

Against this background, it is no mystery why the description of facts underlying the first superseding indictment of 23 May 2019 was broadly framed and only partially relevant to the eighteen counts of the indictment, and why the alleged facts were once more significantly expanded more than a year later, in the second superseding indictment of 24 June 2020. This suggests that, in the event of Assange's extradition and trial in the United States, the US Department of Justice intends to further expand its indictment. The current charges focus on criminalizing the obtention, reception and disclosure of national defence information, all of which are standard journalistic activities. The indictment is therefore vulnerable to counterarguments based on constitutional press freedoms that may well prevail before the US Supreme Court. In order to ensure that Assange would be silenced behind bars for the rest of his life, the government therefore had an interest in providing the trial judge with broad factual allegations permitting the identification of additional offences unrelated to press freedom protections – such as computer crimes and endangering life and property.

It is noteworthy that the US indictment focuses exclusively on conduct that is alleged to have occurred in 2010 – as if there had been no WikiLeaks publications before or after. In fact, Assange had continued his work with WikiLeaks even from the Ecuadorian embassy, at least until March 2018, when his ability to communicate was effectively suppressed after the change of government in Ecuador and the secret US indictment. Most of these activities do not appear to be fundamentally different from those described in the US indictment or to pose a lesser threat to official secrecy and impunity.

The decisive difference seems to be that, for the WikiLeaks revelations of 2010, the US Department of Justice possesses actual correspondence between Assange and his source inside the US military – Chelsea Manning – who had indisputably violated her own duty of non-disclosure and thus made herself liable to prosecution under US criminal law. Only this correspondence enabled the US government to charge Assange with conspiring to commit a crime: that of Manning. In most other cases, there is no evidence of direct contact with the source. Assange himself has often emphasized that WikiLeaks does not know its own sources and that the documents are transmitted anonymously. This makes criminal prosecution of WikiLeaks personnel virtually impossible, because the mere publication of classified information has long been recognized as a journalistic activity protected by international and constitutional press freedom guarantees.

Accurately understood, therefore, Assange is charged with assisting Manning in violating her own duty of non-disclosure and inciting her to deliver further classified documents. At first glance, even this reads like the job description of any moderately motivated journalist. Should we not expect of investigative journalists to enquire exactly what information a source has to offer, to dig deeper wherever possible, and to not be satisfied too quickly?

Admittedly it may not be part of a journalist's job to help his source crack a password hash, as Assange allegedly attempted to do, even for the purpose of source protection. But then, even if this allegation were true, all it refers to is an unsuccessful attempt. As is well known, every single day, millions of attempts are made to decode sensitive passwords or password components on government computers throughout the world. In the vast majority of cases, these attempts fail or otherwise remain harmless, just like the one Assange is alleged to have been involved in. But no government spends millions of dollars on surveillance and extradition proceedings for more than a decade simply to investigate and prosecute a single inconsequential conspiracy like the one alleged in the US indictment against Assange. Provided such isolated attempts are not carried out, are unsuccessful or otherwise remain harmless, they are generally regarded as petty offences that are not worth prosecuting. In Assange's case, however, the US Department of Justice was desperate to find a pretext for his prosecution. The problem was not Assange's alleged conspiracy to commit computer intrusion, of course, but that he had exposed war crimes and other dirty secrets, creating transparency in places where the powerful wanted nothing but obscurity. Unlike the whistleblower Manning, however, Assange's journalistic activities were protected by press freedom and could not be prosecuted. At least, this seemed to be the view taken by the Obama administration.

The Trump administration's superseding indictment of 23 May 2019 performed a dramatic U-turn and, for the first time since the Pentagon Papers scandal of the 1970s, tried once more to use the Espionage Act to criminalize and suppress journalistic publications. At the time of the Pentagon Papers, the Nixon administration had obtained a federal court injunction preventing the *New York Times* from publishing secret documents proving that the US government had deliberately deceived the American public and Congress about, among other things, its illegal expansion of the Vietnam War into neighbouring Cambodia and Laos. The injunction was ultimately overruled by the Supreme Court. In its landmark decision of 30 June 1971, the court held that: 'Only a free and unrestrained press can effectively expose deception in government. And paramount among the responsibilities of a free press is the duty to prevent any part of the government from deceiving the people and sending them off to distant lands to die of foreign fevers and foreign shot and shell.' The court's lifting of the publication ban set a precedent that would protect the free press from a power-hungry executive for exactly five decades. With its indictment of Assange for espionage, the US government was once again using its criminal justice system in an bid to silence a publisher for exposing its secrets. At the same time, by threatening a maximum sanction of 175 years of imprisonment, the US government had forcefully asserted priority for its own extradition request over any competing Swedish interests – 'America first!'

## Medically Prescribed Solitary Confinement

Already during my prison visit in Belmarsh, Assange's health gave rise to serious concern, and we warned the authorities that, unless urgent safeguards were put in place, his medical condition was likely to deteriorate rapidly. Little did I know how quickly our fears would become a reality. Just nine days after my visit, on 18 May 2019, Assange was permanently transferred to Belmarsh's health care unit. In addition to significant weight loss, his mental health had reportedly deteriorated to the point where he could no longer attend court hearings and had to be stabilized with medication – the tragic but predictable medical culmination of years of relentless psychological trauma. At the health care unit, Assange initially shared a cell with three other inmates, but was transferred to a single cell soon thereafter, where he would be held from June 2019 to January 2020 in conditions de facto amounting to solitary confinement: locked in his cell for twenty-three hours a day, under permanent video surveillance due to an alleged suicide risk, and without any contact with other inmates.

According to the UN Standard Minimum Rules for the Treatment of Prisoners, known as the 'Mandela Rules', solitary confinement refers to any confinement of a prisoner without meaningful human contact for twenty-two or more hours a day. The Mandela Rules state that solitary confinement may be used only in exceptional cases and as a last resort, for as short a time as possible, and subject to independent review. Moreover, again according to the Mandela Rules, solitary confinement should be prohibited whenever its use would exacerbate a prisoner's mental or physical condition, and any prolonged solitary confinement for more than fifteen consecutive days would violate the absolute prohibition of torture or other cruel, inhuman or degrading treatment or punishment under international law. Such are the international minimum standards of humane treatment applying to all and any persons deprived of their liberty throughout the world. For Assange, however, this form of ill-treatment very quickly became the status quo.

From a legal perspective, there can be absolutely no justification for imposing any form of detention amounting to prolonged solitary confinement on a non-violent inmate posing no threat to anyone. In the case of Assange, it is difficult to escape the impression that the necessary medical measures were used as a welcome pretext to isolate him. Whatever the situation, the prison administration always had a handy excuse. When Assange's health stabilized, any progress was said to confirm the positive medical effect of his isolation, which therefore had to be extended. Conversely, whenever his health deteriorated, his isolation and constant surveillance had to be extended for his own protection. A torturous Catch-22 was underway by which Assange's silencing and abuse could be perpetuated indefinitely, all under the guise of concern for his health.

To make matters worse, throughout his detention in Belmarsh Assange was denied meaningful access to his court documents, his meetings with lawyers and independent medical doctors were severely restricted and systematically obstructed, and external visits from family and friends were kept to a minimum – all under the convenient pretext of bureaucratic constraints. Thus, Assange was deliberately prevented from adequately preparing for his upcoming court proceedings in multiple jurisdictions, above all for the complex US extradition trial. Although this situation evidently constituted a grave and sustained violation of Assange's most basic rights as a defendant, all complaints by his legal team were shrugged off by the responsible judge. In her view, the responsibility for Assange's conditions of detention lay exclusively with the prison administration and therefore beyond her jurisdiction. What she failed to explain, however, was how this was compatible with her duty to ensure that any trial in her courtroom would be conducted in full compliance with fundamental procedural guarantees, including the defendant's right to adequately prepare his defence.

# 5

# Crossing the Rubicon

## Preliminary Observations

By the end of May 2019, the time had come for me to present my preliminary observations and recommendations in the case. Originally, I had intended to address my official letter only to the British government, which currently had Assange in its custody. However, my inquiry had revealed that at least four states had actively contributed to Assange's persecution and were legally co-responsible for causing his current situation: the United Kingdom, Sweden, Ecuador, and the United States. I therefore decided to write separate letters to all four states, in order to transmit my findings, request explanations and make recommendations.

By mid-May, I had already completed first drafts, but new information kept arriving almost every day, which needed to be cross-checked and then integrated or discarded. In addition, translation errors, contradictions and other inaccuracies came to light, which required further inquiry, corrections or amendments. Also, the medical report, whose final version had been co-authored by Professor Vieira and Dr Pérez-Sales, had to be incorporated in such a way that while the doctor–patient confidentiality of the diagnosis was preserved, it could still serve as an objective medical basis for my legal findings. In addition, the Secretariat of the High Commissioner's Office kept raising questions of protocol and procedure which had to be duly taken into account.

Over the past decade, a veritable mountain of evidentiary material had accumulated in multiple languages, including judicial and administrative decisions, investigative files, official and unofficial correspondence, emails and text messages, testimonies by medical doctors, legal experts, and other witnesses, as well as countless press reports promoting various contradicting narratives. Clearly, this material could not be comprehensively addressed within the limited form and space of official letters to the responsible governments. But then, my role was not that of an investigative judge or prosecutor expected to submit unassailable courtroom evidence. As the UN special rapporteur, my mandate was to alert states to possible violations of the prohibition of torture and ill-treatment, to seek to clarify these allegations, and to remind governments of their international legal obligations to prevent, investigate, punish and redress such crimes. As a matter of treaty law, the governments concerned had to act ex officio to launch a prompt and impartial investigation, as soon as they had 'reasonable grounds to believe' that an act of torture or ill-treatment may have been committed or contributed to by persons acting within their jurisdiction. Given that my findings were based on a personal prison visit, numerous witness statements and a specialized medical examination, the 'reasonable grounds' threshold clearly had not only been met, but far exceeded. It was therefore sufficient for my letters to summarize my preliminary observations, make further inquiries and recommend urgent measures.

My aim was to provide the involved governments with a clear and coherent description of how their alleged acts and omissions had contributed to Assange's psychological torture and why his extradition to the United States would be incompatible with the UN Convention against Torture. My letter started out with a general assessment of Assange's current conditions of detention and expressed my alarm at his deteriorating state of health. It then established the causal link between Assange's current medical symptoms and the treatment and conditions to which he had previously been subjected: years of arbitrary confinement, surveillance and harassment in the Ecuadorian embassy; the abuse of Swedish investigative and judicial proceedings for the purpose of political persecution; and his sustained and unrestrained public mobbing, intimidation and defamation by authorities, political leaders and the press. I therefore called on each government to investigate its own contribution to Assange's abuse and to ensure the compensation and redress of any harm unjustly inflicted on him.

But dealing with past misconduct alone was not enough. If extradited to the United States, whether directly from Britain or indirectly via Sweden, Assange would almost certainly face an unfair trial, as well as a draconian sanction and conditions of detention which could only be described as cruel, inhuman and degrading. In light of this risk, Assange's extradition would be absolutely prohibited under the principle of 'non-refoulement' enshrined in Article 3 of the UN Convention against Torture. However, even the strictest extradition ban can only be effective when it is actually enforced, in a fair and transparent extradition trial. All of the previous and ongoing British judicial proceedings against Assange strongly suggested that the United Kingdom could not be relied upon in this regard.

The wording of my letter may have been unusually harsh and uncompromising, but not without good reason. By now, the Assange case had been dragging on for more than nine years, during which the involved governments had repeatedly acted in bad faith and blatant violation of both international and domestic law. I certainly did not want to find myself in the same situation as the UN Working Group on Arbitrary Detention a few years earlier, when their expert opinion in the Assange case was self-righteously ignored by both Sweden and the United Kingdom, simply because it confirmed the unlawfulness of Assange's continued siege in the Ecuadorian embassy. So far, all of the evidence I had seen strongly suggested that Assange's deteriorating state of health was not the result of an unintended chain of unfortunate circumstances, but of deliberate collusion for the systematic persecution, silencing and destruction of an inconvenient political dissident.

I knew that, if I wanted my findings to be taken seriously and to receive more than just a few evasive platitudes in response, a diplomatic expression of concern would not be sufficient. Instead, I had to sound the alarm, alert the public and send an unmistakable message to the responsible states: Get your act together! You may have legitimate concerns about the activities of Assange and WikiLeaks and, if you have evidence for criminal conduct, then by all means hold him accountable. But all of this needs to be done in fair and transparent proceedings governed by the law, and must not be misused for political purposes. The persecution of Assange must end here and now!

I wrote in the hope that, by being so blunt, I would rock the boat sufficiently to achieve some results. Sweden had just reopened its preliminary investigation against Assange, but had not yet requested his extradition from Britain, and the US extradition proceedings had not yet begun. Perhaps, I thought, there was still time to turn this ship around. Perhaps the involved governments would want to avoid too much dirt being dug up and might prefer to find a face-saving way out. Like in the case of Augusto Pinochet, the British government could decline to extradite Assange on medical grounds, or the British courts could come to the same conclusion, in both cases without having to adjudicate the legal admissibility or extraditability of the US espionage charges. In such a 'pre-cooked' scenario agreed by all involved governments, Assange could be repatriated on humanitarian grounds to Australia, London could point to 'medical imperatives' or, respectively, to the 'independence of the judiciary', and Washington could pretend to only grudgingly accept while making clear that any return of Assange to WikiLeaks would immediately trigger a new extradition request. To achieve this, I could not rely on diplomacy, but had to build up sufficient public pressure to force the involved governments out of their comfort zone. So, I decided not to mince my words, but to call a spade a spade and to throw both the political weight of my mandate and my personal and professional credibility into the balance in order to make myself heard – first of all by the states in question, but also by the media and, hopefully, the broader public.

On 27 May 2019, my first letter went out to the British government, at that time my most important interlocutor in the Assange case. The letters to Ecuador, Sweden, and the United States followed the next day. The four letters were identical as far as my observations were concerned and differed primarily in terms of the respective government's current responsibilities, my follow-up questions and my specific recommendations, all of which were tailored to each state. All letters contained the standard closing formula announcing that the letter and any response received from the government would be published online within sixty days. All of them also contained the following sentence summarizing my most important conclusion: 'I am therefore gravely concerned that, starting from August 2010, Mr Assange has been, and currently still is, exposed to progressively severe pain and suffering, inflicted through various forms and degrees of cruel, inhuman or degrading treatment or punishment, the cumulative effects of which clearly amount to psychological torture.'

## Going Public

How could life in an embassy with a cat and a skateboard ever amount to torture? What business does the UN special rapporteur on torture have to even occupy himself with Julian Assange? Doesn't he have worse cases of torture to address? How often have I been challenged by people questioning the legitimacy of my entire investigation into the Assange case. My answer has always been the same. Yes, there are worse cases. There are always worse cases. But that is not the point. Torture is torture, and any victim of torture is as important as any other, regardless of the gravity of the abuse, their socio-economic status, celebrity, origin, gender or age.

The Assange case is relevant to my mandate in three distinct ways. First, as we have already discussed in detail, the four states involved have jointly exposed Assange to various forms of ill-treatment whose cumulative effects amount to psychological torture. Second, there is a great risk that Assange will be extradited to the United States and imprisoned there in conditions that not only my predecessors and I, but also Amnesty International and many other human rights organizations, have consistently described as amounting to torture or other cruel, inhuman or degrading treatment or punishment. And third, Assange has published evidence of state-sanctioned war crimes, including torture, through WikiLeaks. Yet it is Assange who is prosecuted, whereas the torturers and other war criminals enjoy complete impunity. Under the Nuremberg Principles and international criminal law, the US government's refusal to prosecute its own torturers not only violates the UN Convention against Torture and the international law of armed conflict but amounts to a separate war crime on the part of the responsible military commanders and government officials. Each of these three aspects of the prohibition of torture – investigation of past and present violations, prevention of future violations, and prosecution of perpetrators – is relevant to my mandate and warrants my intervention.

What makes the case of Julian Assange particularly important is that it sets a dangerous precedent and demonstrates systemic failures that not only reach far beyond one man's individual fate, but also far beyond all of the individual states involved. In the case of Julian Assange, so-called mature democracies of the West are systematically disregarding the rule of law and directly undermining fundamental constitutional rights indispensable to any democratic system: the prohibition of torture, the freedom of the press, the presumption of innocence and the right to a fair trial. Those who justify their own indifference by pointing to the existence of 'worse cases' are making a fatal mistake that will exact a high price from all of us. At best, they miss the big picture of what really is at stake here – the proverbial 'elephant in the room'. At worst, they deliberately bury their heads in the sand while investigative journalism is being ruthlessly criminalized, persecuted and annihilated. Only the day that they themselves are arbitrarily arrested will they pull their heads back out of the sand and realize that there is no one left to speak up for them.

Given the emblematic importance of the case and the foreseeable reluctance of the involved states to change their abusive conduct, it was not sufficient to simply report my findings to these governments: I had to sound the alarm in public. Assange's health was an urgent concern, and the threat scenario of an irregular deportation to Sweden or the United States escalated almost daily. At the same time, the British authorities and the mainstream press were outdoing each other in displays of self-righteous delight mixed with indifference. In these circumstances, it would have been irresponsible to wait a full sixty days before informing the public about my alarming observations. I therefore decided to issue a press release and to offer individual interviews to the media.

In my official letter to the governments, I announced my intention to publicly express my concerns 'in the near future', and, as per standard procedure, I transmitted an advance copy of my press statement for their information. The headline was released on 31 May 2019: 'UN expert says, "collective persecution" of Julian Assange must end now.' On less than two pages, I summarized my conclusions, condemned serious human rights violations and, here too, deliberately did not mince my words. This was no longer about diplomacy – I needed to reach the broader public with clear-cut wording that was sufficiently alarming to challenge the very same deep-rooted prejudices that had clouded my own perceptions of this case. I strongly criticized the continuing failure of the involved states to protect Assange's human rights and said that 'by displaying an attitude of complacency at best, and of complicity at worst, these governments have created an atmosphere of impunity encouraging Mr Assange's uninhibited vilification and abuse.' Should any doubts about my stance still linger, I certainly dispelled them with this concluding statement: 'In 20 years of work with victims of war, violence and political persecution I have never seen a group of democratic States ganging up to deliberately isolate, demonise and abuse a single individual for such a long time and with so little regard for human dignity and the rule of law.'

I was fully aware that, with this statement, I had figuratively crossed the Rubicon and there was now no turning back. With my starkly uncompromising stance, I put not only my credibility at risk, but also my career and, potentially, even my personal safety. If nothing else, I certainly would not win any new friends among states. But what would have been the alternative? Should I have acted against my better judgment and expressed my 'confidence' in the judicial authorities of the countries involved? Should I have expressed lukewarm concern about Assange's 'self-inflicted' state of health, sweeping all the dirt under the carpet with a few half-hearted recommendations? I was painfully aware that both speaking out and remaining silent would come at a price. But I did not really have a choice. I knew that I would rather be wrongly perceived as a liar, failure, and traitor by the entire world, than rightly by myself. The price of my silence would have been my integrity – a price I was not willing to pay.

Until that moment, I had never been a man of the limelight. Exposing myself in this way made me feel very uncomfortable and triggered a full-blown personal crisis. In so doing, I both outwardly and inwardly broke with my residual trust in the system. With my trust in Western democracies as states governed by the rule of law. As states which, when confronted with irrefutable evidence for human rights violations or war crimes, would unquestionably take the necessary measures of investigation and redress. Now I suddenly found myself with my back to the wall, defending human rights and the rule of law against the very democracies which I had always considered to be my closest allies in the fight against torture. It was a steep and painful learning curve which forced me to question and rethink my entire worldview.

Not even thirty minutes after my press release, the then British Foreign Secretary Jeremy Hunt shot back on Twitter: 'This is wrong. Assange chose to hide in the embassy and was always free to leave and face justice. The UN Special Rapporteur should allow British courts to make their judgments without his

interference or inflammatory accusations.' The superficial asser-
tiveness of Hunt's message scarcely concealed to what extent I
had caught the British government off guard. It was of course
absurd for the foreign secretary to accuse me of 'interference'
with the British judiciary when, in fact, I had been formally
invited by his own government to investigate the case of Julian
Assange from the perspective of the prohibition of torture and
ill-treatment. In any case, having chosen the weapon, Hunt also
relieved me of the diplomatic *bon ton* to not conduct my own
official correspondence with government officials on Twitter. My
reply followed on the spot: 'With all due respect, Sir: Mr Assange
was about as "free to leave" as a someone sitting on a rubber
boat in a shark pool. As detailed in my formal letter to you, so
far, UK courts have not shown the impartiality and objectivity
required by the rule of law.'

# PART II

---

## ANATOMY OF A PERSECUTION

# 6

# Swedish Judicial Persecution

## Turning Point from Fame to Shame

By the summer of 2010, Assange is at the peak of his popularity. Everything seems to be going his way that year. In April, he presents the 'Collateral Murder' video at the Washington National Press Club, and at the end of July, the Afghan War Diary follows, with 90,000 field reports issued between 2004 and 2010. As the founder and face of WikiLeaks, Assange has become a veritable 'rock star'. A man who dares to confront the powerful in politics and business and, at the same time, manages to overhaul the entire media landscape. In August 2010, he travels to Stockholm to give a lecture at the invitation of the Swedish Social Democrats.

He also intends to explore the possibility of obtaining a residence permit for himself, which would allow him to establish WikiLeaks as an officially recognized Swedish publisher. The resulting status of a legally protected press organization could give WikiLeaks formal legitimacy and virtually unassailable protection under the Swedish constitution. This would provide the organization with one of the world's strongest safe havens for

publishing activities – a definite game changer, of decisive importance for the huge releases planned for the autumn and winter
2010/2011 and beyond.

At the same time, much is at stake for Sweden's political establishment. A small country of 8 million inhabitants, Sweden has in
the past century managed to stay out of two world wars and the
Cold War. After the fall of the Berlin Wall in 1989, however, the
country rapidly gave up its traditional neutrality and became a
de facto member of the Western security, intelligence and defence
community led by the United States. Come 2010, Sweden is now
a close ally of the United States in Afghanistan and the broader
'War on Terror', with a security policy that can only be described
as subservient to US interests. This development does not sit too
well with most of the Swedish population, so that politicians
constantly have to go out of their way to sweep it under the
carpet. On 10 August, the US news website 'The Daily Beast'
reports US officials as saying that the Obama administration is
pressing Britain, Germany, Australia, and other allied Western
governments to consider opening criminal investigations against
Assange and to severely limit his ability to travel across international borders. Without any doubt, having WikiLeaks established
in Sweden as a constitutionally protected publisher would put
the Swedish government's transatlantic relations under considerable strain, and constitutional protections combined with public
sympathy for the organization would make any interference
with its activities exceedingly difficult.

This is the background to Julian Assange's visit to Sweden in
August and September 2010, which will become the most dramatic turning point in the public perception of him as a person.
It is no exaggeration to say that, on the day Sweden issues an
arrest warrant against Assange for the alleged rape and harassment of two women, his fame turns to shame and his success
story into a story of persecution. Even more importantly for an
accurate understanding of the Swedish dimension of the case,
however, these allegations cause vital Swedish supporters for
the institutional establishment of WikiLeaks in Sweden to hesitate or pull back; Assange's Swedish residence permit is refused;

and the Swedish government's worst nightmare is averted in the nick of time.

Significantly, as a matter of legal procedure, the Swedish allegations never managed to evolve beyond the initial stage of a preliminary investigation, where they were left to simmer for nine years before finally being dismissed for lack of evidence. Nevertheless, they set in motion a dynamic of vilification and arbitrariness that continues to this day. As will be demonstrated in this book, it was the refusal of the Swedish authorities to guarantee against Assange's onward extradition to the United States, and not the allegations of sexual misconduct, that led him to resist extradition to Sweden and request diplomatic asylum in the Ecuadorian embassy in June 2012. Assange's escape to the embassy, in turn, violated British bail conditions in connection with the Swedish extradition proceedings. For this bail violation, committed only to seek protection from serious violations of his human rights, Assange was sentenced to fifty weeks in prison seven years later – the only 'offence' he has been convicted of so far. Finally, while serving that sentence, the proceedings began for Assange's extradition to the United States, where he faces a political trial and almost certainly a life sentence without parole.

The rape allegations initiated by the Swedish authorities became the starting point of a sustained and concerted campaign of judicial persecution and public mobbing that would systematically corner and dehumanize Assange. The resulting prejudice had caused even me – a mandated human rights expert of the United Nations – to carelessly swipe off my screen Assange's initial appeal for help. It was only in November 2019, after nine years of extreme procrastination and arbitrariness, that the Swedish Prosecution Authority finally admitted to the lack of evidence and dismissed all remaining allegations. Nine months later, in August 2020, the final statute of limitations came into effect, thus drawing a line under what must have been the longest 'preliminary investigation' in Swedish history. Throughout the entire proceedings, Sweden never came up with sufficient evidence to press charges against Assange, let alone to convict him of any offence. Throughout the entire proceedings, Assange should have been presumed innocent as a matter of law, and he certainly must be considered innocent now. In stark contradiction to this requirement, the aggressive bias and arbitrariness with which the Swedish authorities pursued these allegations, and the carefully ambiguous rhetoric they maintained, even when they finally closed their investigation in 2019, ensured that the 'rapist' stigma would remain forever branded on Assange's forehead and prevent his case from being seen for what it is: a story of political persecution.

## My Investigation of the Rape Allegations

My investigation of the Swedish rape allegations is a particularly sensitive dimension of this case, because it concerns not only Julian Assange and the responsible state authorities, but also affects the personal privacy and human dignity of A. and S., the two women involved. In examining these allegations, I therefore had to adhere to particularly high standards of responsibility and care towards all parties. In principle, I consider all three individuals – Assange, A. and S. – to be equally credible. As we know from numerous scientific studies comparing witness accounts, depending on the circumstances, different people can perceive the same events very differently. In my view, to the extent relevant for determining criminal culpability, the discrepancies between the respective accounts given by Assange, A. and S. are by no means unusual or suspicious but fall within the normal range of varying perceptions that could be expected to arise in intimate encounters between strangers. Particularly in the presence of very strong influencing factors such as the clash of the women's admiration for Assange with the potentially impaired interpersonal sensitivity caused by his diagnosed autism spectrum disorder (ASD), but also the distorting effects of powerful third-party interests and involuntary media exposure.

The comprehensive criminalization and systematic prosecution of sexual offences of all kinds is of great importance and does not allow for any compromise, regardless of the identity, status, or origin of the suspect and without regard to his or her political, professional, humanitarian, or other achievements or merits. Every allegation of rape and other sexual offence must be rigorously investigated, and every prosecutable case vigorously pursued, to a far greater extent than occurs now. Even in modern democracies, the prosecution rate for reported rapes is often unacceptably low, which speaks volumes about the level of priority given to such crimes by the responsible authorities. As will be shown, contrary to public perception, the Swedish authorities did everything to prevent a proper investigation and judicial resolution of their rape allegations against Assange. In so acting, they demonstrated a shocking indifference to the rights and dignity not only of Assange, but also of the two women involved. Moreover, justice requires the professional and reliable determination of individual culpability in accordance with the fundamental principles of due process, including the right to a fair and expeditious trial, the presumption of innocence, and the principle of *in dubio pro reo* according to which the accused receives the benefit of the doubt. Throughout the Swedish investigation against Assange, none of these principles was even remotely respected.

As special rapporteur, I am mandated to monitor the compliance of UN Member States with the prohibition of torture and ill-treatment. Clearly, therefore, the aim of my investigation cannot be to determine what actually happened between Assange and the two Swedish women, to speculate about individual guilt or innocence, or to express my opinion on the character traits or moral conduct of private individuals. That said, reconstructing relevant acts and omissions by key protagonists in this case may still be necessary for the purposes of my mandate, because the handling of these facts by the authorities allows me to draw conclusions as to their good faith and compliance with due process principles.

For example, when contradictory or exculpatory evidence inconsistent with the official narrative is deliberately disregarded or even suppressed by the authorities, this may not prove Assange's innocence, but it is certainly a strong indicator for an arbitrary and corrupted proceeding. Official arbitrariness almost always constitutes a central element in political persecution and related ill-treatment and therefore clearly falls within the scope of my mandate. All evidence cited in this book, as well as my conclusions, must be understood and evaluated exclusively in this light. Materials of a purely personal nature, irrelevant to the outcome of my investigation or where personal privacy is paramount, have not been included in this book, even if they are not disputed and are publicly available through other channels.

Since I began working on the Assange case, I have collected some 10,000 pages of court files, witness statements, trial assessments and analyses, emails, SMS transcripts and handwritten notes, as well as photographs and video. Despite my requests, the authorities did not provide any reliable evidence or explanations. Thus, even official documents, which constitute the bulk of the evidence and should have been made available to me by the authorities themselves, had to be painstakingly compiled through other sources. The most commonly accessible pieces of evidence I obtained through my own research, whereas others were passed to me by numerous independent sources and through a variety of channels. Also, most key documents were received from several sources in parallel, often of varying quality and completeness. My knowledge of the Swedish language was of great advantage in the process.

Although the four governments made sure to classify, suppress and even destroy almost all the most decisive evidence, they did not completely succeed in keeping the lid on their collusion and misconduct. First, anyone who knows what to look for and has the necessary language skills will be able to find the most important pieces of evidence somewhere in the bottomless memory of the internet, and very extensive materials have also been made publicly available by WikiLeaks and its supporter groups. Second, through freedom of information requests and related litigation, investigative journalists and human rights activists have forced the authorities to hand over thousands of pages that are not – or not in full – available on the internet. In most cases, however, these materials have been excessively censored, thus all but defeating the very purpose of any freedom of information legislation. It would have been more honest to flatly decline a freedom of information request involving official correspondence, witness hearings, expert opinions or internal memos, than to hand over a pile of blacked-out papers showing nothing but the document title, the date and the page numbers – and to claim with a straight face that this obvious mockery amounts to anything remotely similar to 'freedom of information'.

Given that, under current legislations, freedom of information requests can be refused only in exceptional circumstances, public authorities usually prefer to hand over hundreds of completely redacted documents, along with an invoice based on the total number of pages, and to assert that any redactions have been strictly limited to what is required by law – a claim that remains as unverifiable as it is unconvincing in the face of a heap of black paper. Even in mature democracies such as Sweden, the United Kingdom, Germany and the United States, this widespread, clearly abusive practice is employed to prevent the transparency and oversight pursued by applicable freedom of information legislation, thus effectively suppressing the public's right to know the truth about the exercise of governmental power.

This means that in investigating the case of Julian Assange I found myself confronted with countless pieces of a puzzle, some of which I had received in multiple copies while others are still missing. Even now, therefore, I have no way of knowing with certainty how many pieces the whole puzzle actually comprises. The reason for this continued uncertainty is that the involved states not only refuse to 'fully cooperate' with my mandate as required by the relevant UN resolutions, but also openly violate their international obligations under the Convention against Torture and other applicable human rights treaties. States are not only called to respond to all queries transmitted by a UN special rapporteur, but they are also legally obliged to conduct a prompt and impartial investigation whenever they have reasonable grounds to believe that torture or ill-treatment have occurred within their jurisdiction, to prosecute violations, and to provide redress and rehabilitation for the resulting harm. With their blatant sabotage of my investigation, these states deliberately undermine the purpose of my UN mandate and, at the same time, demonstrate the lack of credibility of their own human rights policies.

As a result, my reconstruction of the facts relevant to the case of Julian Assange may still have a couple of blank spots, and, on specific issues, may allow for other interpretations of the acts and omissions attributable to the involved States, their authorities and individual officials. Whichever way they are assembled, however, the available puzzle pieces always yield the same conclusive picture, namely that the trial of Assange is not about the rule of law, but about political persecution, and that investigative and judicial institutions are being deliberately abused for that purpose. Victimized by this abuse are not only Assange but also the two Swedish women. From the very beginning, their legitimate interests were systematically disregarded by the authorities and they were ruthlessly exposed and instrumentalized for the purposes of a political persecution. The upshot has been that their public lives have been largely destroyed; they were made to fear for their own safety, have been vilified as secret agents, honeytraps and liars, and have received no redress for the harm so wantonly inflicted on them by the authorities – two sacrificial victims of Swedish *raison d'état*.

## The Case of A.

Assange arrives in Stockholm on 11 August 2010. As usual, to reduce the risk of surveillance, he will not be staying at a hotel, but with private hosts. This time it is A., a political activist involved in organizing his seminar, who has offered to accommodate him in her studio in the Södermalm district of Stockholm. A. herself plans to spend a few days outside the city and to return only on 14 August, the day of Assange's lecture. Before leaving, she hands the keys to journalist Donald Boström, who welcomes Assange and takes him to A.'s apartment. But A. returns one day earlier than expected, on Friday, 13 August, and meets Assange in her studio. The two go out for dinner and then return to her apartment, where A. invites Assange to spend the night with her.

During her interview with the police one week later, A. will recount her version of events. According to the written summary filed by the police, A. stated that Assange had tried to initiate sex; that his attempts were rather clumsy at first but then grew increasingly demanding; that she eventually allowed him to undress her but did not want to have unprotected intercourse; that Assange initially held her arms and pushed her legs down, which prevented her from reaching for a condom. Eventually, he asked her why she was resisting and, when she explained, agreed to use a condom. Nonetheless, A. sensed a 'strong unspoken reluctance by Assange to use a condom, and immediately became suspicious when, during intercourse, he 'withdraws from her and begins to adjust the condom. Judging from the sound, according to [A.], it seemed that Assange removed the condom. He entered her again and continued the copulation.' But when she reached down, she was reassured to feel the lower edge of the condom with her fingers. She therefore allowed intercourse to continue until Assange ejaculated inside her. Afterwards, when Assange withdrew and removed the condom, A. saw that it did not contain any semen and she noticed that something 'ran' out of her body. A. then became 'convinced that when he withdrew from her the first time, Assange deliberately broke the condom at its tip and then continued copulating to ejaculation'. Assange himself confirmed during his police interview a few days later that he had had consensual intercourse with A., but denied damaging the condom. He also said that he had no recollection of the condom having been damaged and that A. had not made any comment to that effect, but that she first made this allegation one week later, on the same day she visited the police station together with S.

The morning after this first night at A.'s apartment, Assange gives his lecture 'The First Casualty of War Is the Truth', concerning the Afghan War Diary, which had just been published by WikiLeaks. A. sits next to him on the podium and serves as his press secretary during the subsequent discussion. In the front row of the audience sits S., a young woman often described as wearing a bright pink cashmere sweater. She works in a museum in the city, is a big Assange fan and has been eagerly anticipating the event. According to several witnesses and her own testimony, everyone wonders where this woman comes from, whom no one knows and whose appearance and manner do not quite fit in with the rest of the audience. When Assange needs a charging cable for his laptop during the seminar, she offers to get one from an electronics store, and hands it to him personally. After the seminar, she joins the large group gathered for lunch and comes to Assange's attention. They later spend the afternoon together and end up at the cinema, where they touch each other intimately.

In the evening, A. honours Assange with a traditional Swedish crayfish party in her garden. A friend of A.'s later testifies that, during the party, A. told her that she had had intercourse with Assange and the condom had broken, albeit without accusing him of bad intentions. In the middle of the night, with the party still going on, A. posts an enthusiastic tweet: 'Sitting outside at 2 am and barely freezing with the coolest, smartest people in the world, it's just amazing!' Donald Boström, who was also at the party, said that A. told him a few days later that she was 'proud as a peacock – the world's most awesome man in my bed and living in my flat'. The night of the crayfish party they again share A.'s bed, although several acquaintances have already offered to host Assange in view of the cramped conditions in A.'s apartment. According to witnesses, A. declined these offers saying that Assange was welcome to continue staying with her. Johannes Wahlström, one of Assange's primary contacts in Sweden, testified that he checked with A. every day whether Assange should be accommodated elsewhere. According to Wahlström, A. had complained jokingly about her 'adoptive child's' nightly laptop sessions in the bathroom and his careless hygiene, but always confirmed that everything was fine, and that Assange could continue to stay with her.

## The Case of S.

On the following Monday, 16 August, Assange receives a call from S., with whom he had spent the afternoon two days earlier. They meet late in the evening and decide to take the train to Enköping near Stockholm, where S. lives. The next morning at 9:40 a.m., A. receives a message on her cell phone: Johannes Wahlström asks her to please remind Assange of a meeting at the journalists' union which is scheduled for noon that day. During his subsequent questioning by the police, Wahlström will read out the SMS correspondence directly from his cell phone to the interviewing officer. A. texts in reply, 'He is not here. He has been planning every night to have sex with the cashmere girl but has not been able to find the time. Perhaps he managed to do so yesterday?' A. does not have S.'s phone number but gives Wahlström her email address instead and says that S. works at the Museum of Natural History – 'That's all I know.' This correspondence suggests that, in his conversations with A., Assange had made no secret of his intention to seek a sexual fling with S. It also suggests that A. was not particularly worried about that prospect.

It is midnight when Assange and S. arrive at her apartment. According to S.'s testimony and her irritated text messages to two friends between 1:14 and 1:43 a.m., Assange first wants unprotected sex, which S. refuses, and then falls asleep after long foreplay. S. is disappointed and complains that he 'generally behaves weirdly', but eventually falls asleep as well. Sexual intercourse occurs only later during the night, sometime before her next text message at 5:15 a.m. When S. insists on the use of a condom, Assange accepts, albeit rather reluctantly, according to S.'s account. On the morning of 17 August, between 7:22 and 7:46 a.m., another text message chat takes place in which S. expresses her annoyance at Assange's snoring next to her. Within the following hour, S. leaves the apartment to buy breakfast, then serves Assange oatmeal porridge, milk, and juice and returns to bed with him, where they again have protected sex. In an SMS chat between 8:42 and 8:59 a.m., S. writes, clearly put out, that Assange had been reluctant to use a condom, that he even 'ordered' her to serve him orange juice, and that he was snoring again. Her next message follows exactly ninety minutes later, at 10:29. It is during these ninety minutes that the alleged rape is said to have occurred.

According to the written summary prepared by the police of S.'s interview, after their – protected – sexual intercourse earlier that morning, both Assange and S. had 'dozed off'. After some time, Assange allegedly tried to penetrate S. again, but this time without a condom. The police summary states that 'she awoke and felt him penetrating her'. Immediately, she asked him, 'Are you wearing anything?' to which he replied, 'You.' She said: 'You better don't have HIV', and he replied, 'Of course not.' The summary continues: 'She felt that it was too late. He was already inside her and she let him continue [*lät honom fortsätta*]. She didn't have the energy to tell him one more time. She had gone on and on about condoms [*tjatat om kondom*] all night long. She has never had unprotected sex before. He said he wanted to come inside her; he did not say when he did, but he did it. A lot ran out of her afterward.'

It should be noted that, under the domestic legislation and case law applicable in Sweden in 2010, mere physical contact between the sexual organs of two persons is already considered sexual intercourse, regardless of penetration; that being asleep is considered a state of helplessness; and that deliberately exploiting such a state of helplessness to initiate sexual intercourse amounts to the crime of rape and cannot be excused by the victim's subsequent consent. Any form of rape, in turn, must always be prosecuted ex officio, regardless of the victim's agreement with such prosecution, and carries a penalty of at least two years in prison. The broader definition of 'rape' which is in force today, and includes any sexual intercourse without the full consent of the involved parties, was not introduced in Sweden until the 2018 revision of the Criminal Code. The same applies to the newly introduced offence of 'negligent rape', so that, in 2010, the crime of rape in Sweden still requires proof of the perpetrator's culpable intent.

S.'s nocturnal text messages in which she repeatedly expresses irritation about Assange's desire to have sex without a condom make it clear that he could not in good faith assume her consent to unprotected intercourse. However, the conversation between Assange and S. reproduced in the police summary of her interview, which ends with her 'letting him continue' without a condom, offers no indication of violence, threats, or any exercise of power that could have precluded S.'s freedom of action or decision. Assange's criminal liability under the Swedish law in force at the time therefore hinges exclusively on whether S. had been asleep and, if so, whether he was aware of her helpless state at the moment of the unprotected penetration.

The only piece of evidence which can be considered to provide reasonably reliable indications as to how S. genuinely experienced this incident is a text message sent by her to a friend almost twenty-four hours later, on 18 August at 6:59 a.m., stating that she had been 'half asleep' when Assange had unprotected intercourse with her. This choice of words leaves room for reasonable doubt, as it excludes neither that S. was in a helpless state due to sleep nor that she was sufficiently aware of Assange's attempted penetration that her freedom of action and decision was not completely suspended.

Assange himself later asserted that S. had not been asleep and had consented to unprotected intercourse before it began. Just as in the case of A., particularly coming from a suspect diagnosed with autism spectrum disorder, his own perception of events may be genuine without necessarily constituting reliable evidence for how the situation was experienced by S. But absent a confession, he must be considered innocent until proved guilty beyond reasonable doubt. Just like any other suspect.

S.'s account of the events, in turn, was not transcribed verbatim, nor was it recorded by audio device or witnessed by a second police officer, but merely summarized in the words of the interviewing officer. Moreover, as will be shown, the police summary of S.'s statement was only read back to her and approved by her almost two weeks later, on 2 September 2010. By then, the Swedish authorities had already amended the text without S.'s participation, had seized complete control of the narrative, and had created an almost incontestable fait accompli by aggressively disseminating the rape allegations through the mass media. Within the past two weeks, her case had been opened by one prosecutor on probable cause of rape, discontinued by another for lack of evidence and then reopened by a third, who officially reaffirmed that Assange was indeed suspected on probable cause of rape. Thus, by the time S. was first asked to approve the written summary of her own interview, she was already under massive pressure to conform to the official rape narrative imposed by the authorities, on pain of exposing herself to blame for falsely accusing Assange. Therefore, on the question of whether S. had been asleep at the relevant moment and, if so, whether Assange had been aware of her helpless state, her police interview cannot be considered as reliable evidence either.

All in all, on the only points of fact that were decisive for Assange's criminal liability, there had clearly been reasonable doubt from the start. Objectively, in the absence of a relevant criminal record or a confession on the part of Assange, there was never any realistic prospect of successfully prosecuting him for the rape of S. Whatever may have happened between Assange and S. during those ninety minutes on the morning of 17 August 2010, from an evidentiary perspective, the only conceivable outcome of indicting Assange for the rape of S. would necessarily have been acquittal, based on the benefit of the doubt. Any other outcome would have defeated the presumption of innocence and the requirement of proof beyond reasonable doubt, two universal bedrock principles of criminal law.

The Swedish investigating authorities must have been fully aware of their evidentiary impasse. Assessing the objective likelihood of a conviction is an integral part of any professional criminal investigation: it serves to prevent both the pointless squandering of public resources and unnecessary reputational harm and trauma to suspects and others involved. As soon as it becomes clear that, irrespective of the investigative measures undertaken, there is no realistic prospect of proving an alleged offence beyond reasonable doubt, the case must be discontinued, regardless of the personal preferences of the officials involved. Accordingly, Chapter 23 Section 1 of the Swedish Code of Judicial Procedure states: 'A preliminary investigation need not be initiated if it is manifest that it is not possible to investigate the offence.' The fact that the Swedish authorities continued to disseminate and perpetuate the rape narrative against Assange for more than nine years, when the lack of prosecutable evidence should have been immediately apparent to any experienced prosecutor, strongly suggests that other motives were in play.

## Two Women Insist on an HIV Test

Neither S. nor Assange have claimed that their unprotected intercourse triggered an argument or other disagreement. Rather, they joke about the consequences of a possible pregnancy: S. warns that Assange would have to pay for her tuition fees, and he suggests that the child should be named 'Afghanistan'. But after they part ways, S.'s amusement wanes. She begins to feel mounting anxiety. Not only is she worried about an unwanted pregnancy, but also about a potential infection with a sexually transmitted disease (STD), most notably HIV. Her text messages show how her fear grows and her helplessness turns to anger. 'I feel totally used', she writes, and then, 'I want revenge. But how?'; 'I hope the USA gets him' and 'I wish I dared to make money out of this'. And, again and again, an overwhelming fear of having contracted HIV. Still on Tuesday, 17 August, S. decides to get a prescription for the morning-after pill, and on the next day she visits a clinic for advice. Swedish hospitals offer alleged victims of sexual offences immediate and free testing for STDs. During the night from Wednesday to Thursday, her text messages become increasingly distraught: should she undergo a four-week preventive HIV antiviral therapy? She wants her test results – now!

When S. wakes up on Friday morning, 20 August, she knows: the only quick way to get clarity on a possible HIV infection is for Assange himself to get tested. If he had been infected more than three months ago, it would already show in his blood. So, if Assange tested negative now, the probability of her having contracted HIV from him would be close to zero. She sends an email to A. asking how she can get in touch with him.

That morning, S. travels to Stockholm's main hospital, Södersjukhuset, to receive strong medication as HIV post-exposure prophylaxis. The counsellor at the clinic contacts the police, and an officer speaks with S. by phone. When she tells her story, the officer explains that what she has experienced is not rape, apparently based on the – clearly inaccurate – assumption that the crime of rape requires some physical resistance on the part of the victim. But S. does not appear to be concerned with criminal law – what upsets her is that the result of her HIV test will not be available for another three months.

Then, at 11:16 a.m., A. finally sends an SMS responding to S.'s earlier email: 'Hi, here is my mobile number. [A.].' And so the two women, whose contact thus far had been merely superficial, start talking, initially by phone. They speak about their respective experiences with Assange and want to convince him to get tested for HIV. In her police interview of 2 September 2010, S. asserts that it had been A.'s idea to involve the police. According to S., A. had suggested they go to the station together and file a criminal complaint. However, they would not sign the complaint, but only use it as leverage against Assange. If he then agreed to get tested, they would simply withdraw the complaint. According to S., at the time of this phone conversation, Assange is still with A. in her small apartment, but he does not understand Swedish. Shortly thereafter, S. receives an angry call from Assange. He says that A. has asked him to call S. and told him that she, S., intends to go to the police because of the HIV test. S. begs him to just do the test, explaining that it would take him a mere thirty minutes to relieve her from a three-month wait for her own results. But Assange allegedly replies that he has to take care of Guantánamo, of human lives, and therefore has absolutely no time for such trivialities. A veritable telephonic battle ensues between all involved parties, with Donald Boström trying to mediate and get Assange to take the women's concerns seriously. When Assange finally agrees to take the test, but wants to meet S. first; it is already too late. S. no longer believes he is serious and decides to involve the police to make sure he gets tested. With that in mind, S. steps onto the escalator leading up to Klara police station, at Stockholm's main train station.

## The Police Impose a Rape Narrative

According to S., she first enters the police station around 2 p.m. At the reception, she briefly explains her concerns and then agrees to return together with A. at 4 p.m. for a meeting with a police officer experienced in the field of sexual offences. A. is still at work and cannot join earlier. Although the initial police memorandum indicates that both women arrived at the police station 'around 2 p.m.' (*vid 14 tiden*), during her police interview of 2 September 2010, S. is clear that their meeting with the police did not begin until 4 p.m. – time enough for the police to give the matter some thought. Strikingly, when S. first enters the police station at 2 p.m., the officer present at the reception appears to be keen to register a criminal complaint against Assange. Only twenty-six minutes later, at 2:26 p.m., while S. is still waiting for A. to arrive at the police station, she sends the following text message to a friend: 'I am with the police. The "sosse" [slang for social democrat, meaning A.] and I are pressing Julian via his assistant to go and get tested. The police officer appears to like the idea of getting him [*att få tag på honom*].' While I have found no direct evidence that the police were notified in advance of S.'s visit to the station, it seems to be extremely unusual, to say the least, for a law enforcement officer to demonstrate such individualized prejudice spontaneously.

S. herself has consistently emphasized, both during her police interviews and in her text messages, that she had no intention to report a crime, but visited the police station only to seek advice on how to obtain an HIV-test from Assange. She had inquired by phone about a police service specialized in such matters but was told that such a service did not exist. According to S., after her visit to the clinic at Södersjukhuset, she therefore simply went to the nearest police station. Klara police station does seem like a natural choice for S., being located in the central train station serving Enköping, her place of residence. However, Klara police station is also where Inspector Irmeli Krans is on duty at the time, a Facebook friend of A.'s with whom she has been in personal contact since at least 2009 – mere coincidence, according to A.

Be that as it may, at least the initial conversation with S. and A. is conducted by a different police officer, Inspector Linda Wassgren. S. recounts her version of the events. When A., sitting next to her, hears S.'s story, she immediately intervenes and asserts a similar experience of her own. She now tells her own story about unprotected sexual intercourse with Assange, claiming that he deliberately ripped his condom. Thus, no more than a few minutes into the conversation, the issue is no longer about pressuring Assange to take an HIV test, but takes a different turn, at least in the perception of the police. According to S., Wassgren very quickly comes to the conclusion that what has happened constitutes rape and that she, Wassgren, is therefore obliged to file a criminal report, regardless of their consent. Revealingly, Wassgren's internal memo summarizing her conversation with A. and S. focuses exclusively on justifying the opening of an investigation for rape. The women's original query regarding the possibility of forcing Assange to take an HIV test is not mentioned anywhere, and, for Inspector Wassgren, does not appear to have any relevance whatsoever. The women are confused, anxious, and reluctant to go along with a criminal report, but Wassgren makes it clear that they have no say in the matter. At the same time, she also reassures them that there will be no inconveniences and that nothing will be made public unless and until Assange is formally charged and tried in court. Wassgren's memo does not reflect the women's reluctance and legitimate concerns but immediately rewrites history. In particular, Wassgren notes that, 'from the beginning' (*inledelsevis*), the crime of rape was mentioned and that both women had been victims, which is inconsistent with the women's version of events. Therefore she, Wassgren, 'obviously' decided to talk to the women separately and ask each one for a 'detailed description' of their experiences.

While the decision to speak to the women separately is correct, of course, this should have been done from the outset. The reliability of mutually influencing witness statements has a notoriously short half-life, especially in politically exposed cases that are influenced by strong third-party interests. By the time Wassgren decides to separate the two women, they have not only discussed their respective experiences privately and come up with a joint plan on how to address their shared concerns. They have also listened to each other at the police station and have seen the initial reactions of the police officer, the suggestive effect of which can hardly be overestimated in view of their own sense of insecurity. They know, of course, that they are dealing with a celebrity. They are angry, confused and vulnerable, and they have also very quickly understood what the police wants them to say. From their point of view, it is still all about the HIV test. But the Swedish police has a different agenda.

What follows looks like a hastily prepared choreography being played out according to the script, but much too rushed to resemble a natural unfolding of events. Contrary to what her memo seems to suggest, Inspector Wassgren does not, in fact, bother to conduct detailed interviews with either woman but acts immediately. Already at 4:11 p.m., a first criminal report for rape is registered in the system, containing the – demonstrably untrue – assertion that S. herself has reported Assange for rape. Conversely, S.'s real concern – the HIV test – is not even mentioned in the report. Here too, S.'s declared needs and primary concerns appear to be perceived as completely irrelevant. All that seems to matter to the Swedish police is getting a rape allegation against Assange registered as quickly as possible. Perhaps too quickly. The electronic timestamp on the criminal report, 4:11, raises serious questions not only because it is registered only eleven minutes after the beginning of the initial meeting between Inspector Wassgren and the two women, but also because it is not recorded in the name of Wassgren but in that of

Inspector Irmeli Krans, who conducts the full interview with S. after Wassgren's initial conversation with the two women. While it is highly unlikely that Wassgren could – or would – have electronically registered a criminal report in her colleague's name, Krans's interview with S. undisputedly does not begin until ten minutes later, at 4:21, and lasts until 6:40. Needless to say, in any natural sequence of events, a criminal report by Inspector Krans would be filed at the end of her interview with S. and certainly not before it has even started. Unless, of course, the decision to report Assange for rape has been taken already in advance and Krans merely played out a plot predetermined by authorities who 'appeared to like the idea of getting him'. The electronic timestamp on the criminal report for the rape of S. certainly is yet another indicator that, from the perspective of the authorities, her visit to Klara police station may have been less spontaneous and coincidental than it has been portrayed.

A second criminal report is recorded at 4:31 p.m., this time in the name of Wassgren, again containing the – demonstrably untrue – assertion that A. had come to the police station with the intention of reporting Assange for sexual harassment. After her initial conversation with Wassgren, A. returns to work without a protocolled interview being conducted. With two registered criminal reports against Assange for sexual offences, the police seem to have obtained all that matters to them. Collecting reliable evidence in support of these allegations appears to be perceived as a formality that can be taken care of at a later stage.

To sum up, in both cases, criminal reports were registered by the police before the women had been formally interviewed, and in the case of S. before the reporting police officer had even spoken to her. In both cases, it was falsely asserted that the women themselves had intended to report a sexual offence against Assange, although this demonstrably had not been their intention. As if to cover her back, Wassgren detailed in her memo that she had consulted with various departments and that 'everyone' had been 'unanimous' that this was rape.

Both women later confirmed that Wassgren had immediately made very clear to them that the alleged facts amounted to the crime of rape and must be prosecuted ex officio, regardless of their own preferences or consent. By confronting the women with their own juridical powerlessness and the inescapability of the official rape narrative, the Swedish authorities swiftly hijacked the women's personal stories and experiences for their own purposes. It seems that they wanted to create a fait accompli as quickly as possible and without the women's interference. A. had just left the police station, and S. was still relating her version of events to Inspector Krans, when Inspector Wassgren picked up the phone and informed the public prosecutor on duty, Maria Häljebo Kjellstrand, of the two newly registered criminal reports. The prosecutor, too, struck immediately and, at 5:00 p.m., issued an arrest warrant against Assange on probable cause of rape. No written report or witness statements required, no need for clarification, no questions asked. Once the deed was done, Wassgren entered Krans's office, where S. was still being interviewed, and announced that an arrest warrant had been issued against Assange.

Let this sink in for a moment. A public prosecutor issues an arrest warrant on probable cause of rape against a politically controversial public figure, solely on the basis of a phone call from a police inspector who has spoken to two women, neither of whom intended to report a crime, but whose real request was not even taken note of? Without any recorded interview with the women, with no other evidence, and no attempt to obtain a statement from the suspect? A suspect who poses no danger whatsoever, who is not violent and who does not threaten anyone? Why so much haste? Because Assange is not a Swedish citizen, because he is a flight risk, and because he must be prevented from interfering with the investigation, the Prosecution Authority explains in a press release on the following Monday, 23 August. But then, if this was the case, why was Assange not arrested? Why was he left to find out from the press about the allegations against him? All we know for sure is that when he did find out, Assange did not try to escape, but voluntarily postponed his departure from Sweden, which had originally been planned for 25 August, by a full month and made himself available for questioning by the police and the Prosecution Authority.

When S. receives the news about the arrest warrant, she seems to be caught completely off guard. At 5:06 p.m., still sitting in Inspector Krans's office, she sends a text message to A. to inform her of the news. She is 'shocked' that they wanted to arrest Assange, S. writes, when all she wanted from him was an HIV test. In subsequent police interviews, S. recalled the 'incredible shock' and confusion of that moment, explaining that she had never intended to file a criminal complaint against Assange, that the arrest warrant was far beyond anything she could ever have imagined, and that it was the opposite of what Inspector Wassgren had promised, namely, that nothing would happen for ages, so she should not worry but try to relax. At 6:30 p.m. she writes another text message, this time to a friend: 'Did I do the right thing going to the police? He has been detained [i.e. through an arrest warrant in his absence] for raping me and sexual assault (I think) against the Sosse girl.' This friend will later testify that S. 'felt that she had been run over by the police and others.' According to Inspector Krans's closing remarks in the protocol, after learning about the arrest warrant against Assange, S. can hardly concentrate. Therefore, at 6:40 p.m. Krans decides to suspend the interview with her. S. leaves the police station without reading or approving the written version of her interview as summarized by Inspector Krans – the same police officer who had registered a criminal report for the rape of S. in the computer system before even talking to her and who, six days later, would modify S.'s statement without consulting her. At this point, right after her interview, S. still seems to desperately cling to the original plan proposed by A., namely, to try and prevent the opening of a criminal investigation by refusing to sign her own statement.

According to A.'s own account, Krans is keen to question her immediately after S. and asks her by phone to come back to the police station for a formal interview. A. responds that she is already on a train to Uppsala and would prefer to do the interview another day. Krans cautions that, in this case, it might not be her who conducts the interview. While A. seems to prefer not to be interviewed by a police officer who is also a friend or acquaintance, Inspector Krans does not appear to perceive her personal relationship with A. as presenting a potential conflict of interest. In the course of the following weeks, Krans repeatedly expresses extreme bias against Assange in social media, which eventually triggers a formal conflict-of-interest complaint against Inspector Krans to the Swedish ombudsman for the judiciary. In a breathtakingly superficial, naïve and self-defeating decision of 23 May 2011, the ombudsman dismisses the complaint, stating that the police and Prosecution Authority themselves had found Inspector Krans's conduct to be without fault and that, therefore, the ombudsman has no reason to further investigate the matter.

## Suppression of Exculpatory Evidence

Chapter 23, Section 4 of the Swedish Code of Judicial Procedure states: 'At the preliminary investigation, not only circumstances that are not in favour of the suspect but also circumstances in his favour shall be considered, and any evidence favourable to the suspect shall be preserved.' In the light of this provision, it is particularly revealing how the Swedish authorities suppressed or sidelined text messages sent by A. and S., the content of which often diametrically contradicts the official narrative disseminated by the authorities. While it is on record that the text messages stored in the personal mobile phones of the two women were seized by the police – for S. on 10 September 2010, for A. on 27 January 2011 – these messages were subsequently classified as 'secret' by the prosecutor and not even handed over to Assange's defence attorneys. The standard response of the prosecutor was that releasing the text messages would jeopardize the investigation. It took more than a year for Assange's lawyers, Thomas Olsson and Per Samuelson, to gain access to the messages and, even then, the modalities and restrictions imposed by the prosecutor were so prohibitive that the effective use of these messages as exculpatory evidence was rendered virtually impossible.

On 8 December 2011, Olsson and Samuelson were invited to the office of Chief Police Investigator Mats Gehlin to inspect several hundred printed messages he had pre-selected for them from S.'s cell phone. However, the two lawyers were not allowed to copy the messages, to transcribe them by hand or to make any notes on their content except for the date and time they were sent or received. According to the prosecutor, these restrictions were necessary for reasons of data protection and privacy – rights to which the Swedish authorities attached considerably less importance vis-à-vis Assange. This led to the bizarre situation that, in a modern democracy like Sweden, Assange's attorneys were forced to memorize exculpatory text messages and try to write down their content immediately afterwards, naturally without being able to reproduce the exact wording in every case. In view of these difficulties, the precision of their transcripts, some of which I have been able to compare with original sources, is remarkable.

Even four years later, on 16 July 2014, Assange's lawyers were prohibited from filing a printed copy of these messages as evidence to the Swedish District Court on the grounds that they had been classified by the Prosecution Authority. The same pretext for suppressing the text messages was given – and accepted – at the Court of Appeal. In consequence, even the Swedish judges, tasked with deciding on the extension of the arrest warrant against Assange, were not given access to these text messages and so had to reach their verdict relying on unverifiable claims of the prosecution. One does not need to be a law professor to understand that tactics such as these severely undermine due process safeguards and fair trial guarantees.

It was only in 2019, after their investigation had been reopened for the third time, that the Swedish Prosecution Authority produced an official English translation of those text messages from S.'s mobile phone which it acknowledged to be 'relevant for the investigation'. However, from the index numbers of the listed messages, it can be seen that there are numerous gaps where one or several messages were withheld. Most importantly, twelve messages sent or received by S. between 2:32 p.m. and 6:30 p.m. on 20 August (index 3994-4005) are missing. This is precisely the period when S. was at the police station and very upset about the rape narrative imposed on her. As mentioned earlier, we know from the transcripts made by Assange's lawyers in 2011, and from S.'s own testimony during her second police interview of 2 September 2010, that S. sent a message to A. at 5:06 p.m., expressing her shock at the news about the arrest warrant. Despite its obvious importance for Assange's defence, this message was deliberately suppressed by the Swedish Prosecution Authority. There is a second, particularly significant gap of sixty-six messages sent or received from 7:36 a.m. on 21 August (when the women started exchanging messages expressing strong disagreement with the official rape narrative published in the media) until 3:31 p.m. on 23 August when the women finally had been assigned a legal counsel fiercely promoting precisely that narrative (index 4018-4083).

By deliberately withholding exculpatory or mitigating evidence, the Swedish authorities not only violated Assange's procedural rights as set out in the Swedish Code of Judicial Procedure but, in conjunction with their aggressive dissemination of the rape allegations, may even have committed the criminal offence of false accusation.

## Headline: 'Julian Assange Hounded on Suspicion of Rape'

But Friday, 20 August 2010, the day of the women's visit to the police station, is not over yet. In the evening, a journalist – who was attending a crayfish party with the inner circle of Sweden's political leadership at the time – learns of the arrest warrant against Assange on probable cause of rape. It is not known who leaked the information and whether it was leaked directly to the journalist, or whether the police or Prosecution Authority informally alerted key figures in the political leadership, who then tipped off the journalist at the party. Either way, the circle of possible culprits for the original leak is small.

The journalist immediately passes the information on to a colleague at the tabloid *Expressen*, and *Expressen* does what any tabloid paper would do: they call the prosecutor, Maria Häljebo Kjellstrand, that same Friday evening. Is it true that she has issued an arrest warrant against Julian Assange? The inconceivable happens: Kjellstrand loquaciously confirms to *Expressen* not only that an arrest warrant has been issued against Assange, but also that there is probable cause of rape (*på sannolika skäl misstänkt för våldtäkt*) involving two victims. Has she spoken to the women? No, she has not. Nor does she know when the rape complaint was made – she herself received it from the police just an hour ago. No, she has no idea where Assange is and whether he is being searched for, but she hopes and assumes that this is the case. Having said all that, Kjellstrand then concludes that, in consideration of all those involved, she can say 'absolutely nothing' (*inte nånting*) about the case at this time.

*Expressen* further specifies that the women allegedly did not want to file a criminal complaint. 'The women are scared to death [*är livrädda*] and therefore do not dare to cooperate. In this case, the police believe that the reason for their fear is the position of power of the perpetrator [*gärningsmannen*].' And so, with the stroke of a pen, the non-violent 'suspect' has become a menacing 'perpetrator'. No mention of mere suspicion, no hint of the presumption of innocence and, above all, no resemblance to what the women had reported to have experienced. Another source, described by *Expressen* as a 'person close to the women' (*person nära kvinnorna*), seemed to have a great deal of detailed knowledge, namely that the alleged victims were aged between twenty and thirty, that they know each other, and that one of the alleged offences was committed on Tuesday morning in Enköping and the other on the previous weekend in an apartment in Södermalm.

To make matters worse, two days later, on Monday, 23 August, the police releases part of their investigative case file to the Swedish press in prompt response to a freedom of information request. The thirty-nine-page fax, sent between 4:28 and 4:30 p.m., includes the original summaries of the interviews with S. (from p. 7) and A. (from p. 18). While sensitive information has been largely redacted, the police have failed to redact A.'s name and surname from the title of her interview summary, thus revealing her full identity to the press. But the publication of all this information now also makes it impossible for S. to remain anonymous, and soon the identities of both women are common knowledge.

The Swedish authorities know, of course, that their indiscretion will expose both Assange and the two women to a relentless media circus and needlessly undermine the objectivity of the investigation. However, neither the privacy and protection of the individuals concerned nor the effectiveness of the investigation seem to be a priority for the officials in charge. According to Sven-Erik Alhem, former chief prosecutor and director of public prosecution in Stockholm and Malmö, the authorities' indiscretion clearly violated the applicable Swedish Secrecy Act (2009:400), according to which the identity of those involved in a preliminary investigation must be kept confidential unless and until charges are brought. The same opinion is shared by Brita Sundberg-Weitman, a former law professor, appeal judge and president of the Solna District Court, who, like Alhem, has written an expert report for Assange's defence lawyers detailing some of the most notorious due process violations that have tarnished the Swedish preliminary investigation against him.

The legal situation is clear – the Swedish authorities violated not only their specific duty of confidentiality, but also their general duty of care as expressly set out in Chapter 23 of the Swedish Code of Judicial Procedure: 'The investigation should be conducted so that no person is unnecessarily exposed to suspicion or put to unnecessary expense or inconvenience.' From the start, the authorities themselves seriously undermined the objectivity and effectiveness of the investigation. They publicly disclosed Assange's identity without any evidence for his criminal culpability, without any imminent danger or temporal urgency, without having formally interviewed either the suspect or the alleged victims, and without any consideration for the harm likely to result from their indiscretion to everyone involved. This course of action also disproved the credibility of their purported justification for the arrest warrant, namely that Assange was a flight risk. Had such a risk really existed, no prosecutor in their right mind would have publicly announced the arrest warrant in the mass media, thus giving the suspect an advance warning he could not possibly miss. Unless, of course, their real intention was to provoke Assange's flight as a means of obtaining probative evidence for his culpability.

In any case, neither Prosecutor Kjellstrand nor anyone else was ever held accountable for a breach of duty, nor were any disciplinary measures taken. A complaint was reportedly filed with the Swedish ombudsman for the judiciary who, once again, swiftly found a boilerplate excuse for evading his official responsibilities – this time, he reportedly did not wish to interfere with an ongoing proceeding. Given that all the judiciary really does is to conduct investigative and judicial proceedings, it is rather hard to conceive of a case where the ombudsman could exercise effective parliamentary oversight over the judiciary without 'interfering' with an ongoing investigation or proceeding. As already demonstrated in the cases of Inspector Krans and the unlawful rendition of Agiza and Al Zery, the ombudsman's record of ex post facto investigating and confronting official misconduct does not seem any brighter, at least not when overriding national security interests are involved.

Early on Saturday, 21 August 2010, the day after the police interview, around 5 a.m., *Expressen*'s headline reads: 'WikiLeaks Julian Assange hounded on suspicion of rape in Sweden' [*Wikileaks Julian Assange jagas misstänkt för våldtäkt i Sverige*]. Within minutes, the news rockets around the world. Assange himself learns it from the press and reacts at 9:15 a.m. on the Twitter channel of WikiLeaks: 'We were warned to expect "dirty tricks". Now we see the first one.' By now, at the latest, the two women must have understood that control over their own story had been snatched from them. Within less than twenty-four hours, their attempt to use the police to pressure Assange into taking an HIV test had backfired and triggered an avalanche of unforeseen events that could no longer be stopped. The SMS correspondence of the two women bear witness to the tremendous pressure they suddenly find themselves exposed to. Already at 7:09 on Saturday morning, S. writes to a friend, 'I feel awful. It's already in the news even though it was supposed to be confidential. I have to choose a lawyer, "a reputable name, criminal lawyer, preferably a man", the police said. Help!' And then, when asked what was in the press, she writes: 'That one of the offences was committed in Enköping. Bloody police! It was supposed to be confidential and we said we didn't want to submit a report.' Almost simultaneously comes a text message, whose sender is blacked out, but which only A. could have written: 'It's in the media now, check out Expressen. Bloody hell. I don't know what to do other than be quiet and turn off my phone.' S. replies at 7:33 a.m., 'I know, I am in a total panic. Fuck, I don't want to be part of this. I wish I could flee the country.' A. replies at 7:36, 'Take it easy dear, no one knows you are involved, right?'

As indicated earlier, the next sixty-six text messages sent or received by S., some of which reportedly provided clear evidence for S.'s disagreement with the official narrative imposed on her, have been deliberately withheld from Assange's defence lawyers by the Swedish Prosecution Authority. The official trail of messages picks up only fifty-seven hours later, once the two women had been assigned a legal counsel bent on aggressively pursuing precisely that narrative. A small number of messages transcribed by Assange's lawyers nevertheless testify to the fundamental transformation of attitude forced onto A. and S. during this period of radio silence.

Not surprisingly, after the initial shock, the two women soon realize that they have no choice but to come to terms with the new reality. On Saturday evening, 21 August, at 10:25 p.m., S. still complains in a transcribed text message that it was the 'police who made up the charges'. But by Monday morning, 23 August, her tone has changed. Again according to the lawyers' own transcription, at 6:43 a.m., A. wrote to S. that it was important that she – S. – went public with her story so that they could mobilize public opinion for their case. Then on Thursday, 26 August, at 1:38 p.m., A. suggested to S. that they ought to sell their stories to a newspaper, and on 28 August, at 12:53 p.m., reported that they had a contact at the largest Swedish tabloid. S. reportedly replied on the same day, at 3:59 p.m., that their lawyer was negotiating with the tabloid. Caution should be exercised when interpreting this correspondence. Given the circumstances, I do not believe that the motivation for these messages was primarily monetary, but rather that they reflect a desperate attempt by the women to somehow keep the 'upper hand' in a situation where they had already been effectively stripped of all influence and control – a common compensatory pattern shown by people who have been cornered.

Given the scandalous headlines and the official confirmation given by the authorities, a differentiated account of what the women had experienced with Julian Assange was no longer possible. In the eyes of the broader public, Assange was either a rapist or he had been falsely accused – there was no longer any space for grey zones, for misunderstandings, for accidents, or for alternative explanations. A. and S. had to choose: would they jump on the bandwagon of the official rape narrative and, in return, be able to count on the full support of the public authorities? Or would they challenge the official rape narrative, inevitably raising questions as to why they had visited the police station in the first place and, possibly, inviting criminal complaints for false accusation or defamation as well as financial claims? In the latter case, the two women would have to face not only the wrath of Assange and his devoted entourage, of which they themselves had been an integral part just twenty-four hours earlier, but they would also be abandoned by the Swedish authorities and exposed to severe criticism by the press, if not the entire world public.

When evaluating the behaviour and statements of A. and S., therefore, due consideration must always be given to the fact that, through no fault of their own, they have been under enormous pressure to conform to the official rape narrative ever since the first *Expressen* headlines and until today. Accordingly, from this point on, the women's original concern – the HIV test – all but disappears, even in their private text messages and correspondence. Their primary trauma now no longer seems to be a possible HIV infection, but the relentless media hype and the threats and abuse they receive on social media. Had the authorities complied with their duty of confidentiality as required by Swedish law, this investigation would have disappeared into the archives of the Swedish Prosecution Authority after only a few days. But that was not what the Swedish authorities appeared to have in mind.

## The Questioning of A.

Just a few hours after the *Expressen* shock, on Saturday, 21 August, at 11:31 a.m., the first formal police interview of A. takes place – by phone. This is an important detail, because the initial questioning of a possible rape victim should never be conducted on the phone. It is not only a matter of reliably identifying the person being questioned, but also of being able to identify and address situations of anxiety or distress which may not be expressed verbally, but rather through body language, facial expressions and gestures. It must have been clear to the police that A. was under intense pressure at the time of the interview and could not be properly questioned over the phone. By this point, the authorities had already informed the whole world in no uncertain terms how her experience with Assange was to be legally categorized: 'Rape, alternatively sexual harassment' were the crimes referenced at the top of the interview summary written by Inspector Sara Wennerblom.

Just as with S., the initial interview of A. is not witnessed by a second officer and is not recorded on tape but is merely summarized by the questioning inspector in her own words. This is clearly contrary to standard professional practice, as it makes it impossible to verify whether the initial testimonies used against the suspect have been influenced by leading questions or implicit expectations. An unfortunate coincidence? No, because this is exactly how the police will proceed for the initial questioning of all seven witnesses who are either friends or relatives of the two women and, therefore, likely to be supportive of them. None of these statements are made in the presence of a second police officer, none of them are recorded on tape, and none are reproduced verbatim, but merely summarized in the words of the interviewing officer. As the police are very well aware, these witnesses perceive the authorities as acting in the interest of the two women and so are unlikely to question or correct the precise manner or wording in which their statements are summarized by the interviewing officer.

Conversely, Assange's own interview is conducted by the book in the presence of a second police officer, is duly recorded on tape and reproduced verbatim. Assange, of course, is unlikely to accept a freely paraphrased summary of his statement, and he is accompanied by his defence lawyer, who gives the authorities no wiggle room. Likewise, the interviews of Donald Boström and Johannes Wahlström are both conducted in the presence of a second police officer, recorded on tape and reproduced in their original wording. Boström and Wahlström are both experienced journalists, who have a neutral attitude towards the involved parties, choose their words carefully and insist on their verbatim recording.

A. herself does not contradict Inspector Wennerblom's summary of her statement. As noted earlier, she is convinced that Assange intentionally ripped his condom during sexual inter-course. She clearly acknowledges, however, that this is only an assumption, that she did not see Assange actually ripping the condom, and that she has not even verified whether the condom, which she still has in her possession at home, really was damaged. In the police summary of her statement, A. further affirms that Assange initially – that is, before their sexual intercourse – prevented her from reaching for a condom 'by holding her arms and prying open her legs while trying to penetrate her […] without a condom'. But then, 'after a moment, Assange asked [A.] what she was doing and why she was squeezing her legs together. [A.] then told him that she wanted him to wear a condom before he came in her. At that, Assange released [A.]'s arms and put on a condom that [A.] fetched for him.' The telephone interview of A. ends at 12:20 p.m.

Just three and a half hours later, at 3:55, another major Swedish newspaper, *Aftonbladet*, publishes an interview with A. in which she partially corrects the *Expressen* article: 'It is absolutely wrong to say that we did not want to report Assange because we were afraid of him. He is not violent, and I don't feel threatened by him.' A. emphasizes that she sees herself as a victim of sexual coercion or harassment, but not of rape. Contrary to S.'s own testimony and text messages, however, A. consistently claims that S. wanted to file a criminal report for rape, while A. had merely accompanied her in order to support S. with her own testimony. According to A., the allegations against Assange were not orchestrated by the Pentagon, of course, but were the responsibility of a man with a 'distorted image of women' and difficulties 'taking "no" for an answer'. However, at least according to the written summary of her police interview given earlier that morning, 'Assange made sexual advances to her every day after the evening when they had sex' and A. 'had rejected him on every such occasion, which Assange had accepted' in each case – that is to say, her 'no'.

## First Discontinuation of Investigation

Barely half an hour after A.'s interview in *Aftonbladet*, the case takes another dramatic turn. The Swedish attorney general, concerned that the case was too sensitive to be left to a duty prosecutor's care until Monday, transmits the written summaries of the two police interviews to Eva Finné, chief prosecutor for Stockholm, for review. Finné reacts quickly. Around 4:30 on Saturday afternoon, she cancels the arrest warrant issued by Kjellstrand the evening before and releases a press statement: 'I do not believe there is any reason to suspect him of rape.' Given that the Prosecution Authority had already caused a worldwide media flurry by publicly confirming both the arrest warrant against Assange and the probable cause of rape, Finné must have been very confident in her assessment to perform such a rapid and dramatic U-turn. She knew, of course, that her decision was sure to be painstakingly scrutinized by powerful stakeholders with vested interests. Therefore, based on the original written summaries of the police interviews with A. and S., it must have been plainly evident to any experienced prosecutor that the crime of rape, as defined in the Swedish criminal code in 2010, could be excluded in both cases. For the time being, Finné does not want to rule out sexual harassment in either case, but this reduces the minimum sentence below the threshold of one year's imprisonment, which is generally required for an arrest warrant.

In the case of S., Finné even proceeds to drop the investigation altogether only a few days later, on 25 August 2010. The official press release reads: 'As previously announced, the information obtained from interviewing [S.] is such that the suspicion of rape no longer exists. This does not mean that I do not believe her statements. I have studied the content of the interview to see whether there is any suspicion of another offence, primarily harassment or sexual harassment, but my analysis shows that this is not the case. The investigation is therefore closed as far as this complaint is concerned, as there is no suspicion of a crime.' The communiqué concludes by affirming that, in the case of A., 'the suspicion of molestation remains. I will instruct the investigator to interview the suspect'.

Finné's impending discontinuation of S.'s case had become foreseeable with her lifting of the arrest warrant over the weekend. Accordingly, on Monday, 23 August, S.'s text messages begin to express growing concern. Already during her interview on Friday evening, the police had recommended that she take a lawyer, 'a reputable name, a criminal defence lawyer, preferably a man'. Now, on Monday, S. and A. will be assigned a legal counsel fitting this description perfectly. Claes Borgström is an ambitious lawyer who has earned his political credentials as the Swedish government's equality ombudsman and is standing for the Social Democratic Party in the upcoming parliamentary elections of September 2010.

However, earlier that year, he had received disastrous press coverage and later would even be subjected to an – ultimately inconsequential – disciplinary investigation by the Swedish Bar Association for his controversial role as defence counsel in what has been described as the biggest judicial scandal in Swedish history. Borgström's client, Sture Bergwall, aka Thomas Quick, a drug-addicted psychiatric patient, had voluntarily confessed to thirty-three unresolved murders – each of which he had, it later transpired, read about in the newspapers. He was convicted in eight cases and considered the biggest serial killer in Sweden. Despite the lack of reliable evidence and motives, the credibility of Quick's confessions was never questioned by the police, the prosecutor or the courts, and not even by Borgström, his own defence counsel. In a spooky preview of what was to come in the Assange investigation, police interviews were manipulated, and contradictory or exculpatory evidence was suppressed in order to support the authorities' preferred narrative of Quick as the mentally deranged serial killer. It took a ninth murder prosecution, the tireless work of investigative journalist Hannes Råstam, and the sober eye of an experienced chief prosecutor – Eva Finné – to expose and terminate this grotesque travesty of justice in May 2010. As a result, Bergwall withdrew all his fantasized confessions, replaced his defence counsel, was acquitted on all counts and, after twenty years of confinement, was released an innocent man. Clearly, this outcome was bad press for Borgström and bad news for his political ambitions. In August 2010, then, he urgently needed a high-profile case with which to rehabilitate and polish his reputation with a view to the upcoming parliamentary elections, which were just weeks away. The Assange case, with Chief Prosecutor Eva Finné on the opposing end, must have been a perfect match.

On the Monday following the Friday police interview, 23 August 2010, at 4:31 p.m., S. sends the following text message: 'Claes Borgström is my lawyer now. Hope he can help me get out of this shit.' In Sweden, it is standard practice for the state to assign a public legal counsel to alleged crime victims, at least in more complex cases. Invited by the court to comment on Borgström's request, Chief Prosecutor Finné only writes: 'I have no objections to the appointment of legal counsel to the injured party. This is justified in view of mass media attention.' Finné's unequivocal abandonment of the rape narrative must have been deeply unsettling to the two women. After all, only twenty-four hours earlier, the same rape narrative had been forcefully imposed on them at the Klara police station, only after having been dismissed by another police officer via telephone a few hours earlier. Given this dizzying back and forth, the women cannot be blamed for being confused. For them, however, the primary burden does not appear to be any alleged misconduct by Assange, but their unwarranted public exposure in conjunction with the uncertainty resulting from the constantly changing official narrative. Tellingly, in her text message, S. does not express the hope that Borgström will help her to obtain 'justice', or to make Assange take an HIV test, but that he will get her 'out of this shit'. Given that both criminal reports falsely state that it was the women who, on their own initiative, filed a criminal complaint against Assange, they may also have become worried about a possible complaint against them for false accusation, defamation or other legal claims relating to reputational damage.

On Monday, 23 August, Inspector Mats Gehlin, to whom the case has just been assigned, writes a memo stating that, in S.'s case, the elements of rape are fulfilled. However, in A.'s case, he notes that there might be a 'deception' (*vilseledande*), and that it is unclear whether there is any offence at all. The reason for this assumption is redacted. Exactly one week later, on 30 August, Chief Prosecutor Eva Finné issues an order stating that a criminal complaint for false accusation will not be acted upon, for lack of sufficient evidence of the crime. The complaint was submitted the day after the *Expressen* headline, on Sunday, 22 August, and assigned the file number belonging to the preliminary investigation against Assange. The Swedish authorities have not disclosed who had lodged the complaint and against whom.

Still on that Monday, in the afternoon, the following text messages are exchanged between S. and a friend: 'No. My lawyer takes care of everything so I can't comment. Will try to work this week.' Unfortunately, we are not told what exactly S. cannot comment on – the immediately preceding text message (index 4087) has been picked out and suppressed by the Swedish Prosecution Authority. In any case, her friend writes back, 'Oh you've sued him. That's great. I hope the swine gets what he deserves.' S. replies, 'No, the police got it all started, I didn't want to be part of it, but now I have no choice ...' There really is no better way to explain the coercion of the two women into conforming with the official rape narrative than through these desperate words sent out by S. that afternoon.

## 'Necessary changes' to S.'s Interview

On the same Monday, 23 August, Inspector Irmeli Krans wants to edit her summary of S.'s interview. Krans had written the summary with the help of the text creation program in the police's own DurTvå system immediately after the – rather abrupt – end of S.'s interview on Friday evening. But when she returned to the office after the weekend, the system denied her access to her own summary. Inspector Gehlin provides the explanation the same morning at 10:26 a.m. in an email to Chief Prosecutor Finné: 'Hello Eva, I have been given the honour of handling this case. [...] Journalists are calling from all corners of the world!!! I have extended access protection in DurTvå. Need a secrecy stamp on the case. Everyone wants the police report'.

Apparently, Gehlin's first official act after taking over the preliminary investigation against Assange had been to restrict internal access in the system and, curiously, to exclude Krans. At 4:28 that afternoon, a redacted copy of S.'s original interview summary is faxed to a Swedish press contact, reportedly in – rather prompt – response to a freedom of information request. On that fax copy, the decisive passages describing the alleged sexual misconduct have been redacted. The original, unredacted version appears to have been eliminated from the official investigative case documents archived by the authorities and – presumably – no longer exists. On the next day, 24 August, Inspector Gehlin logs the following memo: 'Spoke with Eva Finné. She does not believe it is rape. Inform her that I do not agree, but that it is her case. She told me not to take action until she has read through the case documents. Interview of injured party to Claes Borgström.'

So, according to Inspector Gehlin's diary, Borgström obtains a copy of S.'s original interview by the latest on 24 August – something Assange's lawyer will be denied for months to come – and also meets personally with the two women. Borgström's intention is clear. He does not want to accept the impending closure of the preliminary investigation in the case of S. and intends to appeal Finné's decision to the next hierarchical level, the director of public prosecution. But this requires strong arguments. Given the worldwide media attention and the public scrutiny of her handling of the case, Finné would have examined the material particularly carefully before cancelling the arrest warrant and then officially dropping the entire case of S. for lack of evidence of any criminal conduct. Had Finné harboured even the slightest doubt, she might still have dropped the arrest warrant but would certainly have allowed the preliminary investigation to continue for a few days, at least for a less serious offence, until Assange could be formally interviewed. As explained by Kjellstrand on Sunday, 22 August, in an interview with *Expressen*, Swedish prosecutors do not normally reverse each other's decisions except on the basis of new facts.

Borgström's complaint against Finné's decision will be addressed to the competent higher authority: Director of Public Prosecution Marianne Ny in Gothenburg, a personal friend of Borgström's. When Borgström receives the original interview with S., he knows it has not yet been read and approved by S. and can still be amended or corrected. Inspector Krans, who is tasked with editing the text of S.'s interview, will on 25 August appear on Facebook describing the discontinuation of that case by Chief Prosecutor Eva Finné as a 'SCANDAAAAAAAAL!!!!!', and expressing her delight that 'our dear, eminent and highly competent Claes Borgström will hopefully bring some order.'

Inspector Gehlin, her superior, has also made clear in his diary that he disagrees with Finné's decision.

It is against this background that the following email exchange between Inspectors Gehlin and Krans takes place from 23 to 26 August, and for which the Swedish authorities have refused to provide any explanation. On 23 August, at 8:27 a.m., Krans writes: 'Hello, I hope I have done it right now and the document reaches you as it should. Please send me a confirmation. Regarding the verbal report to the prosecutor, I only know that it was made by Linda Wassgren by phone sometime during the interview [i.e. the original police report to Prosecutor Kjellstrand on the afternoon of 20 August while S. was still being interviewed by Krans]. What was reported is unknown to me, as Wassgren did not want to communicate with me. There was no opportunity to discuss the crime classification with the prosecutor, but I was told that it should be classified as rape on the instructions of the prosecutor.'

Why didn't Wassgren want to communicate with Krans? Why was Krans excluded from the investigation of this case, despite the fact that she was the only officer who had actually spoken with S. in detail and had heard the precise words of her original statement? Despite? Or perhaps rather because of it? It is not until one day later, at 9:33 a.m., that Gehlin responds: 'Good morning Irmeli! Proceed as follows. Copy this into an interview and sign the interview. It would look strange if I signed it. I attach the old interview.' Krans, an experienced police officer after all, is at a loss. At 1:38 p.m., she replies: 'I may be dim, but I don't really understand what you mean.' Gehlin replies just six minutes later. 'Create a new interview. Add the text and assign the interview to the case file. Sign the interview, too.' Krans's confusion persists: 'Sure, but then there are two interviews. But only one formal interview has been conducted, by me anyway. So where does the second interview go? If everything is to be done correctly, I suppose I must make the changes in the original interview and then sign it. At the risk of appearing to be difficult, I do not want an unsigned document with my name on it circulating in DurTvå space. Especially not now that the matter has evolved in this way.' It is not until two days later, on Thursday, 26 August at 12:30 p.m., after an email exchange with Claes Borgström, that Gehlin concludes his correspondence with Krans with the assurance, 'Yes, but I'll write a memo about it.' Two hours later, Krans generates S.'s new interview in the DurTvå system, replacing the original document. The next day, on 27 August, Borgström will join this revised interview to a complaint submitted to Prosecutor Marianne Ny requesting the case of S. to be reopened and the allegations in the case of A. to be extended.

While the correspondence between Gehlin and Krans may remain cryptic to outsiders, there can be no doubt that Gehlin asked Krans to do something very unusual, if not suspicious. Krans, whose access to the original interview had been blocked by Gehlin, appears to be confused, reluctant and nervous about not acting correctly. This feeling does not seem to have lessened even several days after Krans had completed her task. When the preliminary investigation in S.'s case is reopened on 1 September, thus making it likely that S.'s interview will be subjected to judicial review, Krans makes sure to attach a memo to the interview at 4:45 p.m. The memo explains that, on Gehlin's instructions, a new interview with the 'necessary changes' was created on 26 August 2010, at 2:43 p.m.; and that this timestamp was automatically adopted by the system as the beginning of the interview, although it had actually been conducted on 20 August, between 4:21 and 6:40 p.m.

What changes exactly were made and why they were 'necessary' cannot be determined with certainty, since the original interview has been heavily redacted. In any case, it cannot have been a matter of pure spelling corrections, which would never have triggered such an extensive correspondence and so much discomfort. When one compares the original (but redacted) interview with the revised (but unredacted) version, both of which were printed in the same font and format, it is quite evident that the text has become slightly longer. Depending on whether the black censorship bars extend beyond the text lines printed underneath or reflect their exact length, a total of between one and three lines of text appears to have been inserted in the paragraph describing the alleged sexual misconduct. Where did these 'necessary changes' come from? S. had not been consulted, no tape recording had been made of her statement, and no other officer had witnessed the interview. Moreover, six days after the interview, too much time had already passed for reliable corrections to be made based on Inspector Krans's personal recollection. Why did Gehlin's request make Krans so nervous? Had someone perhaps suggested alternative wording that would increase the chances of the case being reopened? To encourage a different appreciation of the case by the director of public prosecution, it would not be necessary to substantially change the entire story – slight adjustments in the wording could be enough.

Let us remember that, according to the Swedish criminal code in force at the time, the alleged conduct of Assange could only constitute rape if, at least at the beginning of the sexual act, S. had been asleep, and therefore incapable of giving free and full consent to unprotected sexual intercourse. Thus, whether S.'s interview described her state at the time as being 'asleep', 'half asleep', or 'sleepy', and whether it said that Assange 'initiated', 'attempted', or had already 'penetrated' S. at the relevant moment, are not semantic quibbles, but could have tipped the scales so as to justify – or not – resuscitating the rape allegation against Assange. Given that the original text of S.'s interview was not transcribed verbatim from a tape recording, but had been summarized in Krans's own words, a subsequent manipulation cannot be ruled out. As long as the Swedish authorities are allowed to hide behind a convenient veil of secrecy, the truth about this dubious episode may never come to light.

## Shadow Boxing around Condoms and DNA Analyses

In parallel, a bizarre sideshow arises in connection with the condoms used by Assange with the two women and their suitability as evidence to substantiate the rape allegations against him. During her initial phone interview on 21 August, when asked by Inspector Sara Wennerblom, A. says that she believes she still possesses the condom used by Assange during sexual intercourse with her eight days earlier. A. acknowledges that she has not verified whether it is damaged at all but promises to check. She also says that she probably still has the unwashed bedsheet on which Assange's sperm might be found. On the same day, at 6:21 p.m., Wennerblom personally knocks on A.'s front door and takes the following items into police custody: 'a sheet, cotton, blue, taken from the laundry basket' (Exhibit 2010-0201-BG20840-1) as well as a condom, torn, 'found in the wastepaper basket and put in a box' (Exhibit 2010-0201-BG20840-2).

S. takes even more time and waits a full sixteen days from the date of the alleged rape before handing over to Inspector Gehlin, during her second interview on 2 September, a torn piece of a condom, which she says to have found under her bed. According to her initial interview twelve days earlier, however, she had returned home to 'clean up and wash everything' immediately after Assange had left. She mentioned the presence of semen on the bedsheets but, at least according to the summary written by Inspector Krans, does not appear to have found the piece of condom at that time. According to a memo written by Gehlin another six weeks later, on 20 October 2010, S. allegedly had not noticed in the darkness that a condom had been damaged, but she heard a sound as if he were 'pulling a balloon' when he put the condom on. It is striking to see how the stories of A. and S. begin to converge over time. In the original interview, only A. had spoken of a torn condom and strange sounds of snapping latex. Now, with the Prosecution Authority running out of promising investigative steps to be taken in support of their allegations against Assange, the same elements suddenly start appearing in the case of S. as well.

Such 'evidentiary harmonization' is a form of confirmation bias resulting from deliberate or inadvertent suggestive questioning, or from mutual witness influence. It is quite common in investigations where the same officials are tasked with interviewing several witnesses and tend to use leading questions to elicit the elements they are looking for. In the present case, it suggests an attempt by the authorities to strengthen the evidentiary value of the two interviews by 'harmonizing' some of their components. Such manipulative methods of questioning had reportedly been used extensively during the police investigation of the Bergwall/Quick case in order to gloss over serious evidential contradictions and confirm the misdirected 'mass murderer' narrative favoured by the authorities.

On 24 August, Chief Prosecutor Finné requests a forensic examination of the condom submitted by A. with a view to determining how it had been damaged. Inspector Gehlin hands the condom over to the technical service of the police. The service is unable to answer the question and passes the task on to the State Forensic Laboratory, SKL. The condom fragment submitted by S. is likewise handed over to the laboratory to determine how exactly it was damaged. In its report of 25 October 2010, SKL offers the initial results of its analysis. At the same time it issues an express disclaimer clarifying that it lacks the accreditation – required under the industry standard (ISO/IEC17025) – for investigating the actual question before it, namely the cause of the damage done to the latex material of the condoms. As the laboratory will confirm in an extensive letter sent to the police on 20 June 2012, it essentially investigated a matter for which it lacked the required standard procedures and specialized expertise. Instead, the laboratory staff intentionally damaged the condom submitted by A. with a knife, with scissors, and by ripping off its lower part. When comparing the three types of damage under the microscope, the one resulting from ripping off part of the condom showed the greatest similarity with the pre-existing damage. The same opinion was reached about the condom fragment submitted by S. The official conclusion was that, in both cases, the observed damage had been caused by the condom being ripped. The probability level for this hypothesis was said to be '+2', which means that there is a 'small' probability that the laboratory's conclusion is wrong. On the scale of forensic probative value, this is situated at the lower medium level of strength: one level above mere circumstantial evidence

(+1), and two levels below evidence capable of excluding other hypotheses (+4). As would be expected, however, the laboratory was unable to determine who had ripped the condoms, at what point in time, and whether the damage had been caused deliberately or accidentally.

Equally unsurprisingly, on the condom fragment provided by S. the laboratory found S.'s DNA, as well as that of a man. Although the authorities continue to keep the identity of this man secret, it can reasonably be assumed to be Assange. After all, neither Assange nor S. have disputed that they had repeatedly and voluntarily engaged in sexual intercourse during which condoms had been used. Both also agree that, during their last sexual intercourse, which gave rise to the rape allegation, Assange did not wear a condom from the beginning. So, whatever had happened to the condom fragment submitted by S., it was entirely irrelevant to the rape allegation made against Assange. In the case of S., the only question to be investigated was whether their unprotected intercourse was initiated by Assange while S. was helpless due to sleep – a question which even the best forensic expert could not be expected to answer.

The laboratory had significantly more trouble finding DNA on the condom submitted by A. According to Inspector Gehlin's memo of 20 October 2010, the laboratory initially could not detect any DNA whatsoever. Eight days later, on 28 October, Gehlin corrects himself in another, much more elaborate memo: he had now had the opportunity to discuss the results of the DNA analyses with the SKL. The forensic scientist had explained that it was not correct to state that no DNA had been found on A.'s condom, because 'something' had been seen, but it had not been possible to interpret it. Gehlin goes on to list a number of possible reasons for these interpretative difficulties which, according to the scientist, included: interference with the analysis due to contamination, etc.; small amount of DNA; people leaving varying amounts of DNA substrate; the material under examination having been washed, dried or otherwise affected after it was used. Gehlin made sure to mention that these were just some examples, and other factors could also have affected

the result. In view of the nature of the item here – a condom
that allegedly had been worn and torn during intercourse – these
explanations seem rather far-fetched and reveal preferences that
can hardly be reconciled with objective fact-finding. In any case,
as Gehlin noted, the laboratory decided to carry out an additional, more refined DNA analysis which would take another
two weeks to complete. The methodology to be followed was the
highly complex 'Low Copy Number' (LCN) procedure, which
can be applied to extremely small trace elements and incomplete
DNA fragments, but which often produces much less reliable
results and is therefore not accepted as forensic evidence in the
courts of most states.

The projected two weeks turn into more than eight months
before the laboratory finally renders its final report on 15 July
2011. The report states that on one side of the condom, DNA had
been detected that could be matched to a person. The next three
explanatory lines are crossed out with a thick censoring pen and
followed by the indicated probability level of '+2'. Again: one
level above circumstantial evidence (+1), and two levels below
evidence capable of excluding other hypotheses (+4) – in any
case much weaker than a standard DNA analysis, where probative values of 99.999 per cent and above are quite common.

Before getting carried away with forensic technicalities,
however, let us pause for a moment and use our common sense.
In the cases of both A. and S., it is worth asking exactly what
factual allegations or circumstances these DNA analyses were
supposed to prove. Just as in the case of S., Assange acknowledged that sexual intercourse with A. had occurred and that
a condom had been used. He only denied having ripped the
condom intentionally. Therefore, even a perfectly reliable DNA
match based on an abundant DNA substrate – which would
have to be expected on a used condom – would only prove
that A. had actually submitted the condom that had been used
together with Assange. Whether the condom was torn intentionally or accidentally, by whom and at what time, are questions
that defy forensic determination – certainly within the param-
eters of the given circumstances. In this respect, Assange claims

that he was not even aware that the condom had been damaged, whereas A. is sure that he ripped it on purpose. A. acknowledges, however, that this is a mere assumption and that she did not see him destroy the condom. Even during her police interview, one week later, she still does not know whether the condom is damaged at all, although she still has it in her possession. It is quite clear that, until her police interview on 21 August, neither Assange nor A. seem to have been sufficiently preoccupied with this question to at least verify whether the condom – which for a whole week lay in the trash can of the apartment where they were staying together – was damaged or not.

The police also task the laboratory with examining the stain on A.'s bedsheet for DNA and semen. Here, too, the evidentiary added value remains unclear. During their interviews, both A. and Assange have confirmed that they noticed and commented on this stain shortly after sexual intercourse, but did not give it any importance and so did not pursue the matter further. As the police know very well, the decisive question of whether the condom was ripped intentionally or accidentally cannot be clarified by this analysis either. It is therefore no coincidence that Gehlin did not request the laboratory to conduct this analysis until six months after the alleged events, on 1 March 2011.

The trigger for the belated request must have been that, one week earlier, the Swedish extradition request for Assange had been approved by Westminster Magistrates' Court in London. Depending on whether the High Court would accept to hear Assange's appeal, his imminent extradition to Sweden had become a realistic possibility. This had abruptly increased the pressure on Prosecutor Marianne Ny. Suddenly, she might have now to present sufficient evidence to the court in support of an indictment of Assange, failing which he would have to be released and cleared of all allegations. As a result, the police and Prosecution Authority start scrambling for circumstantial and technical elements which could help to gloss over the precarious lack of prosecutable evidence in support of the official rape narrative. From a professional investigative perspective, the Swedish prosecutor must have been fully aware not only of the evidentiary irrelevance of all these laboratory tests, but also of the fact that, in reality, there had never been any prospect of a successful conviction. The only conceivable motivation for undertaking such pointless efforts is that this forensic hyperactivity was to serve as a smokescreen to persuade the judges and the public that a serious criminal investigation was underway which required Assange's extradition, detention and indictment.

Let us recall that, regardless of whatever took place between Assange and the two women, in both cases his criminal liability depended entirely on factors that objectively could not be proved beyond reasonable doubt. In the case of S., the only decisive question was whether she had been asleep or awake at the first moment of sexual contact initiated by Assange. In the case of A., Assange's criminal culpability depended exclusively on whether, during sexual intercourse with A., he had ripped his condom intentionally or accidentally. As soon as Assange had publicly denied these allegations in response to the *Expressen* headlines, Chief Prosecutor Finné knew that a criminal investigation would be futile. In the absence of a confession from Assange, who despite his rumoured promiscuity had no history of sexual offences, it was objectively impossible to corroborate the decisive facts. Therefore, a criminal trial would inevitably result in an acquittal based on the benefit of the doubt – most likely followed by claims for reputational damages or even criminal complaints. Indeed, a related criminal complaint for false accusation was filed the day after the *Expressen* headlines, on 22 August 2010. In light of the given evidentiary circumstances, any reasonably experienced prosecutor would have immediately understood that the allegations reported by the police could not be successfully prosecuted. The fact that, nevertheless, the Swedish criminal investigation against Assange was being artificially kept alive by pointless investigative action and endless procrastination strongly suggests that the authorities were not pursuing justice in this case but a completely different, purely political agenda.

Indeed, for years, Sweden will cite the need to take a DNA sample from Assange as one of the main reasons why he cannot be questioned from London by phone or video link but must be extradited to Sweden at all costs. And yet, as early as 7 December 2010, Assange voluntarily gave to the British police a DNA sample which was then stored in the National DNA Database and could be requested by Swedish authorities through mutual legal assistance at any time. But Paul Close from the British Crown Prosecution Service, in an email dated 25 January 2011, specifically advises Marianne Ny against obtaining a DNA sample in the United Kingdom. He begins by stating the obvious: 'I am not sure if this evidence is really critical.' Furthermore, he cautions that 'the obtaining of such evidence could have a greater propensity for harm or mischief by the defence, than it would benefit the prosecution case.' For the British, too, truth and justice do not seem a priority in this affair: any potentially exculpatory evidence is framed as 'harm' or 'mischief'.

It is not until six years later that Marianne Ny finally brings herself to take this step, when Sweden's Supreme Court indicates its willingness to lift the arrest warrant against Assange on proportionality grounds due to the lack of progress in the investigation. On 15 December 2016, Sweden finally sends a mutual legal assistance request to the British Central Authority, asking to compare four Swedish DNA profiles with Assange's personal DNA profile stored in the British registry since 7 December 2010: the first comes from A.'s ripped condom, the second from the stain on A.'s bedsheet, the third from S.'s condom fragment, and the fourth from S.'s vaginal swab. The British carefully peruse the Swedish Supplemental Letter of Request, along with the description of Assange's alleged offences, but do not seem to grasp the investigative purpose of the Swedish request. They politely write back to the Swedish prosecutor, asking for clarification: 'It would assist us if you could please send me a line setting out the relevance of this measure to the investigation.' Marianne Ny gives the only response that is convincing from an investigative perspective: 'We seek a comparison of the crime stain profiles to find out whether the DNA on the broken condoms is from [Julian Assange]. These pieces of evidence are of importance for the trustworthy [sic] of witnesses.' So, it is purportedly about clarifying the credibility of the two women as witnesses. In her public statements, of course, Marianne Ny never even hinted that the credibility of A. and S. could be in doubt. This would not only have undermined the official narrative of Assange the rapist but would also have been disingenuous, given that this entire narrative had originally been imposed on A. and S. against their wills.

On 30 January 2017, the test results arrive by email from the United Kingdom: the DNA profile found on A.'s bedsheet matches Assange's profile stored in the British National DNA Database. However, the two DNA profiles found on the two damaged condoms and the one taken from the vaginal swab are not mentioned, implying that none of the three could be successfully matched with Assange's DNA profile. The wording of the message is final and does not suggest that any further results may be expected. The accompanying official report by the British authorities, dated 2 February 2017, is almost entirely redacted. But the structure of the text shows that four different points or sub-points are being discussed, likely corresponding to the four requested profile checks. Of these four points, only one seems to be illustrated in detail with tables and figures. The annexed search results are also fully redacted but seem to refer to only one of the profiles under examination.

The fact that Assange's DNA profile was confirmed in a stain which both he and A. had expressly mentioned in police interviews as resulting from their intercourse can hardly be regarded as revelatory. The same would have to be said if the three other profiles, taken from the two condoms and the vaginal swab, also matched that of Assange. The fact that this may not be the case, in turn, raises questions that cannot be resolved without access to the unredacted laboratory results. In any case, based on the available evidence, the endless shadowboxing of the Swedish authorities around DNA profiles and condoms appears to be nothing but a masquerade to cover up the obvious lack of prosecutable evidence for their allegations of sexual misconduct against Assange.

## Headline: 'The Interrogation of Assange – Word for Word'

For the time being, Assange is still in Stockholm. He has cancelled his departure, originally planned for 25 August 2010, and voluntarily placed himself at the disposal of the Swedish authorities. On the day Chief Prosecutor Finné closes the case of S., she announces that she will instruct Inspector Gehlin to interview Assange concerning the case of A. The following day, on 26 August, Assange is assigned a public defender of his choice – Leif Silbersky – and a formal interview is scheduled for the coming Monday, 30 August. This is surprisingly late for the first interview of a prominent suspect. After all, the rape allegations against him have been in the press for days and triggered a worldwide media hype. Given that Finné has already formally closed the investigation in the case of S., Assange is only questioned about the case of A. The interview is recorded on tape and conducted by Mats Gehlin in the presence of a second police officer, an interpreter, and Assange's lawyer, Silbersky. Early on in the interview, Assange expresses concern about the confidentiality of his statements. 'Before I answer that, shall I assume that this is going to go to *Expressen*?' he asks. Mats Gehlin hastens to reassure him: 'From us? I am not going to release anything. And the only ones who are here, that's we three at this interview, plus a stenographer who will write it out afterwards. And I am the only [*sic*] who has access to the case file. So if it comes out in *Expressen*, you can quarrel with me.' Three days later, on 2 September, *Expressen*'s headline will proudly proclaim: 'Here is the Interrogation of Assange – Word for Word'.

It is during this interview that Assange is first formally notified of the allegations against him: 'During the period from 13 to 14 August 2010, in [A.]'s residence at [xx]-gatan in Stockholm, Assange molested [A.] during an act of copulation – which was begun and conducted under the express condition that a condom would be used – by purposely damaging the condom and continuing the copulation until he ejaculated in her vagina.'

Assange denies this allegation. Although he confirms that he had sexual intercourse with A. several times that evening, always with the same condom, he denies having damaged it and states that he had not even been aware that the condom was damaged. According to Assange, after this first night, he continued to share A.'s bed for a week. During this period there were several sexual encounters, albeit without intercourse. Assange says that it was not until Friday, 20 August, that A. accused him of having removed the condom during their sexual intercourse on the first night. But, so far, she had not accused him of damaging the condom – this was the first time he heard this allegation. Assange remembers that, after their sexual intercourse, A. pointed to a wet spot on the bedsheet and asked, 'Look at that. Is that you?' He replied, 'No, it must be you.' After that, he had no further thoughts about it, especially since it was not brought up again by A. until the day the women went to the police. At the end of the interview, Assange begins on his own initiative to comment on the case of S. as well, but Gehlin does not appear to be interested and concludes the interview. Assange acknowledges that this second story may no longer be relevant, but states for the record that he is available to be questioned about that case as well. 'We can always continue if it is needed,' he says to Gehlin. Now that Assange has denied the allegations made against him, and since no investigative measures could realistically prove those allegations beyond reasonable doubt, the time has come for the Swedish Prosecution Authority to also close the case of A. – due to lack of evidence and based on the presumption of innocence. But things turn out differently.

## Reopening and Expansion of the Investigation

On Friday, 27 August 2010, Director of Public Prosecution Marianne Ny receives Borgström's complaint against Chief Prosecutor Finné's decision to drop the case of S. Ny needs no more than two working days to give Finné the opportunity to reconsider her discontinuation order – which she declines – and then to examine the case file herself and come to the opposite conclusion. On 1 September, she reopens the preliminary investigation in the case of S. and expands the suspicion in the case of A. to include more serious offences. In her decision, she merely states that, based on the case file, there is reason to assume that the crime of rape has been committed in the case of S. and the crimes of sexual harassment and sexual coercion in the case of A. She further finds the available materials to be insufficient and decides that all relevant investigative measures must be carried out before coming to a final conclusion. At the same time, Marianne Ny announces that she herself is taking over the case: she relieves Finné of her responsibility for the matter and assigns another prosecutor to conduct the preliminary investigation on behalf of Ny. In her decision, the director of public prosecution leaves no doubt as to her personal prerogatives: 'Matters of greater importance – such as orders for coercive measures, etc., and the completion of the preliminary investigation – shall be examined by me.'

Strikingly, however, something very important is missing from Marianne Ny's decision: she does not issue an arrest warrant against Assange. Chapter 24, Section 1 of the Swedish Code of Judicial Procedure expressly requires that any person suspected on probable cause of an offence punishable by imprisonment of two years or more – such as rape – be placed in detention 'unless it is clear that detention is not warranted'. Given that her decision of 1 September 2010 did not offer any justification for an exception from the general rule, Ny was legally obliged to issue an arrest warrant against Assange. It was not until 24 November 2010 that the Svea Court of Appeal reduced the categorization of the alleged crime to rape of 'lesser severity', for which an arrest warrant is not mandatory.

In her decision of 1 September, however, Ny explicitly suspects Assange of a crime carrying a minimum penalty of two years. Initial interviews of all those involved have already taken place. So, unlike the premature decision taken by Kjellstrand on 20 August, there now is a reasonable basis for an arrest warrant – always presuming that Ny genuinely suspects Assange on probable cause of rape. Besides, the circumstances adduced for the necessity of the first arrest warrant of 20 August – namely,

Assange's foreign nationality and lack of residence in Sweden, as well as the risks of flight and collusion – are just as relevant now as they were ten days earlier. However, just like ten days earlier, the Swedish authorities seem more interested in planting sensational headlines than in actually arresting and interrogating the suspect. Because to do so would force their hand, obliging them to formally charge Assange and expedite a trial, which, almost certainly, would result in a quick acquittal for lack of evidence. Such an outcome does not fit with their agenda. As we will see, the prosecutor prefers to wait for Assange to leave the country, and then to accuse him of trying to evade justice.

On 1 September 2010, Director of Public Prosecution Marianne Ny takes control, reopens the preliminary investigation into the alleged rape of S. and expands the case of A. to include both sexual harassment and sexual coercion. From a procedural point of view, this means that Ny must now examine whether there is sufficient evidence for a formal indictment of Assange. To this end, it is necessary to conduct additional interviews with all involved parties, at least in relation to new or reopened allegations that were not covered in previous interviews. Accordingly, within a few days of Ny's reopening and extending the investigation, fresh interviews are conducted with both women, on 2 September (S.) and 7 September (A.). Julian Assange, meanwhile, the sole suspect and the person most affected by this investigation, is neither arrested nor interviewed. No one seems to be interested in his version of the story. To former Director of Public Prosecution Sven-Erik Alhem, this is a clear breach of prosecutorial duty: 'It is also imperative according to the Swedish legal procedure that the accused shall have the opportunity to respond to the accusations at the earliest possible time when he still remembers the intimate details.'

## Denial of the Right to Be Heard

On 8 September, after Assange had heard nothing from the Swedish authorities for a whole week after Ny's decision, his new lawyer, Björn Hurtig, telephones the director of public prosecution and requests that his client be given the opportunity to be heard in a formal interview. 'Not just yet', Ny replies. She knows, of course, that Assange is not a national of Sweden, that his business in the country is finished and he can be expected to leave at any time. She re-interviews the women, but almost demonstratively declines to schedule an interview with the one person she imperatively needs to question before she can decide on formal charges – at least in the case of S., which was not covered by Assange's previous interview. As will be seen, what appears completely nonsensical for the purposes of criminal prosecution will prove highly effective for the purposes of political persecution, and fit neatly into the ever-growing puzzle of my own investigation.

Another six days go by without Assange hearing back from the authorities. No arrest warrant, no assigned residence, no obligation to report to the police, not even a ban on travel, although all of these measures are expressly provided for in chapters 24 and 25 of the Swedish Code of Judicial Procedure. On 14 September, Assange's lawyer Hurtig sends an email to Marianne Ny requesting access to all procedural files as stipulated by the Swedish Code of Judicial Procedure, including criminal allegations, interview protocols, witness statements, and any documents from the security police. Hurtig stresses that Assange has urgent business abroad and inquires whether his client is permitted to leave Sweden. As Ny will confirm in writing to the Svea Court of Appeal on 24 November 2010, and as will be explicitly acknowledged in the "Agreed Statement of Facts and Issues" appended to the judgment of the British Supreme Court in 2012, she responds to Hurtig on 15 September that there are no formal obstacles preventing Assange from leaving the country and that, at this point in time, several other investigative measures have to be taken before an interview with Assange becomes necessary. She further explains that Inspector Mats Gehlin has fallen ill, and the first investigative task to be completed after his return will be to conduct interviews with two witnesses. In his expert opinion, former prosecutor Alhem states the obvious: 'This [Gehlin's illness] is no excuse for the prosecutor's failure to interview Mr Assange; others could read the file or her [Ny's] assistant could direct them on the questions to ask.'

Moreover, in terms of sequencing, an objective, unbiased investigation requires that, if at all possible, both the alleged victims and the suspect be heard prior to other witnesses. This is the only way to identify discrepancies between the respective testimonies of the alleged victims and the suspect before questioning other witnesses with a view to determining the veracity of contradicting accounts. The fact that an experienced prosecutor such as Marianne Ny deliberately delayed the questioning of Assange strongly suggests that she was less interested in establishing the truth than in instrumentalizing the alleged victims and other witnesses in order to support and consolidate her own preconceived narrative.

Chapter 23 of the Swedish Code of Judicial Procedure also provides that, in principle, investigative interviews should be conducted in the presence of a reliable witness and of the suspect's defence counsel, who 'may put questions to the person who is being questioned'.

However, in this instance the vast majority of initial witness interviews were conducted over the phone, without tape recordings or verbatim transcripts, and without the presence of a second police officer or other witness. In no case was Assange's attorney permitted to attend or ask questions. As any professional investigator knows, without these safeguards, interviewing police officers remain free to summarize testimonies in their own words, and leading questions, manipulative rephrasing and unwarranted omissions will go unnoticed. Experience also shows that witnesses who are re-interviewed tend to avoid contradicting any written summaries of their original statements that are presented to them, because they do not want to be perceived as unreliable by the authorities. As countless studies have demonstrated, human memory and perception of reality can be strongly influenced and distorted by a wide variety of factors, including unconscious emotional needs for conformity, security, acceptance, and credibility.

According to her own testimony to the British judiciary, Prosecutor Ny made no attempt to schedule an interview with Assange until 21 September, a full month after the *Expressen* headline and three weeks after her own decision of 1 September. The first attempt for which there is conclusive evidence dates from the following day. On Wednesday, 22 September at 4:06 p.m., Ny sends a text message to Hurtig. 'Hi. Is it clear whether an interview on Tuesday at 5 pm is feasible?' The date referred to was Tuesday, 28 September 2010. Hurtig replies at 4:48, 'No, I have not had any contact with my client since we last spoke. I will continue to try to track him down and get back to you as soon as I reach him. But I will be available on Tuesday.' Four minutes later, Ny writes, 'Thanks for letting me know. For the time being we are assuming Tuesday 5pm will work. Grateful for definite reply as soon as possible.' The following afternoon, on Thursday, 23 September at 5:46 p.m., Ny asks again, 'Hello! Have you been in contact with your client?' But Hurtig does not respond until 9:01 a.m. on Monday, 27 September: 'Hello, just want to let you know that I have not been able to establish contact with my client.' Ten minutes later, Ny thanks Hurtig for the notice: 'I'll get back to you later today on our further plans.' However, Prosecutor Ny neither gets back to Hurtig nor waits to see whether Assange will turn up for his interview the following day. Instead, she suddenly decides to issue an arrest warrant against him on Monday afternoon at 2:15, purportedly due to a risk of flight and collusion. Less than two hours earlier, Assange booked his flight with Scandinavian Airlines SK2679 at Stockholm Arlanda Airport, which will leave the Swedish capital for Berlin Tegel at 5:25 p.m. the same day.

As a witness in the Swedish-British extradition proceedings at City of Westminster Magistrates' Court, Hurtig will later conceal his text message correspondence with Prosecutor Ny and claim that she never tried to schedule an interview with Assange before his departure on 27 September. This professional oversight is difficult to comprehend and results in a lot of negative press for Hurtig, as well as earning him a reprimand from the Swedish Bar Association. Over and beyond legitimate criticism, Hurtig's mistake is later blown out of proportion and inappropriately exploited by the British judge in order to undermine the personal credibility not only of Hurtig himself, but also of the expert witnesses instructed by him, and to deflect from the much more serious failures of the Swedish Prosecution Authority. As will become abundantly clear, Hurtig's misrepresentation of facts had no significant evidentiary relevance, as it could not have affected the actual scope and gravity of the Swedish prosecutor's malpractice in any way.

For now, let us just note that the text messages exchanged between Ny and Hurtig from 22 to 27 September do not alter the fact that, despite multiple requests on the part of Assange, Prosecutor Ny did not intend to give him the chance to be heard regarding the alleged rape of S. until 28 September 2010. That was six long weeks after the alleged offence, more than five weeks after the unlawful and extremely damaging leak to *Expressen*, and a full four weeks after the rape investigation had been reopened – a massive delay for which there could be no excuse whatsoever. To put this into the context of domestic legislation, here are the standards of expediency set in Chapter 23 of the Swedish Code of Judicial Procedure: 'The preliminary investigation shall be conducted as expeditiously as possible. When there is no longer reason for pursuing the investigation, it shall be discontinued.'

As far as Assange personally is concerned, it is thus objectively established: that he reacted to the rape allegations by voluntarily postponing his departure from Sweden by more than a month; that he voluntarily participated in the earliest possible police interview and responded to all questions asked by the police on the case of A.; that he repeatedly took the initiative also to be questioned about the case of S.; and that he had requested – and received – prosecutorial approval for his departure from Sweden almost two weeks in advance. The fact that Assange was diffi-cult to reach during his stay in Sweden has nothing to do with trying to evade justice. Two days after his arrival, in response to pressure exerted by the US government, all of his credit cards had been cancelled, rendering him unable to book a hotel or buy food, and forcing him to depend on the hospitality of acquaintances, to spend the night in their private homes or offices, and to constantly change his location. For the same reason, he often did not have enough credit on his phone to make or receive calls.

There is no evidence that Assange was aware of the interview scheduled for him on 28 September, or that he left Sweden knowing that the prosecutor still wanted to interview him at all. All the available evidence illustrates that Hurtig was unable to contact him, and that he left Sweden because the most recent information he had was that the prosecutor did not wish to schedule an interview with him and that he was free to leave the country. In the light of these indisputable facts, the widespread myth that Assange wanted to evade Swedish justice can safely be discarded as deliberate misinformation.

## Sweden as a 'Reliable Partner' of the United States

Was it by chance that Assange's interview was scheduled for the exact first day after his departure from Sweden? It seems unlikely. Had Prosecutor Ny really wanted to interview him on that day, she would not have relied on a casual text message exchange with Hurtig but would have served him with a formal summons for Assange, as provided for in Chapter 23, Section 7 of the Swedish Code of Judicial Procedure. After all, this was not about a local pickpocket being questioned by the village sheriff, but a politically explosive case that had triggered worldwide media attention and was affected by strong third-party interests. Moreover, had Prosecutor Ny genuinely intended to interview Assange on 28 September at 5 p.m., she would not have issued an arrest warrant against him more than twenty-four hours before the appointment, but only in the event of a 'no-show'. Unless, of course, she already knew that he planned to depart on 27 September.

So, let's try to put all of this into a real-world perspective. WikiLeaks had just published the biggest leak in Western military history and was perceived as a serious threat to national security by the United States and its allies, including Sweden and the United Kingdom. It would be ingenuous to believe that, in August 2010, Julian Assange could have visited Sweden without, at the very least, being constantly kept on the radar of the Swedish security police, Säpo. On 18 August, the state-affiliated Swedish Foreign Policy Institute went on national television to express its concern that the planned establishment of WikiLeaks in the country would strain transatlantic relations between Sweden and the United States. In an interview published on 8 September, the head of the Swedish Military Security Service, John Daniels, went as far as to describe WikiLeaks as a 'threat to our soldiers'. It also was an open secret that the US Department of Justice, under Attorney General Eric Holder, was already exploring avenues for prosecuting Assange and had asked allied nations to do the same. At that time, the US government was well aware of the planned publication by WikiLeaks of the 'Iraq War Logs' and 'CableGate' and was bent on stopping Assange in his tracks.

More generally, US diplomatic correspondence classified as 'secret' (and later published as part of CableGate) offers conclusive evidence that the Swedish government maintained 'informal information sharing arrangements' with US intelligence services which were deliberately concealed both from the country's parliament and from the wider public. 'Swedish military and civilian intelligence organizations are strong and reliable partners on a range of key issues', the US embassy in Stockholm noted on 1 May 2007. 'Due to domestic political considerations, the extent of this cooperation is not widely known within the Swedish government and it would be useful to acknowledge this cooperation privately, as public mention of the cooperation would open up the government to domestic criticism' (07STOCKHOLM506_a, § 6). In the following year, on 7 November 2008, the US Embassy referred to 'Swedish constitutional restrictions on the use of intelligence' and noted that the Swedish Ministry of Justice team 'expressed a strong degree of satisfaction with current informal information sharing arrangements with the US ... which cover a wide range of law enforcement and anti-terrorism cooperation' and affirmed their 'willingness to continue feeding information to the US through existing informal channels'. At the same time, given that 'this was a particularly sensitive time politically in Sweden for issues involving government surveillance and affecting personal privacy', the Swedish officials expressed concern that these and 'other existing informal information sharing arrangements' could be placed 'at jeopardy' if exposed to parliamentary scrutiny and public spotlight (08STOCKHOLM748_a). Quite evidently, in the absence of any sort of individual accountability, even the scandal exposing the unlawful rendition by Säpo of the Egyptian nationals Agiza and Al Zery into the hands of CIA torturers had done nothing to enhance the Swedish government's sensitivity towards its obligations under the country's constitution and international human rights law.

To the mind of unsuspecting citizens, the blatant lawlessness of international intelligence cooperation might be deeply disconcerting. To anyone even remotely acquainted with the secretive reality of this 'parallel universe', however, none of it comes as a surprise. Given the perceived security threat posed by WikiLeaks, it is virtually guaranteed that Säpo constantly monitored the flight booking system at Stockholm airport for the passenger-name 'Assange' and that they immediately informed the Swedish Prosecution Authority of the imminent departure of its most prominent suspect – through 'informal channels' and without any form of public scrutiny, of course, just like its transatlantic information exchange with the United States.

Assange, for his part, was under no illusions. The surveillance risk had long since become part of his routine. In order not to give the secret services too much advance notice, he bought his flight ticket, as always, shortly before departure and paid with cash, directly at the airport.

On 27 September 2010, Assange arrives at Arlanda Airport around noon. His preferred flight to Berlin is already fully booked, so he has to switch to a later flight and spend a few hours waiting at the airport – longer than he would have liked, long enough to show up in Säpo's data monitoring system and give the authorities time to consult and react. The fact that

Assange is allowed to leave the country even so is not a sign of incompetence on the part of the Swedish authorities, but another puzzle piece suggesting an entirely different agenda. The plan clearly does not appear to be to arrest and interrogate Assange, but to create and perpetuate the public narrative of a fugitive sex offender all the while denying him an opportunity to defend himself. Although Prosecutor Ny was obliged by law to issue an arrest warrant against Assange as soon as she had reopened the rape investigation on 1 September, she only does so once he appears in the passenger monitoring system a few hours before his departure. She then allows him to leave the country and, thereby, gets him to inadvertently confirm the alleged flight risk by his own action.

Should anyone still doubt that the Swedish authorities were fully aware of Assange's travel plans, that they consciously refrained from arresting him at the border and even 'accompanied' his departure in real time, then these reservations will be dispelled by the evidence surrounding the simultaneous disappearance of Assange's luggage.

Assange travelled to Berlin on 27 September 2010 to meet with various journalists, in particular Holger Stark and Marcel Rosenbach of *Der Spiegel*, as well as Stefania Maurizi of *L'Espresso*. Maurizi would later succeed, through an unrelenting freedom of information lawsuit, in obtaining the release of important documents clearly demonstrating the collusion between Swedish and British authorities. For now, however, the focus was on establishing new publication partnerships for the major leaks that were to be released later in 2010: the Iraq War Logs and CableGate. The purpose, location, and date of these meetings had already been agreed between 26 July and 25 August via unencrypted email correspondence, which could easily be intercepted. So, this information was almost certainly already known to the authorities. Again, it would be completely unrealistic to think that, in August 2010 and with the impending publication of enormous amounts of secret information, the US intelligence services would not be systematically monitoring any unencrypted email correspondence received by WikiLeaks.

We can therefore safely assume that the Swedish authorities knew exactly how long they would have to procrastinate the interview with Assange in order to provoke his purported 'escape' from Sweden, while the intelligence services naturally had every interest in intercepting any documents or hard disks which Assange planned to hand over to journalists in Berlin. On this background it becomes clear that it is no coincidence at all that Assange was allowed to leave Sweden despite the existence of a valid arrest warrant and that his luggage disappeared on the journey. Only a short direct flight connects the two capitals, but after landing in Berlin Assange is the only passenger whose checked bag is nowhere to be found. According to Assange, it contained three encrypted laptops and various hard drives containing sensitive records, including evidence of an unpublished war crime.

Assange's boarding pass shows that, in Stockholm, he checked one piece of luggage weighing thirteen kilograms. A slip of the baggage receipt, with a bar code and the registration number 0117 SK 847249 SK 2679/27SEP, is attached to the boarding pass. However, this bag never arrives in Berlin. The files on record include a baggage loss report from Berlin Tegel Airport, dated 27 September at 7:45 p.m., as well as the signed statements of numerous witnesses, all of whom confirm the loss of Assange's luggage. Acciona Airport Services, which provides baggage services in Berlin, contacts the Scandinavian airline SAS, but receives no information. At Assange's request, the journalist Johannes Wahlström inquires with SAS in Stockholm, without any success. Phone calls are also made to SAS from Berlin. The information is always the same: the computer system shows that Assange checked one piece of luggage at Arlanda airport, and that it never left Stockholm, but disappeared inside the restricted area of the airport, immediately after check-in and even before passing through the X-ray. Mysteriously, the bag cannot be found.

Finally, Wahlström calls Inspector Gehlin and confronts him with the fairly obvious conclusion that the Swedish security police might have something to do with the disappearance of Assange's bag. If the security police were involved, Gehlin says, he would be aware of it, but he promises to make inquiries. Not surprisingly, Gehlin never gets back to Wahlström or anyone else, and the luggage remains unaccounted for to this day. No confiscation order, no notification and certification of seizure, and no legal remedy – all in clear contradiction to Chapter 27 of the Code of Judicial Procedure – another weighty piece in the puzzle. In an email to Assange's lawyer Björn Hurtig on 15 November 2010, Prosecutor Ny categorically denies any involvement of Säpo in the case – after all, this investigation relates to sexual offences, not national security offences, she says. That is the official narrative. Just as predictable is the reaction of Säpo itself. In response to a question asked by Swedish Radio on 11 December 2010, Säpo merely says it is following developments but cannot comment on its work in individual cases. 'As usual', the radio presenter comments laconically, but fails to dig deeper. The Swedish press appears content to be left in the dark and so does the public. The strategy seems to work, and where there is no accuser, there is no judge.

With Assange's departure from Sweden, the stage was set for the perfect enactment of a script which, on the day of Assange's first arrest in London on 7 December 2010, was outlined with terrifying precision in an internal mail correspondence of the US global intelligence consulting firm Stratfor: 'Pile on. Move him from country to country to face various charges for the next 25 years. But, seize everything he and his family own, to include every person linked to Wiki.' Indeed, as will become increasingly clear in the course of the next months, during his stay in Sweden Julian Assange's success story had turned into a story of political persecution. The involved governments had successfully snatched the spotlight directed at them by WikiLeaks, turned it around and pointed it at Assange – at him personally, not at his organization, because that would have been too obvious. From that moment and until today, the authorities, the established media and the general public will devote their attention entirely to the alleged misconduct and purported character flaws of Assange. Forgotten are the war crimes and the corruption of the powerful. Mission accomplished!

# 7

# Anglo-Swedish Extradition Trial

## Sweden Refuses to Offer a Non-Refoulement Guarantee

From Berlin, Assange travels on to London. Meanwhile, for Prosecutor Ny, getting him back to Sweden for questioning has suddenly become a matter of utmost urgency. Assange, too, is keen for an opportunity to be heard by the Swedish authorities and willing to return to Stockholm at his own expense. Already on 30 September, three days after his departure from Sweden, his lawyer Björn Hurtig informs Deputy Director of Public Prosecution Erika Lejnefors that Assange is currently abroad, but that an interview with him can be scheduled as early as 10 October 2010 – a Sunday – or any other day of her choice in the following week from 11 to 15 October. Lejnefors declines to schedule an interview on a Sunday, because this would involve police officers working on the weekend. And the week immediately following that Sunday is vetoed by Director of Public Prosecution Marianne Ny personally, apparently because it is 'too far ahead'.

In her submission of 24 November 2010 to the Svea Court of Appeal, Prosecutor Ny will insist that during this period 'we were extremely anxious to interview him'. However, for more than one month, while Assange was still in Sweden, his right to be heard and to defend himself was consistently denied, despite extremely damaging rape allegations unlawfully leaked by the Swedish Prosecution Authority. And now that he had to travel from abroad in order to be questioned in Sweden, prepared to pay his own way and to make himself available for an entire week, the prosecutor categorically refused to schedule an interview anytime in the proposed period of 11–15 October, purportedly because she could not wait for as little as ten days. As we will see, her 'anxiety to interview Assange' would not prevent her from putting off that very interview for another six years while at the same time professing indignation over A. and S. being denied justice.

In truth, of course, Assange's unexpected offer to return to Sweden so quickly must have been very inconvenient. It clearly did not fit the carefully constructed official narrative of the 'fugitive rapist' to see him voluntarily return to Stockholm and respond to the allegations against him. So, when the authorities received intelligence that Assange planned to give a lecture in Stockholm on 4 October, they changed their plans, and instead arranged for him to be arrested in a police raid at the venue. In order to secure the desired media coverage of this spectacular arrest, the press had been proactively alerted. The trap remained unsuccessful – Assange did not come to Sweden on 4 October.

So far, both Assange and his lawyer had interpreted Prosecutor Ny's relaxed manner as indicating that she intended to close the investigation without even bothering to interview him. From a procedural perspective, this seems to be the only good-faith explanation for consistently declining to take Assange's statement and refusing to provide his lawyer with even the most basic information about the precise allegations made against him. But with her obstructive approach becoming increasingly obvious, Assange begins to grow suspicious. Around the same time, reports multiply of a US Grand Jury working on a secret indictment against Assange. In view of the accumulating irregularities in the Swedish proceedings and the country's subservient proximity to

US intelligence services, Assange fears, not unreasonably, that Sweden might surrender him to the United States without any form of due process, as it did with Agiza and Al Zery a few years earlier. To allay these concerns, Assange wants a guarantee: the Swedish authorities should issue a written assurance that were he to return to Sweden, he would not be extradited onwards to the United States, where he could expect an unfair trial for espionage and inhumane conditions of detention. Assange's request is straightforward, but the response he receives is evasive in the extreme. According to the Swedish authorities, no guarantee of non-extradition can be given so long as the United States has not made an extradition request. Moreover, extradition decisions are a judicial matter for the courts, in which the government cannot interfere. After all, Sweden is a constitutional democracy governed by the rule of law!

While this response may seem convincing at first glance, it has no basis in either law or practice. In reality, such 'diplomatic assurances' are a standard instrument of international relations and are widely used around the world, especially in connection with the extradition and deportation of foreigners. The extraditing or deporting state requests written assurances from the destination or transit state that the person to be extradited will not be executed, tortured or otherwise mistreated under any circumstances, that their procedural rights are guaranteed and that – in accordance with the universal principle of non-refoulement – they will not be extradited to a third state in which their human rights protection is not guaranteed. In practice, such non-refoulement guarantees are routinely given, naturally without requiring a prior extradition request by the potentially unsafe third state. Likewise, the all-time favourite smokescreen advanced by Western democracies trying to evade their human rights obligations, namely that the government cannot 'interfere' with pending judicial proceedings, does not stand up to scrutiny. In Sweden, as in most other countries, the government has the prerogative to refuse any extradition on political grounds, irrespective of whether it has been approved by the judiciary. Clearly, the reasons why Sweden consistently declined to offer Assange a guarantee of non-refoulement were not constitutional, but purely political, and Assange had every reason to be concerned, particularly given the longstanding – and unconstitutional – collusion between Stockholm and Washington in matters of national security and intelligence, which WikiLeaks itself had exposed to the world. This is why, on 8 October and 12 November 2010, Assange's lawyer Hurtig proposes to the Swedish Prosecution Authority that Assange be questioned by phone or video conference, on the basis of applicable international mutual legal assistance agreements. In the alternative, he offers that Assange would also be prepared to provide a statement in writing or to attend an interview in person at the Australian Embassy. As expressly acknowledged in the 'Agreed Statement of Facts and Issues' before the British Supreme Court, all of these possibilities are permitted in Swedish law. Nevertheless, all of them are declined as 'inappropriate' by the Swedish Prosecution Authority, Prosecutor Ny insisting that Assange be interviewed in person in Sweden.

## Sweden Refuses to Interview Assange in London

On 18 November 2010, Marianne Ny requests and receives a detention order in absentia from the Stockholm District Court, which is confirmed by the Appeals Court on 24 November. On this basis, the prosecutor issues a European Arrest Warrant against Assange. Officially, this is nothing but a logical consequence of his alleged attempt to evade justice for sexual offences by 'fleeing' from Sweden to the United Kingdom. Ny wants Assange to be arrested in London and subsequently extradited to Sweden. At her request, Interpol further issues a 'red notice' for Assange – a level of worldwide police alert usually reserved for internationally wanted fugitives formally indicted or convicted of a crime. But Assange has been neither indicted nor convicted. He is a cooperative suspect in a preliminary investigation, who has been keen to respond to the rape allegations against him ever since they were illegally leaked by the authorities on 20 August

2010, but who is not prepared to risk his irregular rendition to the United States. On the day of his arrest, the US consultancy firm Stratfor will note: 'Charges of sexual assault rarely are passed through Interpol red notices, like this case, so this is no doubt about trying to disrupt WikiLeaks release of government documents.' Indeed, Prosecutor Ny's decision comes exactly ten days before the planned and announced release of CableGate on 28 November – a truly monumental leak, of global proportions, which has a terrified US Government desperately scrambling for damage control. A mere coincidence? Certainly not.

The director of public prosecution knows, of course, that her aggressive action will foment another media hype and further damage Assange's reputation, not only in the eyes of the public, but also in the eyes of all the governments that are about to be embarrassed by the release of a quarter of a million US diplomatic cables. As an experienced prosecutor, she also knows that her approach is grossly disproportionate in this case. After all, Assange had clearly cooperated and even repeatedly requested to be interviewed throughout his stay in Sweden; he had expressly requested and received authorization to leave Sweden; he had offered to return to Sweden for an interview on any day from 10 to 15 October 2010; had repeated that offer for a later date on the condition of a non-refoulement' guarantee and, alternatively, was willing to be interviewed through mutual legal assistance in London or by phone or video conference.

A former Swedish judge, Britta Sundberg-Weitman sees this as a clear breach of the principle of proportionality enshrined in European law, which stipulates that public authorities may interfere with individual rights only to the extent necessary and justified to achieve a legitimate purpose. It remains a mystery not only to Sundberg-Weitman why Marianne Ny refused to question Assange personally in London, or by telephone or videoconference, when both would have been possible without any problems under existing mutual legal assistance agreements. Former Swedish prosecutor Sven-Erik Alhem goes a step further: 'In my view, only when it was first shown that it would be impossible to get [Assange] interrogated in England by using

Mutual Legal Assistance from England, should an application for an EAW have been submitted. Since I understand that he has been willing to be interviewed by these means since leaving Sweden, I regard the prosecutor's refusal to at least try to interview him as being unreasonable and unprofessional, as well as unfair and disproportionate.'

In January 2011, Björn Hurtig tries to put pressure on Prosecutor Ny to question his client in London. Her response, which she sends to Hurtig by SMS text message on 11 January at 10:58 a.m., is succinct: 'Hi! For investigative reasons, a request for legal assistance for questioning in England is not relevant. Best regards, Marianne Ny.' In an earlier press interview of 5 December 2010, she had even falsely claimed that Swedish law prevented her from interviewing Assange in London. According to Britta Sundberg-Weitman, 'This is clearly not true.' Sven-Erik Alhem comments that there is 'nothing in Swedish law that I know of to prevent a prosecutor from seeking mutual legal assistance to have a suspect interviewed'. The same is later confirmed in the 'Agreed Statement of Facts and Issues' before the British Supreme Court. Defence counsel Hurtig refuses to give up and, on 9 February 2011, submits a complaint to the Swedish prosecutor-general asking for a legal review of Ny's refusal to question Assange in London. But instead of adjudicating the matter himself, the prosecutor-general refers it back to Ny, asking her to treat Hurtig's complaint as a request for reconsideration. On 14 February 2011, Prosecutor Ny then comes to the unsurprising conclusion that she can find no reason to revise her own decision: 'The interview planned with Assange must take place in Sweden for investigative reasons. These include, among other things, that the interview with Assange must be conducted in the same manner as the interviews with other persons in this investigation and that these interviews are likely to lead to further investigative measures.' This is a rather brazen justification given that the initial interviews with most witnesses and one of the alleged victims had been conducted by phone, whereas Assange had personally come to the police station for questioning on 30 August 2010.

## Assange's First Arrest and Release on Bail

Meanwhile, Assange continues to work from London. In late autumn 2010, he prepares the two largest WikiLeaks releases so far, again in collaboration with some of the world's most prominent newspapers and magazines. On the evening of 22 October, WikiLeaks releases the Iraq War Logs: almost 400,000 American logs covering the Iraq War from 2004 to 2009 and providing an undistorted chronicle of an unlawful war of aggression. Suddenly, everything is out in the open: page after page, log after log, the entire world can read what really happened during six years of 'Operation Iraqi Freedom'. WikiLeaks offers an inside view of a war whose true horrors have been largely concealed or whitewashed by official US statements. The documented atrocity condenses, as it so often does, into unbearable figures: by the end of 2009, the Iraq War has already claimed at least 109,032 deaths, including more than 66,000 Iraqi civilians. At the same time, it is revealed that the United States knowingly exposed thousands of detainees to torture and abuse, abandoning them in the hands of Iraqi security forces and ordering US forces not to investigate such crimes.

With these disclosures, WikiLeaks put a harsh and definite end to any humanitarian myths that may still have lingered about the Iraq War. On 26 October, the then UN high commissioner for human rights, Navi Pillay, called for investigation and punishment of the documented human rights violations, and even the US government did not dispute the veracity of the material. Remarkably, to date, WikiLeaks does not appear to have published a single document that was falsified or even questionable in its authenticity – not a claim many media organizations can make.

Four weeks later, CableGate marks the third and final phase in the journalistic processing of the material leaked by Chelsea Manning. This time, the focus is on US diplomacy. In the last forty-eight hours before the publication begins, an important correspondence takes place between Assange, US Ambassador

Susman in London and the US State Department in Washington. On 26 November, Assange asks the US government to alert WikiLeaks to 'any specific instances (record numbers or names) where it considers the publication of information would put individual persons at significant risk of harm that has not already been addressed'; he assures it that 'WikiLeaks will respect the confidentiality of advice provided by the United States Government and is prepared to consider any such submissions without delay.' However, in his response on 27 November, State Department Legal Advisor Harold Koh makes clear that 'we will not engage in a negotiation regarding the further release or dissemination of illegally obtained US Government classified materials.' On the following day, 28 November 2010, WikiLeaks and its publication partners – the *Guardian*, the *New York Times*, *El País*, *Der Spiegel*, and *Le Monde* – begin the process of publishing what will add up to over 250,000 classified pieces of US diplomatic correspondence.

Importantly, despite the US government's refusal to cooperate in the redaction of these documents, WikiLeaks and its publication partners conduct a rigorous 'harm reduction' process in which every single document is reviewed, and any information is redacted that could have exposed individuals to risk. Initially, only documents that have been selected and redacted by journalists of the aforementioned newspapers are made available on the WikiLeaks website. Contrary to common assumptions, Assange decides to publish the unredacted CableGate materials only nine months later, on 1 September 2011, after they have already been made publicly accessible by combining information published by two *Guardian* journalists and the German weekly *Der Freitag*. Assange tries in vain to convince *Der Freitag* not to publish the relevant information, precisely because he is worried about potentially ensuing risks for certain individuals mentioned by name in the unredacted documents. When *Der Freitag* nevertheless insists on publishing the scoop in late August 2011, Assange alerts the US government in advance, makes clear that this publication would occur without the consent or control of WikiLeaks, and engages with US officials to try and ensure proper harm reduction. We will return to this issue in more detail later.

CableGate comprises primarily confidential diplomatic correspondence between the US State Department and US embassies in various countries. Intended exclusively for internal consumption, the tone of this correspondence is often unvarnished and devoid of diplomacy. The content of the cables ranges from gossip and discourteous portraits of foreign officials to sober assessments of international conflicts, but also includes evidence of collusion between the United States and its allies in extraordinary rendition and torture, as well as other machinations of US power politics. For example, Secretary of State Hillary Clinton's secret 'national human intelligence collection directive' instructed US diplomats to collect intelligence on top UN officials, including biographic and biometrical data, credit cards, passwords and personal encryption keys used for official communications. Other examples include the Swedish government's extensive civilian and military intelligence collusion with the United States, which was deliberately kept secret from the Swedish parliament and public.

Never before have a government's diplomatic practices been exposed on such a scale. For the US government, the reputational damage inflicted by CableGate and the accompanying media coverage is immense. As can be seen from the immediate reactions, the United States feels not only embarrassed, but increasingly powerless and threatened. The long arm of the US government ensures that WikiLeaks comes under serious pressure: its website becomes the target of cyberattacks, Amazon cancels important server capacity rented by the organization, its accounts are blocked, and credit companies as well as financial service providers terminate their cooperation. But the primary target remains Assange. He is the visible head of WikiLeaks; he can be attacked personally without making the assault on press freedom and freedom of information too obvious. Political leaders and journalists outdo each other in condemning Assange and accusing him of espionage, treason and even terrorism. Extrapolating from the CableGate documents, it is not too difficult to imagine how, with each spectacular release, the US government increases the pressure on its allies to take Assange off the streets for good.

At the time, Assange is the guest of Vaughan Smith, staying at his country house, Ellingham Hall, near London. Smith, a former British Army captain, war reporter, founder of the Frontline Press Club in London and WikiLeaks sympathizer, considers Assange a kindred spirit on issues of freedom of expression and press freedom. Approximately one week after the release of the first series of diplomatic cables on 28 November 2010, Assange is informed that the EAW issued against him by the Swedish director of public prosecution has been formally certified by the British authorities. The following day, 7 December, Assange voluntarily reports to London's Kentish Town police station. It is the British police that finally inform Assange of the Swedish allegations against him. Ever since Prosecutor Ny had reopened and expanded the preliminary investigation against Assange three months earlier, she had consistently refused to provide him with this most basic information – another piece in the puzzle. Had he known precisely what misconduct the prosecutor suspected him of, he could have stymied her strategy of procrastination by independently making a public statement responding to each point. But by publicly suspecting Assange of rape while never informing him of the details, the prosecutor deprived him of any effective possibility of defence, without herself having to present any evidence in support of her allegations. The strategy worked brilliantly – the longer the stalemate lasted, the deeper the official narrative of the 'fugitive rapist' took root and crystallized in the collective mind of the world public. As a result, eight years later, even I would initially decline to look into his case.

But on 7 December 2010, Assange voluntarily submits to arrest and is placed in solitary confinement in Wandsworth Prison for nine days, until he is released on bail and allowed to return to Ellingham Hall on 16 December. Numerous prominent supporters have vouched for him and raised the required bail of £200,000. For the next 550 days, as part of his bail conditions, Assange will have to live under house arrest, wear an electronic ankle bracelet and report to the police daily. Most importantly, in February 2011, he will face a hearing at Westminster Magistrates' Court to discuss the Swedish extradition request.

## Anglo-Swedish Collusion

In early January 2011, the Swedish Prosecution Authority shows the first signs of doubt. On 11 January, in preparation for the upcoming extradition hearing, Assange's defence team presents its primary arguments and evidence and also names renowned Swedish experts as witnesses. This may have caused the Swedish authorities to pause for a moment and ponder how far they had already strayed from justice and the rule of law. At least temporarily, it almost seemed as if Prosecutor Ny had changed her mind and was now seriously entertaining the idea of interviewing Assange in London.

But then something remarkable happens. The British Crown Prosecution Service (CPS), which represents Swedish interests in the extradition proceedings, advises against doing just that. 'My earlier advice remains, that in my view it would not be prudent for the Swedish authorities to try to interview the defendant in the UK', Paul Close writes on 25 January 2011 in an email to the Swedish Prosecution Authority. Note that he does not claim that interviewing Assange in London would not be 'permissible' or 'possible' but, rather, that it would not be 'prudent'. He goes on to explain that 'the defence would without any doubt seek to turn the event to its advantage. It would inevitably allege it was conclusive proof that the Swedish authorities had no case whatsoever against him and hence the interview was in the hope that he would make a full and frank confession.' Furthermore, he adds, alluding to the Swedish practice of detaining rape suspects without bail: 'General experience has also shown that attempts by foreign authorities to interview a defendant in the UK, frequently leads to the defence retort that that [sic] some inducements or threats were made by the interviewers (such as the prosecutors' approach to bail on the defendant's surrender to the foreign state). Thus I suggest you interview him only on his surrender to Sweden and in accordance with Swedish law.'

The British official goes on to provide guidance to the Swedes on how to gloss over the most problematic aspects of their entire investigation in the upcoming extradition hearing at Westminster Magistrates' Court: 'As we have discussed your prosecution is well based on the existing evidence and is sufficient to proceed to trial, which is the prosecution's intention.' The following – apparently important – paragraph is redacted, followed by the sentence, 'You have the evidence of the complainants.' The email closes with renewed assurances of support in analysing and responding to the defence arguments in court, and recommends a purely formal line, namely, 'that Marianne Ny can issue a European Arrest Warrant and the Swedish authorities actually still do want to prosecute the defendant'. In other words, any substantive arguments or complaints about Swedish due process violations are not to be addressed, because these matters are not to be adjudicated by the courts in the United Kingdom, but by those in Sweden.

On the face of it, this is not a British case. Neither Assange nor the two women are British nationals, the alleged offences have not occurred in Britain, and the case is unlikely to result in an indictment, let alone a conviction, due to the lack of prosecutable evidence. So why is the CPS so keen to avoid a quick, uncomplicated and cost-effective resolution of this case through mutual legal assistance? Why needlessly lock Assange into a lengthy extradition proceeding that would generate a heavy workload and substantial expenses for the British government and judiciary? If there is one simple truism that has never failed me in my investigations of war crimes and human rights violations, it is that 'where there is smoke, there is fire'. And where there is a lot of smoke, there must be a big fire. From now on, we will see that, whenever the British authorities deal with Assange, they make far more smoke than would be warranted by the issues supposedly at stake. As we advance through the following months, it will become increasingly difficult to escape the impression that the British authorities are pursuing a political agenda that goes far beyond the Swedish extradition request. This impression is confirmed verbatim in another email sent by Paul Close to Marianne Ny on 13 January 2011: 'Please do not think that the case is being dealt with as just another extradition request.'

Over the next eighteen months, Assange's extradition trial proceeds through all three instances in the British judicial system – Magistrates' Court; High Court and Supreme Court. On 30 May 2012, the Supreme Court confirms the permissibility of the European Arrest Warrant issued by the Swedish prosecutor, thus green-lighting Assange's extradition to Sweden. What sounds like a simple and straightforward matter warrants a closer look. To the layman, the following explanations on the EAW may seem technical and dull at first. But they will quickly illuminate the extent to which even the highest British court appears to be prepared to betray the rule of law for the sake of a desired political outcome.

So, here is the European Arrest Warrant in a nutshell. Between member states of the European Union (and the UK was still part of the EU in 2012), a valid, standardized EAW is sufficient to obtain an extradition. Whether there are sufficient evidentiary grounds to suspect, indict or convict a person of a crime does not need to be examined by the extraditing country. In contrast to extradition cases involving destination countries outside the EU, the entire procedure takes place on purely formal grounds. Questions of guilt or innocence, credibility and probative value are not raised in the extradition proceedings, but only during the subsequent criminal trial in the destination country. Therefore, none of these arguments can be raised effectively by Assange's lawyers as a defence against extradition to Sweden.

From this formal perspective, only two conditions must be met to obtain an extradition within the EU: first, under the principle of dual criminality, the offences of which a person is suspected or charged must also be punishable in the country in which he is currently located. This requirement is met, because Assange is suspected of rape and sexual coercion in Sweden, both of which are criminal offences also in the United Kingdom.

Second – and this is the primary bone of contention in Assange's case – the EAW must have been issued by a competent authority. Both the EU Framework Decision of 2002 regulating the EAW system, and the British Extradition Act of 2003, which implement the EU Decision in the United Kingdom, require that an EAW be issued by a 'judicial authority'. This requirement reflects the aim of the Framework Decision to depoliticize the extradition process throughout Europe by withdrawing it from the executive branch of government and placing it under the control of the respective judicial authorities.

This is the point of attack for Assange's defence lawyers. In his case, the European Arrest Warrant has been issued by Marianne Ny – a prosecutor, not a judge. Hence, Assange's lawyers argue, the warrant was not issued by a 'judicial authority' and therefore is not a valid basis for Assange's extradition to Sweden. That also appears to be the British legal position. As the Supreme Court confirms, during the British parliamentary debates surrounding the adoption of the 2003 Extradition Act, it was repeatedly emphasized that the term 'judicial authority' necessarily implied a court or judge, not the police or a public prosecutor, and that this requirement would not be affected by the implementation of the EU Framework Decision. Sweden and a few other EU states have interpreted the term 'judicial authority' more broadly to include prosecutors. But this was not binding for the British judiciary, because, strictly speaking, it was not the wording of the overarching EU Framework Decision that the British judges had to interpret, but the British Extradition Act which had been adopted for the implementation of this decision. What was relevant for the Supreme Court was the interpretation given to the term 'judicial authority' by the British Parliament, and not by other EU states. Thus, in an email to Marianne Ny dated 8 February 2012, her British colleague from the Crown Prosecution Service writes with growing concern: 'The court seems rather troubled by the whole question of other countries having such a wide interpretation of "judicial authority", in particular how it can include prosecutors or officials from Ministries of Justice – I would stress again that it is UK law which [is] under the judicial spotlight not Swedish law.'

According to British legal tradition, Prosecutor Marianne Ny clearly is not a 'judicial authority'. In order to still uphold her EAW and allow Assange's extradition to Sweden, the Supreme Court must now engage in judicial acrobatics that can be better described as legal contortions. In Paragraph 93 of its ruling, the court acknowledges that the British Parliament's explicitly narrow interpretation of the notion of 'judicial authority' is 'certainly disturbing', but then ventures to say that it would be going 'at least one step too far, in constitutional terms, for this court to treat it as determinative'. The majority of the judges are guided by the hypothesis that, regardless of their express positions taken in the legislative debate, members of Parliament could not have intended to legislate contrary to the UK's international obligations but, actually, preferred to interpret their own Extradition Act in conformity with the wording of the EU Framework Decision. The problem is, of course, that the meaning of the wording chosen in the EU Framework Decision only a year earlier was completely uncertain in 2003 when the UK Extradition Act came before the British Parliament – which is precisely why the clarifying parliamentary debate was necessary in the first place. But since then, we learn from the Supreme Court, an inconsistent practice has developed throughout the EU, with roughly one half of the member states restricting the term 'judicial authority' to adjudicating officials and bodies, which excludes prosecutors, whereas the other half interprets the same term more comprehensively and, in some cases, even extends it to prosecutors.

In view of these highly challenging circumstances, the judges find it imperative to ignore the parliamentary genesis of the directly applicable British Extradition Act and, instead, consider the administrative genesis of the EU Framework Decision, even though it is not directly applicable as a matter of law. The original first draft of this instrument having been written in French, the judges further conclude that priority must imperatively be given to the original French wording. The meaning of the French term 'autorité judiciaire', however, has not been defined, nor has it been clarified through uniform practice. Therefore, 'autorité judiciaire' can be interpreted either narrowly, as preferred by the British Parliament, or more broadly, as preferred by the government of Sweden.

For a variety of multi-layered and rather convoluted motives, five out of seven judges then happen to personally prefer the comprehensive interpretation of the French term 'autorité judiciaire', which also includes the public prosecutor. As a matter of logic, they argue, this expansive interpretation must therefore be regarded as binding also for the interpretation of the English term 'judicial authority' – not only in the English version of the EU Framework Decision, but also in the British Extradition Act, even though Parliament had expressly opted for the opposite interpretation. *Et voilà* – Prosecutor Ny's European Arrest Warrant is valid, and Assange can be extradited to Sweden! You couldn't make it up: the honourable Supreme Court of the United Kingdom bending over backwards in deference to political interests, and not hesitating to refer to the French text of an inapplicable EU Framework Decision in order to interpret the original English wording of directly applicable domestic legislation differently than Parliament – and then claiming that this is what Parliament presumably would have wanted in the first place.

Once their decision was in the bag, the judges nevertheless expressed their concern at the fact that the British Extradition Act – contrary to the explicit recommendation of the EU Council – does not require a proportionality test in order to ensure that a draconian coercive measure, such as extradition to another country, is justified in each individual case. In the Assange case, this question arose primarily because Sweden did not request the extradition of a person formally accused or convicted of a crime, but of a cooperative suspect in a preliminary investigation, who had already been voluntarily interviewed and who was ready and willing to respond to further questions, on the spot in London or by telephone or videoconference. Although the Supreme Court conveniently found that it could not examine the proportionality of Assange's extradition in the absence of a corresponding legal provision in the Extradition Act, it made no secret of the fact that this was a formal shortcoming that needed to be addressed – a hint that was duly taken up by Parliament. Two years later, legislation came into force stipulating that, from now on, every single extradition would be subject to a proportionality test and that no person could be extradited before being formally charged with a crime. Both provisions would have prevented Assange's extradition to Sweden and would have allowed him to leave his diplomatic asylum at the Ecuadorian embassy as a free man. But Parliament made sure to add a non-retroactivity clause that prevented the application of these new provisions to extradition cases that had already been decided, but not yet executed. There was exactly one man in the entire United Kingdom to whom this non-retroactivity clause applied. It was a *'lex Assange'*, as it has been poignantly termed, tailor-made by the British authorities for the persecution of a man who is constantly accused of evading justice – but who, quite on the contrary, is constantly deprived of justice precisely by those same authorities.

Assange's lawyers avail themselves of one last legal remedy, requesting the Supreme Court to reopen the appeal, which is rejected on 14 June 2012. This means that Assange has now definitely exhausted the legal remedies available to him in the United Kingdom. The following day, Prosecutor Marianne Ny requests that the Supreme Court permit his immediate surrender to Sweden, thus effectively withdrawing the suspensive effect of a possible appeal by Assange to the European Court of Human Rights in Strasbourg. The court declines and grants Assange a final reprieve of fourteen days. Nonetheless, his extradition to Sweden and – so he fears – his subsequent irregular surrender to the United States are now imminent.

# 8

# Ecuadorian Embassy Asylum

## Australian 'Declaration of Abandonment'

At around 1 pm on 19 June 2012, Julian Assange enters the Ecuadorian embassy in London – the next turning point in the story of his persecution. For the next almost seven years, he will not leave the red-brown brick building with white window frames, centrally located in close proximity to the luxury department store, Harrods. Assange seeks protection from America's wrath and therefore applies for political asylum. His written application states, among other things: 'It is my belief that the country of which I am a national, Australia, will not protect me and the country to which I am due to be extradited imminently from the UK, Sweden, will not prevent my onward extradition to the US. I ask that protection be extended so far as is reasonably possible, to prevent such an occurrence.'

Throughout the Swedish extradition proceedings, from January 2011 to May 2012, Assange's lawyers in London had repeatedly appealed in writing and in person to the Australian government, asking for diplomatic intervention to protect Assange. These appeals were transmitted through the Australian Embassy in Stockholm and the Australian High Commission in London, but also directly to Foreign Minister Kevin Rudd and Justice Minister Nicola Roxon. According to his lawyers, in Sweden, Assange faced not only many months of detention in near-complete isolation and a secret trial for alleged sexual offences, but also the risk of irregular surrender to the United States – a risk that could also materialize in the United Kingdom. Their main request was always the same: the Australian government should urgently obtain assurances from both Sweden and the United Kingdom that Assange would not be extradited to the United States under any circumstances. There, influential individuals in public life had made death threats against him, and he risked a politically motivated trial for journalistic activities that should not be criminalized as espionage in the first place. Of particular concern, they argued, was not only the 'excessive use of extreme isolation' by US authorities, but also the prevailing practice of coercing guilty pleas and supporting testimony through the threat of enormous sentences in case of non-cooperation. For the same reasons, the lawyers also asked the Australian government for assurances that, if repatriated to Australia, Assange would not be extradited to the United States.

These letters triggered an intense internal discussion between ministries in Canberra, especially regarding Assange's possible extradition to Sweden and onward surrender to the United States. Internal assessments were produced, emails went back and forth, and their content differed significantly from official government pronouncements. This correspondence leaves no doubt that the Australian authorities were well aware of the risk of a 'temporary surrender' of Assange from Sweden to the United States for the purpose of criminal proceedings. The Australian officials plainly attached no importance to the Swedish government's assertions to the contrary. In the world of diplomatic relations, the fact that Stockholm refused to issue a non-refoulement guarantee to Assange spoke a clear language and left no room for misunderstandings.

Against this background, Australia's unwillingness to stand up for a politically persecuted national can only be described as shameful. The government's official responses remain formalistic, self-righteous and sanctimonious, but in substantive terms completely distant and noncommittal. The primary smokescreen deflecting from its manifest indifference is the claim that extradition proceedings are always a 'matter of bilateral law enforcement cooperation', governed by the domestic laws and practice of the states involved, in which Australia 'would not expect to be a party'. Nevertheless, the 'expectation that Mr. Assange's case will proceed in accordance with due process' has been expressed to both the Swedish and British governments on several occasions. If Assange were to return to Australia, it would be within the government's discretion to refuse his extradition to the United States, but this would have to be assessed on a case-by-case basis, and no assurances could be given at this time. In effect, Assange's lawyers rightly spoke of an Australian 'Declaration of Abandonment' – he had been discarded by his own government.

## British Plans to Storm the Embassy

Assange's last resort is Ecuador, whose president, Rafael Correa, has proved to be a supporter of WikiLeaks in the past. Assange knows that he can obtain diplomatic asylum solely on the grounds of political persecution, not in order to escape Swedish rape investigations. He is seeking protection from possible extradition to the United States, where he faces a real risk of life in solitary confinement and possibly even the death penalty because of his work for WikiLeaks. For Assange, this is the only reason for his asylum request, and for Ecuador it will be the only reason for granting his request.

On 19 June 2012, Assange has come to the Ecuadorian embassy to stay. The government in Quito reacts quickly and grants temporary protection, pending a detailed examination of Assange's request. During these first days, the diplomatic staff, led by Ambassador Ana Albán, faces major logistical challenges. The embassy has a total of only ten rooms, all of which are located on the same floor. No one is prepared for a permanent guest. A bedroom must be set up for Assange, and the sanitary facilities must be expanded. He will be given a computer and internet access. He can also use the small kitchenette. Step by step, his improvised accommodation becomes permanent. For the time being, Assange is safe – or trapped, depending on the perspective. British police are deployed in front of the embassy and demonstratively block the way out. They, too, have come to stay.

Humiliated by Assange's move, the British government struggles to retain its posture. On 15 August, the day before Ecuador is to render its final decision on Assange's asylum status, a British embassy official in Quito hands the Ecuadorian government a 'note verbale' for the contingency of Assange being granted diplomatic asylum: 'You need to be aware that there is a legal base in the UK, the Diplomatic and Consular Premises Act 1987, that would allow us to take actions in order to arrest Mr Assange in the current premises of the embassy.'

A thinly veiled warning that Britain is prepared to storm the embassy, the note verbale concludes with the words: 'We very much hope not to get to this point.' It later transpires that Foreign Secretary William Hague himself insisted on this unprecedented threat, against the strong reservations of his legal advisers. Predictably, it results in diplomatic upheaval.

Secretary Hague's Ecuadorian counterpart, Ricardo Patiño, has strong words: 'If the measures announced in the British official communication materialize they will be interpreted by Ecuador as a hostile and intolerable act and also as an attack on our sovereignty, which would require us to respond with greater diplomatic force.' Patiño quite rightly considers the British threat a clear breach of the Vienna Convention on Diplomatic Relations. He fears a dangerous precedent that would open the door to the violation of any nation's sovereign spaces, which include embassy buildings. On 24 August, the Organization of American States (OAS), quickly convened by Ecuador for an extraordinary meeting, came to the same conclusion. In their final resolution, the OAS-states declare their solidarity with Ecuador and vigorously reject any attempt 'that might put at risk the inviolability of the premises of diplomatic missions'.

William Hague has made a mistake, and he knows it. He has to row back. The British Foreign Office now asserts that there was never any threat to storm the embassy. It was all just another unfortunate misunderstanding. Even with the risk of a violent invasion banned, however, the siege of the embassy building remains real. One of the Metropolitan Police officers on duty outside the embassy carries a document with handwritten notes under his arm, which is captured by a press photographer with a highly sensitive camera lens. At least parts of the document can be deciphered and reveal instructions that, in case of an exit from the embassy, Assange is to be arrested 'under all circumstances', even if he should be in a diplomatic vehicle or hidden in a diplomatic bag. In both cases, such an arrest would still be a clear violation of the international law on diplomatic immunity. In order to grasp the political magnitude of these events, it must be stressed that no state would dare to blatantly violate the international law on diplomatic relations just to enable a foreign country to interview a man who has repeatedly expressed his willingness to fully cooperate under the terms of mutual legal assistance, who is not violent, and whose case has been stuck at the preliminary investigation stage for two years without any realistic prospect of an indictment, let alone a conviction. The threat to forcibly seize Assange from the Ecuadorian embassy illustrates not only the British government's anger at the unforeseen turn of events but, above all, the immense political dimension of this case. In reality, of course, the British government is not in the least concerned with the Swedish investigation and certainly not with the petty offence of bail violation which Assange committed when seeking asylum in the embassy. No government in the world would consider storming a foreign embassy except in extreme circumstances, such as terrorist attacks, hostage-taking, or other serious and imminent threats to public safety. Apparently, the world power Britain indeed perceives Assange as a threat of this magnitude.

Assange himself is well aware of the big picture. In a brief speech, delivered from the balcony of the embassy building on 19 August 2012, he thanks the Ecuadorian government, embassy staff, and all other supporters, and then appeals to the US president: 'I ask President Obama to do the right thing. The United States must renounce its witch-hunts against WikiLeaks. ... The United States must pledge before the world that it will not pursue journalists for shining a light on the secret crimes of the powerful.' He goes on to demand the same for whistleblowers like Chelsea Manning, who by then has been in American custody without trial for more than 800 days.

## 'Don't you dare get cold feet!'

On 31 August, two weeks after Assange had received formal asylum at the Ecuadorian embassy, an interview is published quoting him as saying: 'The Swedish government could drop the case. I think this is the most likely scenario. Maybe after a thorough investigation of what happened they could drop the case.' The British Crown Prosecution Service is not amused. Less than three hours after the publication, they send an email calling their Swedish colleagues to order: 'Don't you dare get cold feet!' Eighteen months earlier, the British had strongly advised the Swedes against questioning Assange in London or through remote means; now they are warning against dropping the case. Again, one might ask: Why are they doing this? Why are they so invested in a case that doesn't even involve a British national? Should they not be relieved if Sweden no longer wants to pursue the case? After all, there would be no more expenses for the siege and surveillance of the embassy, and no more public protests against Assange's persecution. For the sake of credibility, Assange's bail violation could still be sanctioned with a fine, in addition to the confiscation of the bail deposit of £200,000. After that, the whole case could be closed, and everybody could return to business as usual. But that is not what is happening. Instead, the British authorities seem to have a strong interest in Sweden continuing its investigation and maintaining a threat scenario against Assange. At the same time, the Swedish prosecutor does not seem to be genuinely keen to get Assange extradited to Sweden. When on 29 November 2012 her British colleague jokingly writes, 'I am sure you can guess what I would just love to send to you as a Christmas present', she replies 'I am OK without any Christmas present. In fact, it would be a great shock to get that one!' Just a joke? Perhaps. But every joke contains a grain of truth.

Be that as it may, after more than a full year of standoff, Swedish enthusiasm seems to wane. The arrest warrant issued back in 2010 cannot be maintained forever, and with Assange having permanently settled into his diplomatic asylum, the embassy siege is unlikely to end anytime soon. Prosecutor Ny seems to be under gradually mounting pressure from the Swedish judiciary. Early on Friday, 18 October 2013, she writes an email to the Crown Prosecution Service which – significantly – is entitled 'Question'. But, instead of asking a question, she explains the constraints imposed by Swedish law on open-ended coercive measures: 'There is a demand in Swedish law for coercive measures to be proportionate. The time passing, the costs and how severe the crime is to be taken into account together with the intrusion or detriment to the suspect. Against this background we have found us to be obliged to consider to lift the detention order (court order) and to withdraw the European arrest warrant. If so this should be done in a couple of weeks.' Then, she ominously comments: 'This would affect not only us but you too in a significant way.'

The concluding sentence of the message, which must have contained the 'question' announced in its title, is redacted as it was apparently considered too delicate for the public to know about. Did she ask whether the British authorities had any objections? The tone and content of the ensuing dialogue certainly suggests so. The British response follows in the late afternoon: 'I would like to consider all the angles over the weekend, if that is OK with you.' Why would the British have to 'consider all the angles' of a Swedish decision to lift a Swedish detention order in a Swedish case? This correspondence is odd enough given that, in the Assange case, the British CPS supposedly represents the interests of Sweden in the United Kingdom, and not the other way around. But the correspondence gets even more revealing. First thing on Monday morning, 21 October, Marianne Ny follows up: 'I am sorry that this came as a (bad) surprise. It is certainly OK for you to take your time to think this over. ... I hope I didn't ruin your weekend.' Why on earth would Sweden's director of public prosecution ever apologize to a British mid-level official for 'ruining his weekend', just because she announced that he might soon be relieved of this burdensome case?

On 2 December 2013, Prosecutor Ny seems to refer back to this correspondence when she writes, 'I didn't make myself clear at all, asking for your views', and then specifies: 'The costs that are to be taken into account are those on your side and your views on this are weighty. It has been argued in Sweden that the English police regards the costs getting unreasonably high. I understand from your answer that the costs on your side is not an issue that we should take into consideration at this stage?' Again, the Swedish prosecutor shows a remarkable level of deference to British interests in determining her own handling of this case. On 10 December 2013, the CPS responds: 'Just to confirm that I do not consider costs are a relevant factor in this matter. ... I have certainly not been aware of any adverse comment or concern being expressed by any government departments.' As we now know, from 2012 to 2019, British police spent more than £16 million on besieging the Ecuadorian embassy – far too much smoke for a small fire, and therefore again a clear indication of the political dimension of this case.

## Second Discontinuation of the Swedish Investigation

For the time being, the British pressure works, and the Swedish courts remain complacent, leaving the European Arrest Warrant in place and the preliminary investigation in a dormant state. This enables Prosecutor Ny to maintain and perpetuate a completely artificial impasse by refusing to facilitate a governmental non-refoulement guarantee that would allow Assange to return to Sweden safely for a police interview, while also refusing to interview him remotely by video conference or on-site in London under applicable mutual legal assistance agreements. It is only in March 2015 that the Swedish Supreme Court begins to lose patience with her prosecutorial procrastination and indicates its willingness to lift the arrest warrant against Assange on grounds of proportionality.

For almost five years, Prosecutor Ny has been insisting that her investigation required Assange's personal presence in Sweden: because it would be against the law for her to interview him in London; because a DNA sample had to be taken from him; because of the seriousness of the offences alleged against him; and for unspecified 'technical investigative' reasons. But in 2015, under pressure from the Supreme Court, all these insurmountable obstacles seem suddenly to have vanished into thin air, and the prosecutor agrees to interview Assange at the Ecuadorian embassy in London. Mainly due to formal disagreements between Sweden and Ecuador, however, another twenty months will pass before this interview actually takes place. In the meantime, the allegations of sexual harassment and sexual coercion made against Assange in the case of A. have expired under the applicable five-year statute of limitations. The same applies to the false accusation complaint that was filed in August 2010 but not pursued by Eva Finné, the chief prosecutor for Stockholm. At the end of August 2015, both these issues were definitely off the table.

The fact that the case of A. became time-barred without formal charges being filed is often conveniently blamed on Assange 'hiding' in the embassy. What is generally forgotten is that, in the case of A., Assange had already been interviewed by the Swedish police on 30 August 2010, within a few days of the initial police report. On that occasion, Assange was formally notified of the main allegation against him, namely that he had deliberately destroyed a condom during sexual intercourse, and he responded to all questions asked by the police. Moreover, since 7 December 2010, Assange's DNA profile had been available to the Swedish authorities via British mutual legal assistance and, on 15 July 2011, the State Forensic Laboratory SKL rendered its detailed report on the requested DNA samples. Thus, at the latest by 15 July 2011, the Swedish Prosecution Authority had all the evidence it could conceivably expect to obtain in order to decide whether to press formal charges or to discontinue the investigation for lack of evidence. Instead, Prosecutor Ny needlessly continued to procrastinate for more than four years until, finally, the case of A. was pushed beyond the line of expiry and became time-barred. Of course, as an experienced prosecutor, Marianne Ny must have understood the evidentiary hopelessness of her case against Assange. To her, allowing the case of A. to expire must have been the most elegant and convenient of all solutions, whereas it was probably the worst outcome for Assange. Not only did it perpetuate the criminal suspicion against him without the prosecutor ever being required to offer any evidence, it also allowed her to blame Assange for cheating both A. and the public out of their right to truth and justice. What is hardly ever considered is that, in this way, Assange would effectively be stigmatized as a fugitive sex offender for the rest of his life and there was virtually nothing he could do about it. In my view, that was very likely the real purpose of the entire Swedish investigation.

After the case of A. has been closed and archived, on 13 August 2015, the Swedish preliminary investigation now focuses exclusively on the alleged rape of S. In her case, the applicable ten-year statute of limitations expires in August 2020. The announced interview of Assange by the Swedish prosecutor takes place at the Ecuadorian embassy in London in November 2016. An Ecuadorian prosecutor asks the questions prepared by the Swedish authorities, but Assange's Swedish lawyer is not allowed to participate. After that interview, Assange's lawyers call on the Swedish Prosecution Authority to finally either file formal charges or close the case. But Prosecutor Ny does neither, until Assange's lawyers once again apply to the Stockholm District Court on 3 May 2017 and ask for the arrest warrant to be lifted. The very next day, the court asks the Prosecution Authority to provide a response by 17 May.

Prosecutor Ny knows that she has to act. It has been two

years since the Swedish Supreme Court had signalled its willingness to revoke the arrest warrant against Assange on grounds
of proportionality and, unsurprisingly, the interview at the
Ecuadorian Embassy has not yielded the evidence required for a
formal indictment. The law thus obliges her to admit to the lack
of evidence and close the case, clearing Assange of all wrongdoing. If she does not, the Supreme Court will be obliged to do it
in her place, because the Swedish Code of Judicial Procedure is
clear: 'The preliminary investigation shall be conducted as expeditiously as possible'; 'The investigation should be conducted so
that no person is unnecessarily exposed to suspicion, or put to
unnecessary cost or inconvenience'; 'Upon the conclusion of the
preliminary investigation, a decision on whether to institute a
prosecution shall be issued'; 'When there is no longer reason for
pursuing the investigation, it shall be discontinued.'

On 19 May 2017, Prosecutor Ny chooses the only option that
allows her to circumvent these safeguards of the law and to continue to perpetuate the rape suspect narrative against Assange
without the required evidence. She 'discontinues' the preliminary
investigation into the alleged rape of S. but claims that its proper
conclusion is rendered impossible because Assange remains
under the protection of the Ecuadorian embassy. The prosecutor
explains that 'it is now not possible to take any further steps that
would move the investigation forward' and that 'to continue
with legal proceedings would require Julian Assange's appearance in court', thereby implying that his absence is the only
reason for not proceeding with a formal indictment and trial.

From a procedural perspective, of course, this rationale
is putting the cart before the horse. The decision to formally
charge a suspect never depends on his physical presence, but on
the strength of the evidence against him. Only once the suspect
is formally charged may his physical presence become necessary for the purposes of conducting the actual trial. As we now
know, despite all those years of investigation, Prosecutor Ny
never possessed sufficient evidence to formally charge Assange
of any crime. However, instead of acknowledging this reality,
conceding to the presumption of innocence and rehabilitating

Assange's reputation, the Swedish prosecutor deliberately perpetuates the false impression that the only procedural obstacle to a successful criminal trial is Assange's purported evasion of justice. The official narrative must be protected at all costs. Only through Assange's continued stigmatization can public attention be diverted from the actual elephant in the room: the dirty secrets of the powerful.

The final days before Prosecutor Ny closes the Swedish rape investigation are marked by a bitter culmination. Assange's secret lover and partner Stella Moris is pregnant, and the birth of their son Gabriel is imminent. Per Samuelson, his Swedish lawyer, forwards a personal letter from Assange to Marianne Ny, in which he asks permission to attend the birth of his son at a London hospital: 'Your written agreement to this request will entail the temporary suspension of the effect of the European Arrest Warrant so that I am able to be transported, without publicity, to the maternity unit. I will remain there until my partner and child are discharged from the hospital, after which time I will return to the Ecuadorian embassy. My transport to and from the hospital will occur in a diplomatic vehicle.'

But Prosecutor Ny's answer is unequivocal: 'Request rejected. There lacks the necessary legal prerequisites to temporarily suspend, or make an exception to, the court's decision that you are to be detained in your absence as well as the issued [sic] of the European Arrest Warrant'. On 26 April, the prosecutor sends her decision in Swedish to Assange's lawyer, followed by the English translation on 16 May. By the 16th, of course, Marianne Ny is fully aware that she will discontinue the Swedish investigation against Assange only three days later. Assange pleads with her to reconsider, but to no avail. With this last deed, Marianne Ny bows out from the persecution of Assange. On 19 May 2017, she discontinues the Swedish investigation. But Assange remains confined to the Ecuadorian embassy. All of a sudden, the British authorities have become particularly keen on prosecuting Assange's bail violation five years earlier – the only accusation against him that has not yet been dropped or disproven – and, in the background, the US

Department of Justice ramps up its efforts to indict Assange under the Espionage Act of 1917.

## NSA Scandal and DNC Leaks

Even during Assange's asylum at the Ecuadorian embassy, WikiLeaks continued to work, publishing a wide range of leaked material, not only from Western governments, intelligence agencies and corporations, but also from countries such as Russia, Syria, Angola, Saudi Arabia and Turkey. It was also during this time that the 'NSA scandal' erupted. In 2013, Edward Snowden, an employee of the US National Security Agency (NSA), made the headlines with explosive revelations about global surveillance programmes operated by US intelligence agencies, many in cooperation with British, Australian, Canadian and European partner agencies. For the first time, the world learned about the enormous scale and reach of state-sponsored internet and smartphone surveillance, which involved clandestine access to hundreds of millions of private email accounts and smartphones, and large financial incentives for cooperative technology companies.

Snowden did not seek whistleblower anonymity but affirmed the authenticity of the material by disclosing his identity. This made him a target. The United States accused him of espionage. Assange and WikiLeaks assisted Snowden's escape via Hong Kong to Moscow and helped with exploring options for political asylum in various countries. Bolivia, Ecuador, Venezuela and Iceland were reportedly considered, but Snowden remained in Moscow, where he was granted asylum in August 2013 and permanent residence in October 2020. In the film '*WikiLeaks – Die USA gegen Julian Assange*' (WikiLeaks – The USA vs Julian Assange), aired by German public broadcaster ARD in 2020, Edward Snowden drew parallels between his own case and that of Assange, but at the same time emphasized an important distinction: 'I was the one who actually gathered this material. I am an American, I had a contract with the government. And yet in the case of Assange, he did not gather any material himself. He received it and then merely published it. He signed no contracts. He was not an American. He is by far the weaker case in terms of what the government has against us. And yet, Assange receives less support in terms of opposition to the charges against him.'

The distinction between unlawfully gathering confidential information and publishing it in a journalistic manner is of critical importance with regard to Assange's work with WikiLeaks. It also applies to the so-called DNC Leaks. In 2016, in the middle of the US presidential elections, WikiLeaks published around 20,000 internal emails of key staff of the Democratic National Committee (DNC), as well as of Hillary Clinton's campaign manager, John Podesta. The publication occurred immediately before the Democratic Party convention in Philadelphia, at which Clinton was to be nominated the party's presidential candidate. The published correspondence provided evidence of strong bias within the Committee against Clinton's strongest competitor, Bernie Sanders. Apparently, Sanders's nomination was to be prevented at all costs, including through deliberate defamation. As a consequence, the DNC chair, Debbie Wasserman Schultz, was forced to resign. The second leak occurred on 6 November, only two days before the presidential election, in which Clinton ended up winning the popular vote but losing the electoral college to the Republican candidate Donald Trump.

No other publication has cost Assange as much goodwill in the United States as the DNC Leaks. The American liberal establishment, including many political figures, business leaders, Hollywood stars and other celebrities, struggled to come to terms with this defeat. How could the venerable Democratic Party, with a candidate as prominent as Hillary Clinton, have lost to someone like Donald Trump, widely despised as crude and self-absorbed? The truth is, of course, that all of the compromising emails had been written by Clinton, her staff and supporters – not by Assange. The truth is that Clinton lost the election because of her own conduct and that of the Democratic Party, not that of Assange. The truth is that in any democratic election process, exposing the dirty secrets of political candidates is an indispensable function of journalists. The truth is that even political celebrities such as Hillary Clinton are not 'entitled' to electoral victory but have to earn it themselves. And the hardest truth is that it was not WikiLeaks that gave Donald Trump the presidency, but the American people, in an American election, based on the American Constitution.

All of these truths rose to the surface of public consciousness, but were too painful to face and, therefore, were immediately suppressed back into the subconscious. As the German poet Christian Morgenstern famously said, 'What cannot be, must not be!' A scapegoat was urgently needed, and so Assange was accused of having manipulated the 2016 elections, prevented Hillary Clinton from becoming president, and helped Donald Trump into office. But even a scapegoat could not divert public attention forever from the longstanding misconduct that was the most likely cause for the colossal loss of confidence suffered by both established parties with the American people. What was needed was an external enemy. Sure enough, the mainstream press soon started disseminating the US intelligence agencies' favourite narrative of 'Russian hacking'.

Within days the Democratic Party accused the Russian Federation of stealing the emails and joining forces with Trump, Assange and WikiLeaks to manipulate the election. In 2018 the party filed a lawsuit in the Southern District of New York against all of the above. But Judge John Koeltl's ruling, handed down on 31 July 2019, did not turn out as expected by the Democrats. Koeltl did not have to question Russia's responsibility for the data theft, but simply explained that, due to the principles of sovereign immunity, the Russian Federation could not be sued in the courts of the United States for governmental actions. More importantly, the claims against Donald Trump, his campaign team, WikiLeaks and Assange were also dismissed, this time based on the First Amendment of the US Constitution.

Presumably to the dismay of the entire political establishment on both sides of the aisle, Koeltl described Assange as a 'journalist' and considered the publications of WikiLeaks protected as a matter of press freedom. The judge stressed that 'there is a significant legal distinction between stealing documents and disclosing documents that someone else had stolen previously.' More specifically, he argued, the First Amendment precluded the liability of those who 'publish materials of public interest despite defects in the way the materials were obtained so long as the disseminator did not participate in any wrongdoing in obtaining the materials in the first place'. Importantly for Assange, Koeltl then went on to dismiss the conspiracy rationale: 'The DNC's argument that WikiLeaks can be held liable for the theft as an after-the-fact coconspirator of the stolen documents is also unpersuasive. ... such a rule would render any journalist who publishes an article based on stolen information a coconspirator in the theft.' Therefore, Koeltl concluded, 'journalists are allowed to request documents that have been stolen and to publish those documents.' The DNC's lawsuit had backfired spectacularly and inadvertently prompted a veritable landmark judgment of enormous value for WikiLeaks, Assange and press freedom more generally.

True to his principles, Assange never disclosed his source for the DNC leaks. On 15 August 2017, ex-US Congressman Dana Rohrabacher and his assistant Charles Johnson visited Assange in the Ecuadorian embassy in London in order to propose a deal. According to Assange's lawyer Jennifer Robinson, who was present at the meeting, the visitors made it understood that they were acting with the knowledge and consent of President Trump and that their aim was to explore a possible win-win deal that would allow Assange to leave the embassy without fear of US prosecution. At the time, President Trump was being investigated by Special Counsel Robert Mueller, on allegations that he had committed treason by conspiring with Russian agents in the DNC leaks. The proposed deal was that, if Assange were to disclose his real source for the DNC leaks, disproving the allegation that the emails had been provided by Russian hackers, Rohrabacher would lobby Trump for a presidential pardon on the espionage charges against Assange. Assange declined – and Washington's wrath was not long in coming. On 21 December 2017, the US government transmitted a diplomatic note to

London requesting Assange's provisional arrest; on 6 March 2018, a secret Grand Jury in the United States filed a sealed indictment against him; and within three weeks, Assange's living conditions in the Ecuadorian embassy began to deteriorate drastically. It was the beginning of the end of Assange's diplomatic asylum – made possible by an absolutely decisive event that had taken place ten months earlier: the change of leadership in Quito.

## A New Government in Ecuador

In May 2017, Lenín Moreno replaced Rafael Correa as president of Ecuador. The Ecuadorian people had believed that the election of former Vice President Moreno would ensure the continuation of Correa's progressive policies. They were in for a shock. This was not going to be a simple transfer of power between politicians of the same tradition. Within a few months of taking office, the Moreno government bowed to economic and political pressure and performed a neoliberal U-turn, putting the normalization of the country's relations with the United States at the very top of the agenda. Suddenly, Assange's asylum at the Ecuadorian embassy became an obstacle on the path of US–Ecuadorian rapprochement.

Various options were explored. As the *New York Times* revealed in December 2018, President-elect Moreno received a visit from President Trump's former campaign manager Paul Manafort as early as mid-May 2017. Moreno seized the opportunity to offer Manafort Assange's rendition to the United States in exchange for financial concessions, including debt relief. But Manafort became a primary target of Special Counsel Mueller's 'Russiagate' investigation, which ended his role as a middleman. In the following months, Moreno then apparently tried to get rid of Assange by, first, giving him Ecuadorian citizenship in December 2017 and then appointing him ambassador of Ecuador to Moscow. But the British authorities made clear that they did not recognize Assange's diplomatic immunity and would arrest him as soon as he were to leave the embassy. Three months later followed the secret US indictment on 6 March 2018 and, in late June, US Vice President Mike Pence visited Ecuador to hold 'constructive discussions' with Moreno about Assange. The precise content of these talks was kept secret, but parallel developments inside the Ecuadorian embassy speak for themselves.

Fidel Narváez, consul general of the Ecuadorian embassy in London until the summer of 2018, provides a sober, unexcited, yet largely positive evaluation of Assange's first years of asylum. According to Narváez, the situation was obviously not easy, neither for the embassy staff nor for Assange, but everyone did their best to adapt. Of course, wherever people have to live together in a confined space, there will be occasional situations of stress, he said. Additionally, there was the constant police surveillance, media attention, political pressure, outside visitors, logistical difficulties in securing food, hygiene and medical care, and the indefinite duration of Assange's presence inside the offices of the embassy, which were not designed for that purpose. In view of all these challenges, the former consul found it remarkable that, overall, the co-existence of the embassy staff with Assange had been marked by friendliness and mutual respect for five years. There was a brief exception in October 2016, when the Ecuadorian government temporarily suspended Assange's access to the internet during the US presidential election, in order to mitigate the political tensions caused by the DNC leaks while at the same time reaffirming Ecuador's commitment to shield Assange until his life and integrity could be otherwise secured. In view of Ecuador's military and economic vulnerability, the country deserves to be saluted for its decision to stand up to international pressure and protect Assange from extradition to the United States. In this respect, the then Ecuadorian leadership showed exemplary courage and commitment to fundamental principles of international law, including the universal prohibition of torture and the principle of non-refoulement.

Assange's everyday life at the embassy, which remained largely unproblematic until 2017, was certainly facilitated by a character trait of his which, for lack of a better word, could be called 'resilience'. This man was not accustomed to luxury. For years he had lived out of a suitcase and slept wherever a couch was on offer, the internet was working, and people were willing to support WikiLeaks. In addition, Assange seemed to be strongly focused on his own work, his own person, his own thoughts, keeping the external world emotionally at arm's length. This ability of his is likely to have helped Assange to get through the first few years of his embassy asylum reasonably unscathed – despite the lack of sunlight, despite the uncertainty of his situation, and despite the constant threat of a looming extradition to the United States, knowing that his entire future depended on the decisions of others.

## The Refuge Becomes a Trap

The change of power in Ecuador is another turning point in the story of Assange's persecution. It takes a few months for the fallout of this event to reach the Ecuadorian embassy in London, but when it does, Assange's daily life changes drastically. One by one, reputedly Assange-friendly employees are removed and replaced by others who are willing to implement President Moreno's new policies without criticism. On 8 January 2019, the British minister Alan Duncan notes in his diary: 'Meet the new Ecuador Ambassador Jaime Marchán-Romero. His principal mission is to get Assange out of the embassy – it has been six years – and although he had been aiming for tomorrow, as I'd just learnt it's going to take longer. A tad frustrating, but we'll get there.'

Fidel Narváez was dismissed in the summer of 2018, after eight years of service; late enough to be able to give first-hand information about the increasingly difficult living conditions for Assange in the embassy. The purpose of the instructions received from Quito was clear: to get rid of Assange. To that end, a double strategy was reportedly pursued. Ideally, Assange could be moti-vated to voluntarily leave the embassy, simply by subjecting him to an increasingly restrictive, hostile and arbitrary environment. Alternatively, the intensity of his suffering would be increased to the point where it might trigger a medical crisis necessitating his transfer to a London hospital, where he could be arrested by British police. It was clear that the envisaged escalation would not materialize overnight, and given Assange's strong resilience, the strategy might not succeed at all. In that case, Assange's expulsion would become the only way to end his presence at the embassy, and so the Ecuadorian government started to look for reasons that could be used to publicly justify the termination of his asylum.

As of 28 March 2018, Ecuador begins to increasingly isolate Assange from the outside world. His internet and telephone access are blocked indefinitely, including through the installation of jammers. As has been pointed out, the timing of this measure is hardly a coincidence. It comes less than three weeks after Assange's secret indictment by the US Department of Justice – a move that the US government had deliberately avoided for eight years. Also, from 28 March to 31 October 2018, Assange's right to receive private visitors is severely restricted, with the sole exception of meetings with lawyers and doctors. During the entire period, no more than six private visits have been registered – less than one per month. Moreover, from now on, those visitors who are allowed into the embassy will be denied access to Assange's private rooms. Meetings are now only permitted in a conference room that is monitored through surveillance cameras and hidden microphones. This includes not only meetings with lawyers, politicians or journalists, but also medical examinations and sessions with psychotherapists. Meanwhile, embassy staff and security personnel are instructed to meticulously record anything that can be used against Assange. In the absence of any serious misconduct, they turn to examining Assange's daily routine under the microscope and painstakingly documenting details such as the feeding times of his cat, the cleanliness of the toilet, and any unwashed dishes in the kitchen sink.

On 14 October 2018, Minister Duncan notes in his diary: 'The BBC report that Assange's internet connection has been restored in the Ecuador embassy. The embassy have as good as laid a trap for him. If he misuses it, as he probably will, then they will chuck him out. Let's see.' Indeed, in October 2018, some of the previous restrictions are partially relaxed and replaced by a 'Special Protocol of Visits, Communications and Medical Attention for Mr Julian Paul Assange'. The protocol makes it nearly impossible for Assange not to violate the rules governing his asylum. According to Narváez, the purpose of the protocol is to 'lay out banana peels all over the floor', making sure that Assange will repeatedly slip and thus supply excuses for his expulsion by the Ecuadorian government. In particular, the procedure for admitting outside visitors has become more complicated. In some cases, two weeks pass before the necessary permission is granted. Each visit must be justified in writing, with accurate information about the purpose of the visit, the visitor's current employment situation, and any electronic devices likely to be carried. All visitors must surrender their personal mobile phones while inside the embassy. The same tendency towards arbitrary overregulation can be seen where the protocol addresses medical care, communication devices, and hygiene.

The protocol draws so many lines in the sand that their transgression becomes virtually inevitable. This is the whole point, of course, and so the six-page document concludes with almost gleeful anticipation: 'Failure to comply with the obligations contained in this Special Protocol by the asylee may result in the termination of diplomatic asylum conceded by the Ecuadorian State, in accordance with the relevant international instruments. The Ecuadorian State reserves itself the right to accept or reject the explanations that Mr. Assange may give in writing regarding the breach of the obligations of this Protocol.' In other words, it is made crystal clear that any justification or objection Assange may wish to raise in defence of his right to asylum and the prohibition of non-refoulement will not be considered in a due process proceeding based on the rule of law, but will depend entirely on the whim of the government.

Laying down rules that establish a relationship of unilateral dominance, total dependence and unpredictable arbitrariness is a typical feature in the creation of any torturous environment. More specifically, isolating a person from the outside world and positive social contacts, and over-regulating their daily life with complex, meaningless, and arbitrarily interpreted instructions, prohibitions, and procedures, are two key elements routinely used by torturers around the world to undermine the orientation, self-confidence, and resilience of their victims. But Assange's abuse does not end there.

## Permanent Surveillance

Already in 2017, surveillance measures inside the embassy are strengthened. The control room in the entrance area, where the security personnel and surveillance monitors are located, disappears behind opaque, one-way 'spy glass'. For Assange and his visitors, it is no longer possible to see whether and by whom they are being observed. The existing cameras inside the embassy are replaced by newer, high-resolution models. Officially, they do not provide audio recordings. Officially, Assange's private rooms are also exempt from surveillance. But Assange remains suspicious. He shields documents with his hand while reading or drafting them. He tries to protect the confidentiality of his meetings in the conference room by playing loud music on the radio, switching on his own jamming devices, covering documents, and blinding cameras with bright lights. For the discussion of sensitive legal matters, Assange takes his lawyers to the ladies' room and turns on the water to generate background noise.

While all of this may look like paranoia, it really was well-founded. In fact, as will be shown, Assange's surveillance at the embassy is even more systematic and comprehensive than he imagines. Everything is recorded, documented, spied on: medical examinations, strategy meetings with lawyers, meetings with private visitors. Security personnel are as interested in his state of health and his sleep patterns as they are in his personal notes or the SIM cards in his visitors' mobile phones.

Private documents disappear, medical notes are stolen, phones are opened. Microphones are found in the fire extinguisher in the conference room, in electrical outlets and, yes, even in the ladies' room.

Assange's son Gabriel, who is born in the spring of 2017, arouses particular interest. Stella Moris and Assange have done their utmost to keep the relationship secret. Assange learns that he will become a father from a note that Moris slips to him during one of her visits. After Gabriel's birth, it will never be her who brings the infant to the embassy, but a friend who passes him off as his own. As described above, in April 2017 Assange had entrusted his delicate family situation to the Swedish authorities, in the hope of finding a mutual arrangement that would have allowed him to be present at Gabriel's birth. These were, of course, the same Swedish authorities that had repeatedly demonstrated a complete lack of respect for Assange's right to privacy, and that the US embassy in Stockholm had described as 'reliable partners' in military and civilian intelligence cooperation. Unsurprisingly, therefore, security personnel at the Ecuadorian embassy soon became suspicious and stole one of Gabriel's nappies to conduct a DNA test.

In 2020, German public broadcaster ARD interviews Leon Panetta – CIA director from 2009 to 2011 and then US defense secretary until 2013 – for their above-mentioned film. Confronted with the alleged surveillance of Assange at the Ecuadorian embassy, Panetta is genuinely amused: 'It doesn't surprise me. I mean, that kind of thing goes on all the time. The intelligence business, you know, the name of the game is to get information any way you can. And I'm sure that's what was involved here.' At the same time Panetta condemns Assange and WikiLeaks for what he describes as a 'pretty huge breach of classified information', and opines that 'he should be punished' and 'face trial' in order to 'send a message to others not to do the same thing'. Unlike the CIA, however, WikiLeaks did not obtain any of its information through unlawful methods. No wiretapping, no data theft, no hacking and certainly no torture. Nonetheless, Panetta sees no contradiction in demanding the prosecution of Assange for investigative journalism, while simultaneously tolerating impunity for state-sponsored crimes committed by intelligence agencies. Panetta's genuine amusement and the almost naïve frankness with which he acknowledges the CIA's lawlessness are disarmingly honest. Quite evidently, he is already so accustomed to institutionalized criminality that he no longer even perceives it as problematic – a widespread phenomenon among the powerful and privileged of this world.

A key actor directly responsible for the surveillance measures at the Ecuadorian embassy is the Spanish private security company, UC Global. In 2015 it was contracted to guarantee the security of the embassy's premises and staff, reportedly due to personal contacts with the family of the then Ecuadorian president, Rafael Correa. The owner of UC Global is David Morales, a former Spanish marine. He is behind the massive expansion of Assange's surveillance. Every day, he personally reviews the material collected by his staff at the embassy. Often, these reports reach him in the United States. Morales's trips to America have become more frequent since he participated in a security trade fair in Las Vegas in 2016. He receives contracts from a casino empire that is reported to maintain close links with US intelligence services. After his first return from Las Vegas, Morales reportedly makes cryptic remarks to his staff to the effect that 'we are playing in the big leagues' and that he had 'switched to the dark side' and now worked for their 'American friends'. Did Morales commit the cardinal sin of any security contractor and turn against the interests of his client? Did he take advantage of his position to monitor Assange and then hand the data over to an American intelligence agency? Was he a double agent?

A criminal trial before the National Court of Justice in Spain aims to shed light on this affair. Assange and his lawyers accuse Morales and UC Global of illegal surveillance and, among other things, violating the confidential attorney–client relationship. Apparently, employees of the company have even attempted to blackmail Assange for large sums of money by threatening to publish material showing him in intimate situations. German journalists of the Norddeutscher Rundfunk (NDR) have also filed criminal reports against UC Global for transgressions against privacy and confidentiality during their visits to Assange at the Ecuadorian embassy.

The Ecuadorian government, now headed by Lenín Moreno, terminates the contract with UC Global in 2018 and hires an Ecuadorian security company by the name of Promsecurity. However, this does not put an end to Assange's surveillance. Most notably, his meetings with his lawyers continue to be recorded and, in one case, even the documents brought to the embassy by a lawyer are secretly photographed.

In its official responses to my interventions, the Ecuadorian government has always denied spying on Assange. For example, on 26 July 2019, the Ministry of Foreign Affairs wrote, 'There was no excessive regulation and no recording of private meetings.' This denial is remarkable, given that some of the resulting video recordings have been extensively shown and commented on in the mass media and continue to be accessible on online platforms such as YouTube. On 2 December 2019, the Ecuadorian government followed up with: 'Do not forget that the security cameras inside the Embassy were not installed to record Mr Assange, but to monitor the premises of the mission and to protect all those inside, including diplomatic officials.' This rationale presumably also applies to the microphones in the ladies' room. Further, 'Mr Assange and his lawyers and associates made threats and insulting accusations against the Ecuadorian State and its officials in the United Kingdom, accusing them without foundation of espionage for other nations.' Instead, the Ecuadorian government accuses Assange of making unauthorized recordings in the embassy. On the basis of this one-eyed perception of reality, a constructive dialogue is, of course, almost impossible to achieve.

From a legal perspective, the permanent surveillance of Assange's conversations with his lawyers and doctors renders any proceedings based on information gathered in this manner irreparably arbitrary. Under these circumstances, the equality of the parties before the law simply can no longer be guaranteed. If UC Global cooperated with an American intelligence service, this would fatally affect not only the Anglo-American extradition proceedings, but also the espionage charges of the US Department of Justice on which the extradition request is based. Quite apart from that, permanent surveillance and the associated constant violation of the right to privacy is also one of the standard components of psychological torture. The targeted person is deliberately deprived of the safe space of privacy, something essential for preserving a sense of personal autonomy, emotional stability and identity. One-way surveillance through cameras, hidden microphones, or spy glass suppresses any possibility of human connection, thus further compounding the ensuing feelings of powerlessness.

## Defamation, Humiliation and Demonization

From at least mid-2017, Assange lives under constant observation. Every detail of his daily life is pored over and picked apart, and, as always, truth is in the eye of the beholder. Objectively, there are good reasons to see Assange's resilience and stoic endurance as an impressive feat of resistance. But one can also choose to focus on details that make the scenario look completely different. Not everything about being human is dignified. Some aspects of our lives we prefer to keep private because they are intimate, embarrassing or simply trivial. In the case of Julian Assange, these private aspects increasingly become a topic of public discussion, distortion and humiliation. Ecuadorian officials and political leaders use the disgraceful tool of gossip to launch a new, 'dirty' narrative about Assange. Their tone is aggressive, their language immoderate and their aim is to vilify and belittle. The list of Assange's alleged misconduct is impressive, describing in detail the purportedly unsavoury, inappropriate, and disruptive features of his behaviour. Rhetorically, Assange's asylum is withdrawn months before he is actually arrested by British police.

In March 2018, after the secret US indictment, Ecuadorian officials begin to intensify their slander campaign and receive zealous support from their British counterparts. On 27 March,

Alan Duncan briefs the House of Commons on Assange, saying that 'It's about time that this miserable little worm walked out of the embassy and gave himself up to British justice.' Clearly, public opinion is being groomed across international borders to perceive the impending expulsion and arrest as the logical consequence of a long process of alienation for which Assange himself, and no one else, is to blame.

For any objective observer, the wilful malice of this narrative is easy to detect. Issues that were not considered a problem for years are now suddenly being raised against Assange and cast in the most unfavourable light possible. Everything that can be used against him is exposed, inflated and presented as evidence of a misconduct that can no longer be tolerated. Some of the reproaches are plainly absurd, including claims that he skateboarded and played soccer inside the embassy. We immediately picture Assange as a rowdy teenager, wearing his baseball cap backwards, kicking penalties in the ambassador's office and turning the conference room into a halfpipe. The truth is less jolly. In fact, during our medical examination, we found that Assange showed symptoms akin to those of other long-term detainees. Due to the lack of exercise and recreation, their fine motor skills, sense of balance, and physical coordination are insufficiently stimulated, leading to a regressive overall picture. In fact, Assange's health had already deteriorated to the point where he would have been physically incapable of the escapades he was accused of by the Ecuadorian government. A surveillance video in which he is seen stepping onto a skateboard is still circulating on online platforms such as YouTube. As can be clearly seen, these are not the coordination skills of someone about to wildly skate through the embassy: Assange has trouble keeping his balance even while standing on the board.

Mysteriously, in Assange's meetings with doctors, lawyers and visitors, his surveillance always seemed to have worked flawlessly, and yet the same sophisticated technology has failed to capture any of the misconduct he is accused of. No photographs or audio/video footage of the alleged soccer games, none of the alleged torture of his cat; none of the alleged smearing of toilet walls with excrement. Nevertheless, these allegations are relent-lessly repeated and obediently disseminated by the press until they have taken root in the minds of the public. As a result, when people hear the name 'Assange', they no longer think of the war crimes and corruption he exposed, but only of a tragicomic loser they can treat with pity, ridicule, or disdain.

The media hype that was unleashed by the Swedish authorities in August 2010, and which was then fuelled and escalated for years, especially by the British and American press, now reaches its repulsive finale. Like bloodhounds on a wounded animal, his fellow journalists are now pouncing on Assange, attracted by the lumps of slander thrown their way and meting out vicious blows without the slightest sense of human dignity or professional honour. Rarely do these journalists seem to pause and reflect on who is tossing scoops to them like bloody pieces of meat, and what murky interests they are being instrumentalized for.

A particularly telling example is published in the *Daily Mail* on 12 April 2019. It was the day after Assange's expulsion and arrest by British police – a key moment for the shaping of public opinion. Minister Duncan, who had been in charge of coordi-nating 'Operation Pelican', proudly notes in his diary that he had put the journalist in touch with the Ecuadorian ambassador, 'thus giving the *Daily Mail* their scoop about the "fetid" Assange hovel'. Indeed, the very headline announces hair-raising reve-lations: 'Assange inside his fetid lair: Revealed, the full squalid horror that drove embassy staff to finally kick him out'. And further on, 'EXCLUSIVE: Photos of Julian Assange's "dirty pro-tests" have been revealed. He left soiled underpants in the toilet in the Ecuadorian embassy in a fit of rage. On other occasions he left excrement smeared across the wall and ignored warnings not to leave half-eaten meals in the kitchen'. The photos flanking the article, however, show an empty, used plate as well as three used cups in the sink – no trace of 'half-eaten meals.' And they show a perfectly clean toilet – no soiled underpants to be seen, let alone excrement.

This is not only how tabloid journalism works, but also – and this is one of the most important insights of my professional life – how human perception works in general. Reading the announcement of something repulsive is enough to trigger our feelings of disgust. We add the dirty details in our own minds, because that is what the text suggests to us. Thus, a photo of a spotless toilet becomes the image of a crime scene where something terrible has happened. As long as we only skim through the article, most of us won't notice the deception, and Duncan himself notes in his diary: 'The pictures of his living conditions were beyond repulsive.' The headline is enough for us to know and, once again, the goal of focusing our attention on Assange's personality and supposed weaknesses has been achieved. In consequence, Julian Assange is all we are discussing. Some of us despise him, others defend him; and this diversity of opinion is just fine with the governments. Freedom of expression is guaranteed, after all. At least, so long as we discuss only what is served up to us in the headlines. Only when we start choosing for ourselves what we want to discuss and stray into subject areas that the powerful have declared off-limits, only then does our dissent become a 'conspiracy theory' and our thirst for knowledge criminal 'espionage'.

Admittedly, in addition to the aforementioned trivia there are also accusations that seem to be of a more serious character, at least at first glance. They are repeated, almost word for word, in all three official letters I received from the Ecuadorian government. First, the Ecuadorian government keep referring to a scene from the 58th minute of Laura Poitras's documentary film 'Risk'. According to the authorities, this scene shows Assange attempting to use his laptop in order to break into the embassy's computer system and manipulate the surveillance cameras. Now, let us stop and consider for a moment how likely it is that Assange would really allow himself to be filmed by a documentary team while hacking the Ecuadorian computer system. Moreover, the content of the scene is inconsistent with the allegations made by the government. Assange is shown looking at a desktop screen that is placed on the floor, and not at his own laptop, which was visible in another scene a few minutes earlier. According to several separate and unrelated witness testimonies, the scene in question was recorded in 2012, shortly after Assange's arrival at the embassy, and shows him looking at the embassy's official surveillance camera monitor in a room that was then being shared by Assange and the security personnel. It can therefore be concluded that the Ecuadorian government's hacking allegations against Assange are based on an obvious – and arguably intentional – misinterpretation of the relevant footage, which from a legal perspective may well amount to defamation, if not false accusation.

Equally unconvincing is the official interpretation of another incident that allegedly took place on 27 December 2018. According to the Ecuadorian government's official reply to my office of 26 July 2019, during a conversation with the new ambassador, Assange reportedly said: 'We are on alert here, with hidden activation measures ... we have our finger on the button. We are ready to press it ... several buttons (actually). The decision to press the button it will depend on whether we believe that some threats (made against me) are real' (as translated from the Spanish). From these sentences, the Ecuadorian government constructs another reason for Assange's expulsion from the embassy: 'The aforementioned threat is of significant concern to the Ecuadorian State, as it could even allude to a terrorist attack or other violent event that could endanger the lives of officials and third parties in the embassy building.' While this interpretation may be reasonable in a different context, in the present case it obviously defies common sense. Assange has never been a weapons fanatic, nor has he ever maintained contacts with or expressed sympathies towards terrorist groups or otherwise shown a tendency or inclination to violent crime. Given Assange's background and work for WikiLeaks, the only 'buttons' he could reasonably be referring to are the keys of a computer keyboard. In any case, the alleged statement most likely should be interpreted in a figurative sense as referring to the possible release of leaks. Conversely, it can be excluded with certainty that Assange could have planned the detonation of a bomb, as the Ecuadorian government wanted the world to believe. If the government had even remotely believed in this nonsense, it would not have waited another four months before expelling Assange. Against this background, the Ecuadorian government's adherence to the claim of a terrorist threat can only be seen as ludicrous.

Apart from hacking and terrorism, the Ecuadorian government also accuses Assange of interference with the internal affairs of other states. In the view of the authorities, Assange has through his political statements disturbed the public peace and violated international agreements of non-intervention. The problem with these accusations is that, from a legal perspective, the principle of non-intervention applies only between sovereign states and cannot be violated by asylum seekers and other private individuals. Clearly, when Assange communicated publicly about the 2016 presidential elections in the United States, about the Catalan secessionist movement in 2017, and many other political issues, he did not do so in the name or on behalf of the Ecuadorian embassy, but in his professional capacity as a publicist, journalist, and political commentator. He simply continued to do his work in line with his right to freedom of expression and press freedom. The same work, of course, that had subjected him to political persecution worldwide and which the previous Ecuadorian government had considered deserving of diplomatic protection. To turn Assange's journalistic activities, which had been the justification for his asylum, into a justification for his expulsion is not only contrary to good faith, but also incompatible with international human rights law.

Defamation, humiliation and demonization are key elements of psychological torture. Their purpose is not only to destroy the victim's self-esteem, sense of justice, and trust in the authorities, but also to deprive them of social support within the family, the community, and the broader public, and to trivialize their mistreatment or make it appear morally justified. As with mobbing victims in their private environment, the resulting feelings of isolation, shame, and hopelessness can push torture victims into nervous breakdowns or cardiovascular collapse, or even to suicide. Mobbing is not a trifle – it is a collective, cumulative form of cruelty. Nor is it torture 'light' – it is torture.

## The United States Manifests as the Mastermind

As of 16 October 2018, at the latest, the question is no longer whether Assange will be expelled from the Ecuadorian embassy, but only when. On that day, Lenín Moreno receives mail from the US House Committee of Foreign Affairs. The letter from the House of Representatives makes clear what course of action is expected in the Assange case: 'Many of us in the United States Congress are eager to move forward in collaborating with your government on a wide array of issues, from economic cooperation to counternarcotics assistance to the possible return of a United States Agency for International Development mission to Ecuador. However, in order to advance on these crucial matters, we must first resolve a significant challenge created by your predecessor, Rafael Correa – the status of Julian Assange.'

The letter states that 'Mr. Assange remains a dangerous criminal and a threat to global security, and he should be brought to justice.' Therefore, the envisaged economic cooperation is made contingent on Ecuador taking a significant step: 'We are hopeful about developing warmer relations with your government, but feel that it will be very difficult for the United States to advance our bilateral relationship until Mr. Assange is handed over to the proper authorities.' On 11 December 2018, four senators and two members of Congress follow up in a letter to Secretary of State Mike Pompeo, referring to Assange's stay at the embassy and stressing that 'it is imperative that this situation be resolved swiftly.'

These two letters can be said to formalize the US demand that Ecuador terminate Assange's asylum. Incidentally, in the coming months, the International Monetary Fund (IMF) will have to decide on loans urgently needed by the Ecuadorian government in the amount of $4.2 billion. In the IMF, the United States enjoys veto power and is known to use it very effectively to further its own interests. The resulting pressure on the Moreno government to give in and surrender Assange is enormous, triggering feverish efforts to find reasons that could justify this step in the eyes of the broader public.

In any case, by the time I expressed my alarm at Assange's mistreatment and summary expulsion from the embassy, the Ecuadorian government was well prepared. Their lengthy responses to my official letters of 18 April, 28 May and 2 October 2019 meticulously listed Assange's violations of the 'Special Protocol' and kept repeating the same accusations of interference in the internal affairs of other states, and of levelling terrorist threats against embassy officials.

While each point indicates the inevitability of Assange's expulsion, none of them withstands closer scrutiny. The Ecuadorian government even went as far as professing concern that Assange's health could worsen if he continued to stay at the embassy. In my follow-up letter of 2 October 2019, I rebuked this argument as implausible: 'It is difficult to see how a genuine concern for Mr. Assange's health and liberty could justify expelling him from the Ecuadorian Embassy, against his will, without any form of due process, and foreseeably exposing him to a real risk of lifelong arbitrary imprisonment in the United States marked by cruel, inhuman or degrading treatment, or even torture.' Because that is exactly what happened on that morning of 11 April 2019. Of course, there may be situations in which persons can be lawfully deprived of their asylum. But any such decision must necessarily be taken in a due process proceeding subject to the rule of law, including the right to be heard, the right to legal counsel, and the right to appeal to a judicial body.

Assange does not get the benefit of any of these rights. One morning, the Ecuadorian ambassador simply informs him that both his citizenship and his asylum have been revoked and asks him to leave the embassy within the hour. When Assange refuses, British police are invited to enter the embassy and arrest him there. This is a clear breach not only of Ecuadorian constitutional law, which prohibits the extradition of Ecuadorian nationals, but also of fundamental procedural guarantees and of the absolute prohibition of 'refoulement' under international law. But the legal intricacies of Assange's expulsion and arrest do not seem to be of interest to anyone. Therein lies the advantage of unexpected moves: the public is caught off guard and, by the time the media is up to speed, facts have already been established on the ground, and the focus has moved on.

For years Assange has feared the United States would demand his extradition as soon as he were to set foot outside the embassy – and for years he has been ridiculed as paranoid and unreasonable for it. But on the day of his expulsion from the embassy, Assange's worst nightmare comes true: the United States unseals its secret indictment against him and formally requests his extradition from the United Kingdom. Thus, in terminating Assange's asylum, the Ecuadorian government knowingly exposes him to the very risk they had referred to seven years earlier as the justification for his diplomatic asylum. In their reply to my office of 18 June 2019, the Ecuadorian government claims not to have known anything of the impending US extradition request: 'Ecuador was never officially informed of any procedure of extradition or open court case against Mr. Assange outside British or Swedish jurisdiction.' Forgotten are the 'constructive discussions' with Vice-President Pence, forgotten the letter from the US Congress, forgotten the reasons why Ecuador had granted Assange diplomatic asylum in the first place.

After six years and ten months in the Ecuadorian embassy, Assange is stripped of both his Ecuadorian citizenship and his diplomatic asylum, arrested by British police, brought before a British judge, summarily convicted of a criminal offence, and isolated in a high-security prison to await sentencing and the beginning of extradition proceedings initiated by the United States. Assange's personal belongings, including professional documents and computers, remain in the Ecuadorian embassy. They are not handed over to his lawyers, or to his family, or to the British authorities, but straight to the United States – reportedly in response to a request for mutual legal assistance from the US Department of Justice. Just as with his luggage at Stockholm airport in 2010, Assange's property is confiscated without due process of law. Should any proof be needed to demonstrate who has really been pulling the strings in the Assange case across all these years and boundaries – here it is.

# 9

# A Look across the Atlantic

## Death Threats from America

On 16 August 2012, Julian Assange's request for asylum was officially approved by the Ecuadorian government. He had justified his need for diplomatic protection based on the 1951 UN Refugee Convention: 'This request is made in the belief that I will be sent to the United States where, as a result of my imputed political opinions, I will be persecuted. This persecution will take place in the form of prosecution for political reasons, and excessive punishment if convicted, and inhumane treatment all contrary to the Convention.'

American politicians and journalists have left no room for doubt that Assange would be prosecuted primarily for political reasons rather than for real crimes. Shortly after the WikiLeaks revelations of 2010, which primarily concerned the United States, they begin to prepare the ground for Assange's public prejudgment. Assange's asylum request to President Correa provides a list of accusations, defamations and threats made against him. Among the most salient we find:

- 'I think the man is a high-tech terrorist. He's done an enormous damage to our country, and I think he needs to be prosecuted to the fullest extent of the law. And if that becomes a problem, we need to change the law.' (US Senator Mitch McConnell, 5 December 2010)

- '[President Obama] should put out a contract and maybe use a drone or something. ... I think Assange should be assassinated, actually. ... I wouldn't be unhappy if [Assange] disappeared.' (Tom Flanagan, former chief of staff to Canadian Prime Minister Stephen Harper, 30 November 2010)

- 'Let's be clear: WikiLeaks is not a news organization; it is a criminal enterprise. Its reason for existence is to obtain classified national security information and disseminate it as widely as possible – including to the United States' enemies. These actions are likely a violation of the Espionage Act, and they arguably constitute material support for terrorism.' (Marc Thiessen, former speechwriter for George W. Bush, 3 August 2010)

- 'Why can't we act forcefully against WikiLeaks? Why can't we use our various assets to harass, snatch or neutralize Julian Assange and his collaborators, wherever they are? Why can't we disrupt and destroy WikiLeaks in both cyberspace and physical space, to the extent possible? Why can't we warn others of repercussions from assisting this criminal enterprise hostile to the United States?' (Bill Kristol, journalist, 30 November 2010)

- 'Julian Assange poses a clear and present danger to American national security. The WikiLeaks founder is more than a reckless provocateur. He is aiding and abetting terrorists in their war against America. The administration must take care of the problem – effectively and permanently.' (Jeffrey Kuhner, columnist for the *Washington Post*, 2 December 2010)

- 'Julian Assange is engaged in warfare. Information terrorism, which leads to people getting killed is terrorism. And Julian Assange is engaged in terrorism. ... He should be treated as an enemy combatant.' (Newt Gingrich, former speaker of the House of Representatives, 5 December 2010)

- 'A dead man can't leak stuff. This guy's a traitor ... and he has broken every law of the United States. And I'm not for the death penalty, so ... there's only one way to do it: Illegally shoot the son of a bitch.' (Robert Beckel, journalist and former campaign manager for presidential candidate Walter Mondale, 6 December 2010)
- [Asked whether Assange was a high-tech terrorist or a whistleblower akin to those who released the Pentagon Papers:] 'I would argue that it's closer to being a high-tech terrorist. ... This guy has done things and put in jeopardy the lives and occupations of people in other parts of the world. ... He has made it difficult to conduct our business with our allies and our friends ... It has done damage.' (Joe Biden, vice president under Barack Obama, currently 46th president of the United States, 19 December 2010).

Strikingly, all of these statements are based on arguments of national security and use terms such as 'treason', 'espionage', 'terrorism', 'hostility', 'combatant' and 'warfare'. The preferred solution appears to be Assange's extra-judicial assassination. Asked by Fox News about the WikiLeaks revelations, Donald Trump said on 2 December 2010: 'I think it's disgraceful, I think there should be like death penalty or something.' It was Trump, of course, who, during his term as 45th US president, would finally force the indictment and arrest of Assange.

Equating Assange with a 'terrorist' is not just a question of semantics. Since 9/11, Presidents Bush and Obama had institutionalized a machinery of state-sanctioned assassination through systematic drone strikes against suspected terrorists. Gone was the need for positive identification as a lawful military target, gone the alternative need of an imminent threat, gone the right of every suspect to a fair trial before being sentenced to death. Largely unchallenged by world public opinion, these assassinations conveniently avoided lengthy trials and burdensome due process requirements such as the presumption of innocence, the prohibition of arbitrariness, and public scrutiny by external observers. When confronted with a request under the Freedom of Information Act on whether the CIA had plans to assassinate Assange, the agency on 27 October 2010 responded evasively that 'the existence or non-existence' of such plans could be 'neither confirmed nor denied'. As so often in the assessment of evidence, it is of crucial importance to ask the right questions. In this case, the right question is not, of course, whether the CIA's reply explicitly confirmed an assassination plan against Assange (which the agency would never do), but whether the agency would have given the same answer with respect to someone whose assassination had never been considered. Just as in the case of Hillary Clinton's 'joke' response to allegations that she had contemplated 'droning' Assange, the absence of a firm denial is more revealing than the verbal content of the reply. In fact, according to an extensive investigative article published by Yahoo News on 26 September 2021, several former officials of the Trump administration confirmed that, after WikiLeaks exposed the CIA's worldwide hacking operations in the Vault 7 release of March 2017, various options for direct action against Assange were discussed at the highest level of the US government, including his kidnapping, rendition and assassination. These allegations were corroborated by evidence emerging from court proceedings against UC Global in Madrid.

## Secret State Security Trial

WikiLeaks had confronted the world with truths that were difficult to digest. The war crimes, human rights violations and other machinations exposed in these publications were massive. From the perspective of the rule of law, such revelations called for far-reaching institutional reforms in order to prevent similar violations from recurring in the future, but also for a thorough process of justice and redress for the harm done. Soldiers, officials and political leaders had to be held accountable and innumerable victims and their families compensated. But also, the people of Western democracies were challenged to question their own perception of reality, to give up their comforting illusions and take political responsibility. And, as always when people are involuntarily pushed towards expanding their awareness and acknowledging disturbing truths, they initially respond with strategies of denial. A particularly effective psychological pattern is to deny any responsibility or wrongdoing and to demonize the messenger instead. Accordingly, the entire world was soon slandering Assange as a terrorist, a traitor, a spy and a rapist – all emotional, strongly prejudicial labels that were meant to justify his persecution and distract from the uncomfortable truths he had laid bare.

If the unwarranted demonization of Assange is a fairly straightforward phenomenon from the psychosocial and neurobiological point of view, it does raise major human rights concerns. State-sanctioned threats, humiliation and vilification – whether expressed or merely tolerated by the authorities – are incompatible with human dignity and, depending on the circumstances, may well amount to cruel, inhuman or degrading treatment or, in extreme cases, even torture. Moreover, in view of the strong prejudice that has been publicly expressed by politicians, mass media and commentators, it is almost impossible for Assange to expect a fair trial in the United States. Given that, in any criminal trial, the defendant is presumed innocent until proved guilty beyond reasonable doubt, his acquittal must be at least conceivable. But even the boldest idealist would probably rule out the possibility of Assange being found innocent in the US Espionage Court of Alexandria. The US government and its 'reliable partners' have not spent tens of millions of dollars persecuting and demonizing this man for an entire decade, only to give him the satisfaction of being acquitted of any wrongdoing in an American court.

An aggravating factor are the systemic flaws embedded in the US criminal justice system, which relies heavily on intimidation, coercion and violence to achieve its goals. Central to this is the instrument of plea bargaining, which is used to settle roughly nine out of ten criminal cases throughout the country. A plea bargain is a deal between the prosecution and the defence that comes about when a suspect agrees to plead guilty, usually to a lesser offence, or agrees to testify against another suspect in favour of the prosecution. As a reward for such cooperation – in the case of witnesses it could also be called bribery – the prosecutor then demands a lesser sentence, or drops some or all of the charges altogether. The state thus not only relieves itself of having to prove its accusations beyond reasonable doubt, it also does not risk any compensation claims for unjustified pre-trial detention. The defendant, in turn, does not run the risk of a jury finding him guilty and the court imposing the maximum sentence.

Plea bargains cannot work without a coercive threat scenario that scares defendants into submission. This is often achieved by threatening grotesque prison sentences of up to several centuries or even the death penalty. The purpose is to intimidate defendants to such an extent that they no longer invoke the presumption of innocence but accept a plea bargain, even if it requires a false confession or testimony. It is the exact same rationale that characterizes torture. Defendants know that, in return for their cooperation, they might get away with three years in prison instead of thirty, and with better prison conditions, or that in serious cases they can at least avoid the death penalty. To virtually all defendants, this looks more appealing than the prospect of wasting years in court, accumulating huge legal fees, spending the whole time in prison anyway, and possibly being found guilty by an unpredictable jury. Obviously, the overriding purpose of such a coercive criminal justice system is not to ensure truth and justice, but to force a maximum number of convictions –rightful or wrongful. Equally obviously, it is not conducive to developing or maintaining professional investigative skills; to reducing or eradicating crime, judicial error and arbitrariness; or to alleviating overcrowded prisons. As a result, the United States, with merely 3 per cent of the world's population, incarcerates no less than 25 per cent of all prisoners worldwide.

In trials involving national security, such as the one Assange would face after his extradition to the United States, the threat of draconian penalties is routinely used to break defendants. For example, the sentence demanded for whistleblower and former CIA agent John Kiriakou was forty-five years in prison. In a television interview in 2007, Kiriakou had given detailed information about CIA torture methods, including the notorious 'waterboarding'. This method involves the victim's simulated drowning, interrupted only after unconsciousness has set in and shortly before death by asphyxiation. The victim is then medically resuscitated, and the process is repeated, thirty times, fifty times, 100 times, and in at least one case as many as 183 times. The description of the method as 'simulated' drowning does not mean that waterboarding is less traumatic than actual drowning. The agony is the same. The only difference is that the torturer prevents the victim's physical death from occurring so that their excruciating pain and suffering can be repeatedly inflicted. Kiriakou was accused of having violated his duty of non-disclosure because his testimony allegedly permitted the identification of some of the torturers. In a breathtaking reversal of justice one would sooner expect from a criminal organization than from a democratic state, it was the crime witness who was arrested and charged, and not the criminal perpetrators he had exposed.

Like Assange, Kiriakou was charged at the notorious 'Espionage Court' in the Eastern District of Virginia. In the United States, anyone who is facing a trial by jury and can afford it hires a jury consultant. His job is to go through the list of possible jurors and develop defence strategies tailored to the individual jurors based on their personal profiles. Reportedly, Kiriakou's consultant had previously assisted O. J. Simpson and had never lost a case. But when the consultant went through the documents and saw the list of potential jurors, he had only one piece of advice for Kiriakou: 'In any other district I'd say let's go for it, we're going to win. But your jury is going to be made up of people with friends, relatives at the CIA, the Pentagon, national security, intelligence contractors. You don't stand a chance. Just take the deal.' The context of his assessment is that Alexandria is located in the immediate vicinity of Washington. So, any jury reflecting the average population will be made up primarily of people who work for the government, have friends or relatives in the CIA or the Pentagon, or generally tend to be sympathetic to the national security establishment. While this is unlikely to have much bearing on a standard trial for robbery or embezzlement, it is strongly conducive to bias in national security cases. This may well be the reason why the US Department of Justice seems to systematically try such cases in the Federal District of Alexandria, even though there are theoretically almost 100 such districts available nationwide.

Kiriakou followed the advice and took the deal. He pleaded partially guilty and went to prison for thirty months instead of forty-five years. This made him a convicted felon, and President Obama had achieved his goal of consolidating the illegality of whistleblowing. No president in US history has prosecuted as many whistleblowers as Obama, who not only ensured complete impunity for state-sponsored torture but also prevented any other form of accountability for US war crimes. After World War II, Japanese soldiers who had used waterboarding against American prisoners were convicted of war crimes and sentenced to at least fifteen years by the United States. But when the CIA used the same method against suspected terrorists, the United States lacked the strength and integrity to hold them to account. After taking office, Obama acknowledged that waterboarding was torture and a 'mistake'. But the president now wanted to 'look forward as opposed to looking backwards'. The Nobel Peace Prize laureate reassured the public that he did not want any 'witch-hunts'. No witch-hunts for torturers, war criminals and their superiors, that is. For all those who alerted the public to such crimes, however, the president made an exception. In Obama's view, it was not the torturers and war criminals who had betrayed American values, but those men and women in uniform who – unlike the president – had refused to become complicit in these crimes and had chosen to become whistleblowers instead. In Sicily they call this code of silence omertà.

If Julian Assange is extradited to the United States, his trial will be held at the Espionage Court in Alexandria, before a jury just like the one that would have tried Kiriakou. The proceedings will take place behind closed doors, in the absence of press and public, and based on evidence that will not be accessible to either

Assange or his defence counsel – due to imperative 'national security' concerns, of course. In short: in the United States, Assange would get a secret state-security trial very similar to those routinely conducted in dictatorships and other authoritarian regimes. At the Espionage Court in Alexandria, no national security defendant has ever been acquitted.

## The Case of Chelsea Manning

The case of Chelsea Manning was not resolved through a plea bargain. Manning, who leaked the 'Collateral Murder' video, as well as the material for the Afghan War Diary, the Iraq War Logs and CableGate to WikiLeaks in 2010, pleaded guilty to ten of twenty-two charges – voluntarily and out of principle, not in return for a 'reward' or other bargain. She explained her moral motivation: she wanted to trigger a much-needed public discussion about the misconduct of the US military and thereby contribute to positive change. In July 2013, a military court at Fort Meade in Maryland found her guilty on nineteen of twenty-two charges and, despite her confession, sentenced her to thirty-five years in prison for theft of government property and espionage, among other charges. Prosecutors had demanded an even more extreme sentence of sixty years, but Manning was acquitted of the most serious charge of 'aiding the enemy'.

Clearly, Manning had violated her duty of non-disclosure as a soldier. In so doing she had committed an offence, even though there is no evidence that anyone has been seriously harmed. In terms of motivation, Manning did not seek to enrich herself or to help the enemy, but she wanted to denounce the systematic violation of the values to which she felt committed as a soldier: truth, law and justice. After unsuccessfully trying to do so through internal reporting channels, she first offered the material to the mainstream press. Only when she was met with indifference there as well did she finally reach out to WikiLeaks. She provided evidence of war crimes, human rights abuses and corruption that the public might otherwise never have known about. But the antiquated Espionage Act does not allow for a public interest defence – the duty of silence is absolute, just like in the Mafia. Accordingly, the undisputable public interest in having war crimes exposed and prosecuted was not taken into consideration in the conviction and sentencing of Manning, and the same would apply in any trial of Assange under the Espionage Act.

Manning was arrested on 27 May 2010. For the first two months she was held in a military facility at Camp Arifjan in Kuwait, then, after her repatriation to the United States on 29 July, at Quantico Naval Base in Virginia. In a harrowing article published in the *Guardian* in 2016, Manning described her solitary confinement during that period. She recalled sitting in front of a mirrored wall through which two Marines watched her every move, seventeen hours a day. No sleep was permitted between early morning and 8 p.m., no lying down, no leaning against the wall, no physical exercise. Deprived of her personal belongings, all she could do was to get up occasionally, walk around in her tiny cell, and dance, because that was not considered physical exercise. Occasionally, three guards would take her outside, to a fenced-in area the size of a basketball court, where she was allowed to walk around for twenty minutes. If she stopped even once, the break would end immediately, and Manning would be taken back to her cell. Visits were allowed only for a few hours a month, from family, friends, lawyers. Manning met them behind a thick glass wall, hands and feet shackled, and some of her conversations were recorded. She was not even permitted to sleep through the night. The guards woke her up as soon she tried to turn to the wall.

Finally, in late December 2010, my predecessor in office, Juan Méndez, formally protested against Manning's detention conditions and, in May 2011, requested permission for a personal prison visit with her. Contrary to the standard rules applicable to prison visits by a UN special rapporteur, the US authorities did not permit an unsupervised interview with Manning, which would have been necessary for an objective evaluation of her treatment and conditions of detention; Méndez had no choice but to decline the visit. The same would foreseeably happen to me and my successors if we tried to visit Julian Assange in a US Supermax prison. In fact, since the creation of the mandate of the special rapporteur on torture in 1985, no mandate holder has ever been able to conduct official prison visits in the United States. In December 2016, the Obama administration tried to convince me to carry out a last-minute official country visit to the US before the end of Obama's presidency on 20 January 2017, presumably to provide a bit of window dressing for the outgoing president's human rights legacy. When I insisted that I would visit only on the condition of unrestricted access to all places of detention, including confidential interviews with inmates held under Special Administrative Measures and at Guantánamo Bay, the conversation was over.

Shortly thereafter, on 17 January 2017, President Obama commuted Manning's thirty-five-year sentence, ensuring her release on 17 May 2017. Obama's decision is often described as a generous act of humanity. The reality is less flattering. The president having come under increasing criticism for his 'war against whistleblowers' towards the end of his second term in office, his commutation of Manning's sentence more likely represented another eleventh-hour attempt at mitigating reputational risk. On 11 January 2009, the *New York Times* had quoted then President-elect Obama as reluctant to prosecute the war crimes committed during the Bush administration, because he did not wish for 'extraordinarily talented people' at the CIA to 'suddenly feel like they've got to spend all their time looking over their shoulders'. The president was not too worried, however, about Manning enduring seven years behind bars, almost entirely during Obama's two terms in office, for alerting the public to those war crimes. While Manning's breaches of non-disclosure were an exclusive matter of US domestic law, the Geneva Conventions do not allow the US president any discretion whatsoever with regard to the prosecution and punishment of war crimes. Moreover, as a commander-in-chief refusing to prosecute torture and war crimes committed by his subordinates, President Obama clearly incurred personal criminal liability under the

Nuremberg Principles and the doctrine of command and superior responsibility.

Manning's persecution did not end with her release. In March 2019, she was called to testify against Assange by the secret Grand Jury in Alexandria, Virginia. When Manning refused to give the requested testimony, the judge jailed her for contempt of court for sixty days. A week after her release, she was again subpoenaed. When she again declined, Manning was placed in coercive detention – she was to remain locked up until she gave the requested testimony. Additionally, she would be subjected to a daily fine of $500 beginning on the thirtieth day and of $1,000 beginning on the sixtieth day of renitence. A few months later, on 1 November 2019, I formally protested to the US government against Manning's coercive detention: 'I conclude that such deprivation of liberty does not constitute a circumscribed sanction for a specific offence, but an open-ended, progressively severe measure of coercion fulfilling all the constitutive elements of torture or other cruel, inhuman or degrading treatment or punishment.' It is one thing to punish someone with a defined prison sentence for refusing to testify in court. But it is quite another to subject a witness to indefinite detention in order to force her to testify, thus incrementally increasing her suffering until she breaks. The former is a lawful sanction. The latter is prohibited torture.

Because of the purely coercive nature of the actions taken against her, I demanded Manning's immediate release, as well as the return of any fines improperly obtained. Despite the urgency of my appeal, I never received any reply from the US authorities, and even the publication of my letter and its dissemination in the mass media two months later failed to elicit any official response. Then happened what I had feared the most: on Wednesday, 11 March 2020, shortly after 12 noon, Chelsea Manning attempted to commit suicide in prison. In the end, the severity of the suffering inflicted by her endless coercive detention had simply become too much to bear. She was found in time and survived. But the judge had now seen the writing on the wall and ordered Manning's release, supposedly because her testimony before the grand jury was 'no longer necessary'. She received no compensation for her arbitrary detention, nor was she relieved of her accumulated fine of $256,000. Will Julian Assange, too, have to attempt suicide before the world finally opens their eyes to what is being done to him and, through him, to all of us?

## 'Special administrative measures'

In his June 2012 asylum request to the Ecuadorian government, Assange explicitly referred to Manning's conditions of detention: 'The likely charges, the attitude of the US government towards me and the known circumstances of placement of individuals on comparable charges mean that I will, again with certainty, be imprisoned in conditions that mirror those experienced by my alleged co-accused Bradley Manning.' As became clear during the September 2020 extradition hearing in London, if sent to the United States Assange would not only be held in solitary confinement but would almost certainly be additionally subjected to what are called Special Administrative Measures (SAMs), both pre-trial and while serving his sentence. This euphemism denotes a particularly restrictive detention regime imposed by the attorney general, that is, the head of the US Department of Justice. SAMs can be ordered before, during, or after a trial. They are not a sanction imposed by the judiciary, but a security measure taken by the government. As such, they are not subject to judicial review and cannot be effectively challenged by the detainee. SAMs are used against detainees who, in the view of the attorney general, pose a particular threat to national security, such as suspected or convicted terrorists, spies or whistleblowers.

The main purpose of SAMs is to strictly control an inmate's communication with others inside and outside the prison facility. As we know from numerous reports and witness statements, what this means in practice is near-total isolation. Apart from contact with lawyers, only two short phone calls are permitted per month. If and when family visits are permitted, they take place through a thick glass barrier without any physical contact, and prisoners remain shackled, chained at the wrists, ankles, and to the ground. All visits require fourteen days' advance notice and can take several months to coordinate.

Apart from that, inmates are in total isolation twenty-four hours a day. No communication whatsoever is permitted with other inmates, and even prison staff do not interact with inmates except for opening the viewing slot during their inspection rounds and delivering meals through the secure meal slot in the door. Recreation is limited to one hour daily and takes place in small indoor cages the same size as their cell, without any exercise equipment and often in the middle of the night, when other inmates are sleeping.

Inside the cell: no newspapers, no radio, no television. Showers only three times per week. Violations of the rules are punished immediately. The slightest misunderstanding with prison staff can result in a prisoner being handcuffed in his cell for a week, spending the entire time in complete darkness, with a bag over his head or blindfolded. The government's tight grip on the communication of SAMs inmates means that no email contact is permitted and letters may be written only on rare occasions, to approved addressees only, and subject to elaborate censorship procedures that can delay their delivery for several months. One SAMs detainee – Abu Hamza al-Masri – reportedly broke the rules when he wrote a letter asking his son to tell his one-year-old grandson that he loved him: the grandson was not on the list of approved addressees.

Psychological services are offered primarily through self-help packages and information provided by video; participants in group therapy are kept in individual cages and remain shackled during therapy sessions. Lawyers or family members visiting SAMs inmates can be criminally prosecuted if they talk among themselves or with others about the detention conditions they observe. The SAMs regime makes the abuse of power and arbitrariness easy, beyond control, and absolute. As a last means of resistance, some detainees go on hunger strike hoping to obtain modest forms of relief: to be allowed to call home twice a month, or to read an occasional newspaper. But hunger strikes are brutally suppressed by forced feeding, often carried out in a particularly torturous manner.

SAMs can be imposed for a period of up to one year and are renewable without limit. The government can decline to provide any justification. After all, SAMs are – by definition – a matter of national security. There are convicts who have spent ten years under this particularly cruel, inhuman and degrading regime. In my view, there is no question that these conditions of detention violate not only the prohibition of torture under human rights law, but also the prohibition of cruel and unusual punishment under the Eighth Amendment of the US Constitution. In the world of technicalities, of course, SAMs are not a punishment, but only 'administrative measures'. In the real world, however, the term 'Special Administrative Measures' is nothing but another fraudulent label for torture, and for a detention regime that dehumanizes not only the detainees but also their tormentors, the instructing authority and, ultimately, any society which tolerates and enables such cruelty in the name of justice.

## Press Freedom or National Security?

On 15 October 2019, I participated in a panel discussion at Columbia University in New York. It was entitled 'Press Freedom, National Security and Whistleblowers: From Julian Assange to the White House'. The room was packed, with some people standing or sitting on the floor. In the audience was James Goodale, who had represented the *New York Times* in the Pentagon Papers litigation during the Vietnam War and whose interview on the Assange case had been an important eye-opener for me. During the discussion, the eighty-six-year-old stood up and took the floor. 'Is Assange entitled to the full protection of freedom of the press?' Goodale answered passionately in the affirmative. If the US government wanted to prosecute Assange under the Espionage Act, he said, it would first have to prove that his publications had actually posed a clear and imminent threat to national security. 'It would seem that such proof would create a high bar for the government to jump – particularly when the government has never stated once whether there has been damage to anybody as a consequence of Assange's publication. It has, of course, said such publication caused general damage to national security but has not particularized any harm to anyone such as for example, its Afghanistan sources. ... the government has had ten years to come up with evidence that shows damage to national security but has not.'

Indeed, the claim that Assange's publications have caused serious harm to US national security, endangered American soldiers, and exposed local informants to acts of revenge by the enemy is one of the earliest and least scrutinized myths. On 30 July 2010, just after the publication of the Afghan War Diary, US Chief of Staff Mike Mullen stated: 'Mr. Assange can say whatever he likes about the greater good he thinks he and his source are doing. ... But the truth is they might already have on their hands the blood of some young soldier or that of an Afghan family.' Strikingly, the general seemed to be much less concerned about the blood on the hands of his own soldiers, who in the 'Collateral Murder' video massacred wounded civilians and their rescuers. Nor did it seem to occur to him that war crimes such as that one had destroyed countless Afghan and Iraqi families, driven embittered civilians into the arms of terrorist groups, and provoked acts of revenge against US personnel and civilians. The short-sightedness of the self-righteous is their greatest weakness.

Similarly, US Defense Secretary Robert Gates told Senator Carl Levin in a letter of 16 August 2010: 'The documents do contain the names of cooperative Afghan nationals and the Department [of Defense] takes very seriously the Taliban threats recently discussed in the press. We consider this risk as likely to cause significant harm or damage to the national security interests of the United States.' However, he acknowledged that 'the review to date has not revealed any sensitive intelligence sources and methods compromised by this disclosure.' Three years later, the situation remained unchanged. At Manning's trial in July 2013, Brigadier General Robert Carr, a senior counterintelligence officer who headed the Information Review Task Force that investigated the impact of WikiLeaks disclosures on behalf of the US Department of Defense, told the court that they had uncovered no specific examples of anyone who had lost their life as a consequence of these publications.

Before Assange, no one has ever been charged under the Espionage Act merely for publishing sensitive documents. What, then, would a conviction of Assange mean for the future of investigative journalism? Without a doubt, it would set a precedent by which any journalist publishing leaked material on national security and defence policy issues could face similar criminal charges. If it were not for the establishment of a judicial precedent for the purpose of intimidating investigative journalism, the aggressive prosecution of Assange would make no sense at all. What is at stake, therefore, are not just the personal rights of Assange, but nothing less than the continued ability of the press, as the 'Fourth Estate', to inform and empower the people and, thereby, ensure democratic oversight of governments.

In an interview with *Der Spiegel*, WikiLeaks editor Kristinn Hrafnsson therefore rightly spoke of a 'war on journalism', and Reporters Without Borders called the charges against Assange a 'dangerous precedent for journalists, whistleblowers and other journalistic sources'. Even the former assistant attorney general for national security, Kenneth Wainstein, said in 2010 at a US congressional hearing: 'If WikiLeaks can be prosecuted for espionage for these leaks, there is no legal or logical reason why a similar prosecution could not lie against all of the mainstream news organizations that routinely receive and publish protected "national defence information".' This is no small problem for those who want to see Assange indicted and convicted. Not surprisingly, therefore, they do everything in their power to distinguish WikiLeaks from traditional news organizations and prevent the equation of Assange's work with journalism.

Ultimately, however, the motive behind the aggressive persecution of Assange is always the same: fear. Fear of the WikiLeaks methodology and its proliferation; fear of transparency, truth and new revelations; fear of democratic control and accountability; and, above all, fear of losing power. In the words of Leon Panetta, former CIA chief and US secretary of defense, in an interview with ARD, 'All you can do is hope that you can ultimately take action against those that were involved in revealing that information, so that you could send a message to others not to do the same thing.' To achieve this goal of deterrence, new legal contortions are constantly being attempted. Thus, during a speech at the Center for Strategic and International Studies (CSIS) on 13 April 2017 – shortly after the Vault 7 leak had exposed the CIA's worldwide hacking activities – then CIA director Mike Pompeo claimed that WikiLeaks was a 'non-state hostile intelligence service' and that Assange, as a foreigner, was not entitled to the protection of the press freedom guarantees of the US Constitution. That's how simple it was in Mike Pompeo's world. From a legal perspective, however, interpreting the US Constitution fortunately is not up to the director of the CIA, but to the Supreme Court. But the CIA seems to care as little about the Constitution as it does about the international legal obligations of the United States. These international obligations also include respecting and ensuring freedom of expression, which can be restricted only by law and only for compelling reasons, especially to protect national security. As Goodale had correctly noted, therefore, everything hinges on whether Assange and WikiLeaks actually endangered the national security of the United States – and not just its international reputation and the impunity of its leaders for war crimes, torture and corruption. So far, the US authorities have been unable to provide any evidence for this claim. Indeed, correctly understood, press freedom and national security are not contradictory but symbiotic – and official secrecy is their common enemy.

# PART III

## FIGHTING FOR THE TRUTH

# 10

# Governmental Denial of Reality

In the summer of 2019, my office started receiving the responses to the official letters I had sent on 27 and 28 May to the governments of the United Kingdom, the United States, Sweden and Ecuador. Australia, and a few months later Germany, also reacted to my conclusions, although I had not formally contacted either of these two states in connection with the Assange case. Remarkably, despite significant differences in terms of attitude and content, the reactions of all six governments had one common denominator: the denial of reality.

## United Kingdom: Demonstrative Indifference

Sweden, Ecuador and the United States all replied within the standard deadline of sixty days. Only the British government, which had Assange in its power and from which I had therefore demanded the most urgent measures, made abundantly clear that it was in no hurry to respond. Their letter of reply was not sent until 7 October 2019, almost exactly five months after my visit to Assange, as if to demonstrate the indifference of an overconfident world power. The British response was particularly concise and dispensed with all diplomatic courtesies.

Without preamble, the letter rapped out its points: 'Dear Mr Melzer, The Government rejects any allegation that Julian Assange has been subjected to torture in any form as a result of actions by the UK Government. The UK Government does not participate in, solicit, encourage or condone the use of torture for any purpose. The United Kingdom does not accept that Mr Assange was ever arbitrarily detained; he was free to leave the Ecuadorean Embassy at any time.' Moreover, 'Mr Assange has been convicted under English law of failing to surrender to custody following due legal process. Judges in the UK are completely impartial and independent from Government. ... Mr Assange did not appeal his conviction and has withdrawn his appeal against his sentence. Yours sincerely, [XX].' End of message. No response to the urgent concerns expressed by my medical team about Assange's health. No investigation into British involvement in years of judicial arbitrariness, intimidation, isolation and humiliation. No action to ensure Assange would get adequate access to his lawyers and legal documents. No comment on the risk of serious human rights violations in the event of extradition to the United States. And, last but not least, no 'assurances of highest consideration' or similar concluding phrase – in diplomatic parlance, the equivalent of a slap in the face.

The British government clearly had no intention of answering to a mere UN special rapporteur. This had nothing to do with me personally. In fact, whenever other UN experts had reached conclusions deviating from the British government's complacent self-perception, their reaction had been the same. Whether Raquel Rolnik's critical 2013 report on the right to adequate housing in the United Kingdom; the WGAD's 2015 conclusions on Assange's arbitrary deprivation of liberty in the Ecuadorian embassy; Philip Alston's disconcerting 2019 report on extreme poverty in the United Kingdom; or now my own concerns regarding the persecution and ill-treatment of Assange: every time, the British government had at first voluntarily engaged

with the evaluation process, but then flatly dismissed the inconvenient findings, and aggressively accused the investigating UN
experts of partisanship, 'inflammatory' remarks, and political
motivations. Clearly, a government bent on denying uncomfortable realities would be a difficult interlocutor for constructive
dialogue based on facts.

## Sweden: Bureaucratic Evasiveness

Sweden, too, had difficulties concealing its indignation, but at
least it made a show of maintaining diplomatic countenance. In
my official letter to the government, I had transmitted credible
allegations of serious due process violations on the part of the
Swedish Prosecution Authority. In any functioning system of
democratic checks and balances, this type of allegation letter
transmitted by a mandated UN expert should have automatically
triggered a formal investigation by the parliamentary
ombudsman for the judiciary or similar independent oversight
body. But this obviously was not what the Swedish government
had in mind, because that would have raised too many
inconvenient questions. Instead, the government reminded me
of the constitutional independence of the judiciary, including
the Prosecution Authority, and explained that the government
could not interfere with an ongoing criminal investigation. The
undersigned ambassador seemed rather unconvinced himself,
or else he would not have found it necessary to repeat the same
argument four times on only three pages.

In my experience, the claim that the executive branch cannot
interfere with ongoing judicial proceedings is one of the most
common excuses I receive from democratic governments when
I confront them with allegations of torture or ill-treatment and
remind them of their obligation to investigate, punish, and
redress any violations that may have occurred, and to prevent
their reoccurrence. All these obligations are binding on the state
as a whole and, thus, on all three branches of government. In
practice, it is not only the security forces and secret services

subordinate to the executive branch that are responsible for torture and ill-treatment, but often also the judicial and investigative authorities. The spectrum ranges from interrogational coercion or suppression of statements to the execution of corporal punishment and death sentences, to deliberate judicial arbitrariness and denial of justice, such as in the case of Julian Assange. As a matter of diplomatic protocol, however, I always have to address my official communications to the minister of foreign affairs of the state in question, even if the abuse is alleged to have been committed by officials of the judiciary. It is then up to the Foreign Ministry to forward my allegation letter to the appropriate national oversight body, to ensure that the investigations required by international law are conducted and that my queries are satisfactorily answered. If I were prevented from addressing abuse by investigative and judicial authorities during a pending investigation, my mandate would really be reduced to a toothless tiger with very limited practical relevance. But then, that outcome is precisely what many states would not be too unhappy to see materialize.

The Swedish letter also pointed out that 'the Government does not agree with the WGAD's opinion and its conclusion that Sweden has violated international law. In fact, Mr Assange chose, voluntarily, to remain at the Ecuadorian Embassy, and the Swedish authorities have had no control over his decision to do so. Mr Assange was free to leave the Embassy at any time. He cannot be considered to have been deprived of his liberty while at the Embassy due to any decision or action taken by the Swedish authorities.' Of course, with the requisite dose of cynicism, the same could be said for any other politically persecuted asylum seeker. In the real world, whether someone is 'free' to leave the protection of their political asylum does not depend on whether their presence in the place of asylum is voluntary, but on whether there is a real risk that they will be exposed to serious violations of their human rights once they leave that place. As Assange had correctly predicted, and as has become abundantly clear since his arrest on 11 April 2019, his fears had been well founded all along.

In its response, the government described the possibility of Assange's extradition from Sweden to the United States as 'strictly hypothetical'. Presumably just as 'hypothetical' as the possibility of a US extradition request was said to be by the British government when it responded to my initial visit request on 10 April 2019 – less than twenty-four hours before it ordered Assange's arrest in the Ecuadorian embassy and announced that the United States had formally requested his extradition. A more detailed response to my queries or the initiation of an investigation was not considered necessary by the Swedish government. Overall, the message coming from Stockholm very much resembled the one I would receive from London: no wrongdoing, no culpable omissions, no inconsistencies – complete denial of an unpleasant reality.

## Ecuador: No, No, and No!

Like the British, the Ecuadorian government had difficulties maintaining diplomatic form and composure – but in inverse fashion. In terms of word count, the missive from Quito far exceeded those sent by the other three governments and can only be described as a verbal outburst. The government spotted accusations even where I had not voiced them at all: 'It is regrettable that you refer to the diplomatic asylum granted to Mr. Julian Assange as a 'confinement', a term that denotes the confinement of a person in a closed environment, depriving him of his liberty. In this regard, we would like to remind you that, on 19 June 2012, Mr. Assange entered the Embassy of Ecuador in London voluntarily, of his own accord, and without coercion of any kind.'

I had never claimed otherwise. Any politically persecuted person seeks asylum 'voluntarily'. However, if the place of his asylum measures only a few square metres, which he cannot leave without exposing himself to the risk of serious human rights violations, then his situation unquestionably amounts to deprivation of liberty. As a matter of law, therefore, Assange was indeed confined at the Ecuadorian embassy, albeit not by the Ecuadorian government, but through a threat scenario created by the Swedish, British and – in the background – American authorities. What I had criticized in my letter to Ecuador was not Assange's confinement by other states, but his targeted isolation, defamation and humiliation by the Ecuadorian authorities, and the summary termination of his citizenship and asylum in violation of due process and the prohibition of refoulement.

The main responses of the Ecuadorian government and, most notably, their justification for his expulsion have already been discussed in detail. The progressively derailed tone of their letters showed me that I had hit a nerve. Page after page, their personal attacks increased: 'You, Mr. Rapporteur, and your assistants are obviously free to sympathize with Mr. Assange ... but your opinions on the case distort the facts and promote value judgments that compromise your independence as Special Rapporteur.' Or: 'Your subjectivity is astonishing, Mr. Rapporteur.' Or: 'Zero torture, Mr. Rapporteur. ... All this you already know because we informed you before, Mr. Special Rapporteur, why then ask us again?' Or: 'We repeat it again, but we are discouraged in doing so because we don't know if this time we will be lucky enough to have you read what we wrote.' And finally, 'there is also new content in your letter that you have not addressed before, it still expresses an obvious prejudice against the Ecuadorian state when you merely repeat what Mr. Assange's lawyers and supporters say without any supporting evidence.' In the course of my work, I have rarely received official responses as wordy as this one, but which still left all of my queries unanswered.

## USA: America Does Not Torture!

The reply of the US government, dated 16 July 2019, included a short cover letter and a one-page substantive response. In my letter, I had expressed grave concern at what I described as 'a sustained and unrestrained campaign of public mobbing, intimidation and defamation against Mr Assange, consisting of a constant stream of public statements not only by the mass media and influential private individuals, but also by current or former political figures and senior officials of various branches of government'. In this regard, the government was emphatic: 'The United States rejects the proposition that the types of public statements listed in your letter constitute cruel, inhuman or degrading treatment or punishment, much less torture, as defined by the Convention against Torture and Other Cruel, Inhuman or Degrading Treatment or Punishment (CAT). Further, the United States is deeply concerned by the suggestion that independent reporting or other commentary and discourse on public figures could amount to torture or cruel, inhuman or degrading treatment or punishment. Such a position by the Special Rapporteur has dangerous implications for freedom of expression, democracy, and the rule of law.'

The cynicism of this rationale is striking. On the one hand, the US government justifies the unrestrained defamation, humiliation, and intimidation of Assange based on freedom of expression. But when Assange reveals evidence of war crimes, torture, and corruption, then freedom of expression suddenly ceases to apply, and he is threatened with 175 years in prison.

Furthermore, in the view of the US government, the notoriously inhumane conditions of detention in US high-security prisons have nothing to do with torture or ill-treatment: 'The United States categorically rejects the claims in your letter that the United States will torture or otherwise mistreat Mr. Assange if he is extradited to the United States to face criminal prosecution.' Chelsea Manning has a very different story to tell, and she is not the only one. The failure of the United States to prosecute and punish its own torturers, its excessive use of violence, restraints, and isolation against detainees of all kinds, its practice of extorting confessions and testimony through coercive detention and threats of draconian sanctions, and the notorious overcrowding of American detention facilities reflect a remarkable discrepancy between governmental self-perception and the reality on the ground.

## Australia: The Glaring Absentee

My press release of 31 May 2019 made waves. The interviews piled up, and all of the major media organizations ran at least an online article or a radio interview. Much more difficult were the mainstream television broadcasters. Both BBC World and Sky News, the two most influential British television news channels, initially wanted a live video interview via Skype in the late afternoon. However, both broadcasters took their interviews off the air immediately after the first live broadcast and left no trace of them on the web. My findings that both the British government and the mainstream media had been complicit in Assange's persecution and torture did not appear to fit their preferred narrative. By contrast, the video interview requested by the Australian public television broadcaster, ABC, remained accessible online. While I had described Australia as a 'glaring absence' in the Assange case, I did not have reliable evidence for Australian complicity in his torture and persecution and, therefore, had not included Canberra in my official intervention.

I knew that Assange had been very critical of his home country. Among other things, he had accused Australian authorities of supporting US criminal investigations against WikiLeaks and himself. He had also pointed to media reports that the Australian government had considered cancelling his passport in order to facilitate his prosecution by the United States. Given the military alliance between Washington and Canberra, as well as the country's longstanding membership in the 'Five Eyes' intelligence cooperation between the United States, Britain, Canada, Australia and New Zealand, none of this would have come as a surprise. Assange certainly had reason not to trust his government, and repeatedly rejected Australian offers of consular assistance during his time in the Ecuadorian embassy. As questionable as Australia's abandonment of their own national may be from a moral perspective, I did not have sufficient evidence to speak of legal co-responsibility of the Australian government for the political persecution and ill-treatment of Assange.

So, during an interview with the *Sydney Morning Herald* (*SMH*) published on 31 May 2019, I described the role of the Australian government as follows: 'Australia is a glaring absence in this case. They're just not around, as if Assange was not an Australian citizen. That is not the correct way of dealing with that.' Unfortunately, the *SMH* published the interview with a misleading title: 'Assange a victim of torture and Australia shares blame, says UN expert'. I had never blamed Australia for Assange's torture, but that was immaterial now – the damage was done. The Australian government was irritated and, on the same day, released a press statement of its own: 'We reject any suggestion by the UN Special Rapporteur on Torture that the Australian Government is complicit in psychological torture or has shown a lack of consular support for Mr Assange. The Special Rapporteur has not been in contact with the Australian Government to raise these concerns directly.'

While I had not, in fact, accused Australia of complicity in torture or lack of consular support, my remarks seemed to have triggered the sensitivity of a political leadership that was fully aware of its failure to protect its national from serious abuse. As detailed earlier, the Australian government has never sought to use its considerable political leverage as a major ally of the United States and the United Kingdom to end Assange's persecution. Instead of addressing the case on the political level, where it could have been resolved quickly and effectively, Canberra demonstratively exercised restraint and limited itself to the merely technical and administrative level of consular services. In the world of diplomatic relations, this means that the Australian government needed a modicum of window dressing for domestic consumption, but never intended to fundamentally challenge the dehumanization and persecution of Assange by its allies.

As long as Assange himself did not trust his own government sufficiently to at least accept its consular services, there clearly was no basis for me to try to negotiate a diplomatic solution involving Australia behind the scenes. Whatever the Australian government may have done to protect Assange's interests in the past decade, none of it has contributed anything to fundamentally changing his situation. Although a group of about two dozen Australian MPs have vehemently campaigned for Assange's release and repatriation, and two of them – Andrew Wilkie and George Christensen – even travelled to London in February 2020 to visit him in prison, they were unable to persuade their government to change its mind.

During the extradition hearing at Westminster Magistrates' Court in September 2020, which lasted several weeks, three of the few available public seats in the courtroom had been reserved for diplomatic representatives from the Australian High Commission in London. Outside the court, starting long before dawn, countless journalists, foreign politicians, representatives of Amnesty International and other independent observers waited in vain to be admitted to the courtroom – every single day. By contrast, the cushy Australian seats remained empty – every single day. Given the obvious indifference of the Australian government towards Assange's rights, there clearly was no potential for a constructive dialogue. Here, too, the self-perception of the political leadership had very little to do with reality.

## Germany: Between Appeasement and Complicity

Governments that have no direct connection to the persecution or person of Julian Assange generally do not comment on his case at all, or only very cautiously. Remarkably, this is true even across traditional political blocs, so that Assange receives hardly any public support from countries like Russia, China, Iran or Venezuela, which rarely miss an opportunity to criticize the West. This has nothing to do with Assange's person, of course, but with the fact that the basic idea and methodology of his organization – WikiLeaks – is perceived as an equal threat by all governments alike.

If we have to pick one example to be discussed in this context, Germany is perhaps the ideal choice, both for its commonalities with other countries and for its peculiar specificities. First, Germany is a country with sufficient political, economic and military clout to directly influence the four states involved in Assange's persecution. Second, Germany is a country that has had its own experience of seeing a highly developed society slide into dictatorship, surveillance state and self-destruction. And third, forced to face the consequences of this system failure, Germany has tried to deal legally, morally and politically with the burden of this past with a rigour and resolve which, despite imperfections, remain unique in the world. Tragically, however, Germany remains unable to effectively call out similar developments in allied states or even to publicly express a clear-cut opinion on them.

Berlin, 7 October 2020: during a parliamentary session in the Bundestag, German Foreign Minister Heiko Maas threatens targeted sanctions against Russia over the alleged poisoning of opposition politician Alexei Navalny with a nerve agent belonging to the Novichok group. The minister affirms that the development, production and possession of chemical weapons is a 'blatant violation' of international law, adding that 'Russia itself should have a great interest in solving the crime.' However, according to Maas, Moscow has so far not complied with any of the German government's 'demands and questions' in this case. Unless Russia provides the required clarifications, he says, 'targeted and proportionate sanctions against those responsible will be unavoidable.' The clear messaging from Berlin is widely welcomed, because governments hardly ever find the courage to take such an uncompromising stance.

Later during the same session, Maas is asked about the case of Julian Assange and, in particular, about my official findings that his treatment violates the universal prohibition of torture – another 'blatant violation' of international law. Suddenly, the minister becomes significantly less combative. According to Maas, the German government has 'no information' indicating 'that there have been violations of international law in both the accommodation and the treatment of Julian Assange'. The minister believes that 'Assange deserves a trial in accordance with the rule of law', but sees no reason to 'accuse our British partners of any failure or whatever in this case'. So, unlike Russia, the

United Kingdom is not being confronted with 'questions and demands' from the German government and need not expect German sanctions should it fail to investigate the persecution of Assange and to provide the required clarifications.

Contrary to the minister's claim that he had 'no information' indicating any 'violations of international law' against Assange, I had personally briefed his ministry in the matter a year earlier, on 26 November 2019, during a visit to Berlin. On their own initiative, the Human Rights Division of the German Ministry of Foreign Affairs had invited me for a meeting at their offices to discuss the Assange case. To my surprise, however, my inter-locutors had no intention of discussing the conclusions of my investigation or the measures that could be taken by the German government in order to positively influence the treatment of Assange by the British and American authorities. In fact, no one in the room had read any of my official communications on the case and, throughout the meeting, no one showed the slightest interest in learning about their content. Rather, my interlocu-tors sat there with grave faces and expressed concern that my engagement in the Assange case undermined not only the credi-bility of my mandate but even the continued existence of the UN human rights mechanisms as a whole. For these human-rights bureaucrats, the fact that Assange was being held in solitary con-finement for months on end, that he was deprived of his human dignity and denied the right to prepare his defence, did not seem to arouse any doubts as to the lawfulness of the British proceed-ings. Instead, they met my objections with the same blank stares as the government spokespersons who, at the weekly Federal Press Conference (BPK), dismiss any question about the govern-ment's position in the Assange case with stony faces and tortured phraseology – a veritable reality show in wilful blindness.

London, September 2020: one of the many witnesses who testified in favour of Assange in the US extradition trial was a German-Lebanese dual national named Khaled El-Masri. On 31 December 2003, he was arrested by police in Macedonia and handed over to the CIA. In Skopje and in a 'black site' in Afghanistan, he was humiliated and tortured by CIA agents for four months until they were persuaded of his innocence and abandoned him somewhere on a deserted road in Albania – without any apology, compensation or even sufficient funds for him to travel home. After several unsuccessful proceedings against the Macedonian authorities, the European Court of Human Rights found in 2012 that El-Masri had been tortured by Macedonian and US officials and ordered Macedonia to pay €60,000 in compensation. Torture being a serious crime, the German Federal Prosecutor's Office issued thirteen arrest warrants against the CIA agents allegedly responsible for the abuse of El-Masri.

However, the German government subsequently refused to transmit the required extradition request to the United States – a 'non-justiciable' discretionary decision by the executive branch, the German Administrative Court found. In reality, the German government's refusal was a clear violation of the Convention against Torture. That treaty leaves states no discretion whatsoever in determining whether or not to prosecute torture, but unequivocally obliges them to do so in every single instance. Further investigation of the case by a parliamentary committee of inquiry was reportedly rendered impossible because the German government refused to provide evidence and prohibited other witnesses from testifying. As shown by diplomatic cables of the US Embassy in Berlin that were later published by WikiLeaks (07BERLIN242), the United States put the German government under massive pressure not to allow this extradition request to go forward.

Here too, the German government did not 'ask questions or make demands'. Again, Germany did not threaten the United States with sanctions, despite the 'flagrant violation' of international law. Moreover, the torture of El-Masri was not just an unfortunate isolated blunder, but stood for hundreds of similar cases. It stood for a firmly established policy of serious violations of international law by the United States, from unlawful kidnappings and systematic torture in secret prisons scattered around the world, to countless drone strikes coordinated from Germany's Ramstein Air Base and killing individuals on mere suspicion – an average of two attacks per month under President

Bush, rising to five per week under Obama and three per day under Trump. There is a point at which political appeasement becomes complicity under international law.

How closely German security policy is entangled with that of its Western partners behind the scenes can be seen not only in such individual cases, but particularly clearly in relation to the NSA scandal. After the Snowden leaks revealed the targeted surveillance of top German politicians by the NSA in 2013, there were public protests and calls for a German–American 'no-spy' agreement, for the establishment of an investigative committee, and for criminal proceedings regarding the surveillance of Chancellor Angela Merkel's personal phone. The German government initially pretended to support these demands. Once the dust had settled and public interest had waned, however, realpolitik quietly took over again: the criminal proceedings were dropped for 'lack of evidence', the no-spy agreement was buried without a sound bite, and the investigative committee was prevented from questioning its most important witness, Edward Snowden, in Berlin. In order for Snowden to come to Berlin, he needed a non-refoulement guarantee from the German government against his onward extradition to the United States. Apparently, this would have put too much strain on the German government's sensitive transatlantic relations. This complacent attitude was not even changed by the WikiLeaks revelations of summer 2015, which provided new evidence that numerous top politicians in Germany had been systematically surveilled by the NSA for many years, including verbatim transcripts of wiretapped conversations of the chancellor. In sum, the German political leadership chose to sweep the biggest surveillance scandal in world history under the carpet, along with the right to truth, transparency and privacy of their own people, and to emphasize the indispensable character of the transatlantic partnership instead.

Since the 'Crypto-Leaks' revelations of February 2020, this transatlantic 'partnership' is probably better described as 'complicity' in the field of intelligence collection, too. Via the trustworthy façade of a Swiss company named Crypto AG, which was secretly owned jointly by the CIA and the German Federal Intelligence Service (BND), Germany and the US had been selling manipulated cipher devices for decades to more than 100 countries. This allowed them to systematically wiretap the communications of well over half of all governments in the world. When after more than twenty years the Swiss National Intelligence Service (NDB) finally discovered the German–American espionage scheme, it did not put a stop to it. Instead, the NDB made a deal with the CIA extending access to the compromised devices to Swiss intelligence agents – causing considerable long-term damage to Switzerland's credibility as a neutral, secure and trustworthy country.

It was not until 30 December 2020 that the German government's human rights commissioner, Bärbel Kofler, could bring herself to issue a press release on the Assange case. The commissioner stated that she personally – not the German government or the Ministry of Foreign Affairs, as a government spokesperson hastened to specify – was following Assange's extradition trial 'with concern'; she reminded the United Kingdom of its obligations under the European Convention on Human Rights, 'also with a view to the possible sentence and the conditions of detention'. The commissioner's statement was published on the very last working day before Monday, 4 January 2021 – the day when Judge Baraitser at Westminster Magistrates' Court in London was scheduled to render her first-instance judgment in Assange's extradition case. Too little, too late. Too little to be taken seriously and too late to influence the decision – worlds away from the fighting talk of the German government in the case of Navalny.

## The Common Denominator

My dialogue with the four states directly responsible for Assange's persecution – the United Kingdom, Sweden, Ecuador and the United States – did not end with their initial responses. I was not prepared to accept their excuses, and so wrote an individual follow-up communication to each of the four governments. In these letters, I diligently considered any responses put forward by the authorities, reiterated the need for an official investigation of the case, and explained my findings and reasoning based on more detailed arguments of law and fact. The letters were sent to the United States and Sweden on 12 September, to Ecuador on 2 October, and to the United Kingdom on 29 October 2019. While Quito responded with another verbal volley, Stockholm simply referred back to its initial response and stated that the government had 'no further observations' on the case. London and Washington failed to respond at all.

It was now inescapably clear that nothing more could be achieved through the diplomatic channels at my disposal. The involved states had made it understood that they did not wish to enter into constructive dialogue with my office and that they considered the matter closed. I was about to make it understood that I did not. I had seen too much to be able to simply look the other way and pretend nothing had happened. The dysfunctions I had witnessed went far beyond the Assange case and were indicative of a systemic failure of major proportions.

To be sure: the official misconduct described in this book – from the persecution of Assange by the United States, the United Kingdom, Sweden, and Ecuador, to the evasiveness of Australia and the wilful blindness of Germany – is neither unique to these countries nor proof of an evil conspiracy. The policy of small compromises, where any moral dilemma is always resolved by following the path of least resistance, and where human dignity, transparency, and accountability are always the second (or third) priority, is universal. This is the globally prevailing 'operating system' of any human society, any state, organization or company. This is the unspectacular material from which the most atrocious crimes and the greatest human tragedies are made, through appeasement of the powerful, denial of responsibility and bureaucratic complicity. This is what Hannah Arendt so aptly described as the 'banality of evil'.

As much as we may be tempted to blame and moralize, the cause of the systemic failure of states to uphold the rule of law – whether in the case of Julian Assange or in others – is not moral in nature, but deeply rooted in neurobiology and social psychology. As I argued in my report to the UN General Assembly in October 2020 (A/75/179), even complex political decision-making processes are chiefly driven by unconscious emotions primarily aimed at securing individual and collective self-preservation and avoiding potentially threatening conflicts. Uncomfortable truths and moral dilemmas are suppressed or glossed over through various forms of self-deception. The result of this self-deceptive process is always a moral black hole in which corruption and inhumanity can be practiced without being perceived as such.

In the case of Julian Assange, these uncomfortable truths are, needless to say, the publications of WikiLeaks. They shine a spotlight on the shameful reality of international relations, on the war crimes and human rights abuses, the corruption, the lies and the rotten compromises. The accuracy of the leaked information cannot be disputed, because the documents have been produced by the authorities themselves. But instead of facing this reality and making the necessary corrections, the exposed states preferred to change the subject of the conversation. They teamed up to snatch the spotlight from the hands of the messenger and turn it against him: Assange, rapist, hacker, spy, and narcissist! Not even a proper journalist! A traitor who risked human lives! The world public and the media were grateful, because it is much easier to mock and scapegoat an isolated individual than to question the integrity of one's own authorities and, indeed, of the entire political and economic governance system. It is much harder to take political responsibility and to initiate the enormous global governance reforms that must be undertaken if we are ever to achieve the peaceful, just and sustainable societies envisaged in foundational documents such as the UN Charter and the Universal Declaration of Human Rights.

Given the categorical refusal of the involved states to engage in constructive dialogue with my office, the only way for me to make a difference was to confront the wider public with its own self-deception, the same self-deception which had initially distorted my own perception of the case. This would not be easy because, for the past decade, the official narrative about Assange had become deeply rooted in public opinion and relied predominantly on claims and allegations that could not be easily verified or debunked. But one event would come to significantly facilitate my task: the collapse of the Swedish case in November 2019.

# 11

# Collapse of the Swedish Case

## Headwind from America

Only four days after I had visited Assange in Belmarsh, on 13 May 2019, the Swedish Prosecution Authority reopened its preliminary investigation against him – by now for the third time. Almost nine years had passed since his visit to Sweden, since that fateful day in August 2010 when the two Swedish women visited Klara police station in Stockholm and the Swedish authorities zealously presented Assange to the world as a rape suspect – thus successfully thwarting the imminent establishment of WikiLeaks as a constitutionally protected press organization in Sweden. Since then, Swedish investigators had formally interviewed Assange twice, had heard numerous witnesses and had carried out exhaustive DNA analyses. However, given the persistent lack of prosecutable evidence, the investigation had already been discontinued twice, without Assange ever being formally charged with an offence. Now, the Swedish Prosecution Authority seemed bent on adding a third round to the procedural fiasco of its longest-ever 'preliminary investigation'.

In all these years, no significant progress had been made, but the investigation had been deliberately prevented from progressing beyond the preliminary stage. This was particularly convenient because, in the absence of a formal indictment, the Swedish authorities could continue to publicly portray Assange as a 'rape suspect' without having to disclose their evidence and subject their allegations to judicial review. By May 2019, the allegations in the case of A. had been time-barred almost four years, and the case of S. would expire in fifteen months, in August 2020. Ultimately, the strategy of systematic procrastination on the part of the Swedish Prosecution Authority would deprive not only Assange, but also the two women of any chance to receive justice and redress. But that did not seem to bother the Swedish authorities. They had never shown any genuine interest in prosecuting Assange for sexual offences which they knew could not be proved in court. Instead, these allegations were artificially kept alive for the purpose of Assange's political persecution – not officially, of course, but as part of their 'informal', 'strong' and 'reliable' intelligence cooperation with their transatlantic partner. But that was not something the Swedish people and its Parliament needed to know. Their interference would only have 'jeopardized' these 'successful arrangements' between the intelligence services of Sweden and the United States.

For the Swedish Prosecution Authority, allowing their preliminary investigation in the cases of A. and S. to become time-barred without formal indictment was particularly advantageous. This meant that the case was formally closed and all the evidence – or the lack thereof – sealed, archived and withdrawn from public scrutiny. At the same time, the rape suspect narrative could be perpetuated indefinitely without ever coming before a court. Publicly, this deliberately manufactured outcome could conveniently be blamed on Assange, by accusing him of having evaded justice. The same narrative had been used already in August 2015, when the prosecutor allowed the case of A. to become time-barred, even though she had been in the possession of all the elements required to decide on a formal indictment of Assange since at least July 2011.

On 12 April 2019, one day after Assange's arrest and more than a month before Sweden resurrected its preliminary investigation in the case of S. for the third time, no less than seventy British MPs sent an open letter to Prime Minister Theresa May. They demanded that, in the event of competition between a possible Swedish extradition request and the one already made by the United States, Assange should be extradited to Sweden. 'We must send a strong message of the priority the UK has in tackling sexual violence and the seriousness with which such allegations are viewed', the letter stated.

The hypocrisy of these assertions was revealed when, in the same year, Prince Andrew, the youngest son of Queen Elizabeth II, was suspected in the United States of repeated sexual abuse of a minor as part of the Geoffrey Epstein affair. The US Department of Justice made a formal request to interview the prince as part of its investigation, but His Royal Highness declined. This time, curiously, those same MPs were not moved to send an open letter to the Prime Minister demanding that the prince be handed over to the United States. Forgotten was the need to 'send a strong message of the priority the UK has in tackling sexual violence and the seriousness with which such allegations are viewed'.

In all likelihood, more than anything else, the open letter advocating Assange's extradition to Sweden was designed to woo British voters ahead of the upcoming general election of December 2019. The British people strongly disliked the Anglo-American extradition treaty of 2003, a lopsided agreement that was perceived as being highly unfavourable to the United Kingdom due to Tony Blair's subservient interpretation of Britain's 'special relationship' with the United States. By giving preference to the Swedish extradition request, criticism of British servility towards the United States could be deflated. At the same time, parliamentarians could take a strong public stance against sexual violence without having to lift a finger to improve the notoriously low prosecution and conviction rates for reported sexual offences within the UK. Last but not least, by sending Assange to Sweden, Britain could avoid dealing with the political pressures resulting from the US extradition request and pass the problem on to Sweden.

As patently demonstrated by the British Supreme Court's extradition decision in 2012, however, British realpolitik has long ceased to consider the opinion of Parliament. For years, the United States had regarded the Swedish rape narrative against Assange as a welcome distraction from the war crimes and corruption revealed by WikiLeaks. But now, after the DNC Leaks, US intelligence agencies had managed to portray Assange as the scapegoat for Donald Trump's election victory in 2016, an event that had traumatized very influential segments of the American public. The Swedish 'rape narrative' was no longer needed, because, by and large, the American public had taken the bait and was unlikely to find out about the true purpose of Assange's prosecution in time to prevent the criminalization of investigative national security journalism.

Thus, ten days after the official reopening of the Swedish preliminary investigation into the case of S., the US government doubled down. With the superseding indictment of 23 May 2019, the United States expanded their original indictment on a single charge of 'conspiracy to commit computer intrusion' by seventeen additional counts under the Espionage Act and – crucially – increased the maximum sentence from five to 175 years in prison. Compared to a potentially competing Swedish extradition request for ('lesser degree') rape, which carried a maximum custodial sentence of four years, the US request would certainly take precedence.

## Headwind from London

In Sweden, Marianne Ny had retired from public service and Deputy Director of Public Prosecution Eva-Marie Persson was now in charge of the case. On 20 May 2019, Persson issued a press release announcing that she had applied to Uppsala District Court for a detention order against Assange, based on which she planned to issue a new European Arrest Warrant and obtain his surrender to Sweden. Because – of course – it was still necessary to question Assange in Sweden. On the same day, the Swedish Prosecution Authority also reached out to their British counterpart 'to make clear that the (possible) EAW also includes a request for the temporary surrender'. Persson had probably expected the Crown Prosecution Service to meet her with the same unconditional complicity that Marianne Ny had enjoyed for years. But Paul Close, the man formerly in charge in London, had retired too, and British legislation had since been amended to reflect the proportionality concerns raised by the Supreme Court in Assange's first Swedish extradition trial in 2012.

Most importantly, however, the United States had now openly stepped into the ring with an extradition request of its own and, therefore, no longer depended on its 'reliable partner' Sweden for the execution of its policies. Alison Riley, Specialist Extradition Prosecutor at the CPS, initially responded that extending the European Arrest Warrant to a temporary surrender 'would not be a problem'. But twenty-four hours later, on 21 May, the tone had changed. Presumably, the imminent prospect of a competing extradition request for Assange from Sweden had triggered consultations at the political level.

Now, Prosecutor Riley suddenly confronted the Swedes with far-reaching questions and categorial terms: 'Can you explain why it is still necessary to interview [Julian Assange]? You will be aware of the new section 12A of our law which makes it imperative that there is a decision to charge and try a Requested Person in the Requesting State before an EAW can succeed. If there is any suggestion that those decisions have not been made, or that [Julian Assange] cannot be brought to trial unless he is first interviewed, the Court will not order his surrender.' In short, the harsh message coming from London was that Assange would not be surrendered to Sweden unless it was already decided that he would be formally charged and tried for a criminal offence there. That was a remarkable shift from 2012, when Britain's Supreme Court had bent over backwards and ignored the will of Parliament in order to allow Assange's forcible surrender to Sweden for the mere purpose of an interview in a preliminary investigation.

After almost nine years of comfortable tailwind from London, the Swedish Prosecution Authority was suddenly faced with the requirements of due process and the rule of law. Eva-Marie Persson knew, of course, that she had no chance of successfully prosecuting Assange. She did not even have enough probative elements to back up a formal indictment. There simply was no prosecutable evidence demonstrating Assange's culpability for any offence beyond reasonable doubt. As internal correspondence at the Swedish Prosecution Authority shows, Persson therefore looked for alternatives to his formal extradition. Either Assange could again be questioned in London or – and this was her preferred option – the European Arrest Warrant, which she firmly expected to be issued, could be used to temporarily 'borrow' Assange from Britain through the mechanism of temporary surrender. By proposing this possibility to the British authorities in writing, the Swedish Prosecution Authority explicitly confirmed Sweden's willingness – always feared by Assange and always denied by the government – to circumvent the legal hurdles of formal extradition procedures with the instrument of temporary surrender. Nonetheless, Persson was grappling with what seemed to be British obstruction.

On 21 May 2019, she wrote in an email to a subordinate staff member: 'We have tried to find avenues for the United Kingdom to meet both the wishes of the United States and those of Sweden. But this correspondence [with Alison Riley] seems to indicate that there is no interest in doing so in the UK.' What 'avenues' was Persson talking about here? Was this about Assange's temporary surrender from Britain to Sweden and – given that the same mechanism was foreseen in the US-Swedish extradition treaty – subsequently to the United States? Be this as it may, with its superseding indictment of 23 May 2019 the US government signalled that they were no longer keen or even willing to take the detour via Sweden. They wanted Assange's direct extradition to the United States.

## Headwind from Sweden

But the Swedish Prosecution Authority also faced unexpected headwinds at home. In order to issue a new EAW, Persson had first to obtain a detention order from Uppsala District Court.

On Tuesday, 28 May 2019, two and a half weeks after my prison visit to Belmarsh, I had transmitted my first official letter to the Swedish government, expressing my concern about the alleged complicity of Swedish authorities in the persecution and mistreatment of Assange. On Friday of the same week, 31 May 2019, I released my press statement, temporarily waking even the mainstream press from its lethargy about Assange's human rights. On the following Monday, 3 June 2019, the Uppsala District Court refused to issue a detention order against Assange, on grounds of proportionality. According to the court, Assange was now serving a sentence in a British prison, so it was possible and acceptable for a Swedish prosecutor conducting a preliminary investigation to interview him in London in line with applicable international mutual legal assistance agreements. If and when the prosecutor reached the conclusion that Assange should be formally charged of a criminal offence, his extradition could then still be sought for the purpose of holding the trial.

Of course, for the past nine years, there had never been any legal or practical obstacle to questioning Assange in London. Thus, the exact same considerations of proportionality should already have prevented the initial Swedish detention order and related EAW against him in November 2010. So how come, after almost a decade, the Swedish judiciary suddenly decided to start treating Assange in accordance with the law?

It is probably not too far-fetched to make a causal connection between the decision of the Uppsala District Court and my strong official statements a few days earlier. Like any other officials, judges do not want to end up on the wrong side of history. By deciding not to issue a detention order and to avoid an extradition request for the time being, the Swedish judiciary gained time. They could now wait and see whether the noise created by this UN special rapporteur would be loud enough to trigger a parliamentary investigation in Sweden, or whether it would turn out to be a storm in a teacup they could safely ignore. For once, official self-interest seemed to work in Assange's favour, at least temporarily. However, for the investigation to be dropped altogether, a final element was still missing.

## The Day of Truth

When on 12 July 2019 I received the evasive reply of the Swedish government to my official letter of 28 May, it was immediately clear to me that I was not going to take 'no' for an answer. Too much evidence had piled up for me to be able to sweep the emerging picture of massive judicial arbitrariness under the carpet and continue business as usual.

Instead, I drafted a follow-up letter, which was transmitted to the Swedish Ministry of Foreign Affairs on 12 September 2019 and made abundantly clear that I would not be fobbed off with platitudes. Whereas in my first letter I had asked only five questions, my second letter contained fifty. I confronted the government with a detailed catalogue of perceived due process violations and other inconsistencies and asked them to 'explain, point by point and in detail, the compatibility of each of [these] acts and omissions of the Swedish authorities ... and of the overall impact of the Swedish investigation on the rights and reputation of Mr. Assange, with Sweden's international human rights obligations, in particular with the presumption of inno-cence and with the principles of legality, impartiality, necessity, proportionality, efficacy and good faith, all of which are intrin-sic due process requirements indispensable to justice and the rule of law.' As usual, the Swedish authorities were given sixty days to respond. Their reply arrived on 11 November 2019, the very last day of that deadline. It consisted of three meagre sen-tences, acknowledging the receipt of my letter and informing me tersely: 'In relation to the communication of 12 September 2019, I would like to refer to the Government's response of 12 July 2019. The Government has no further observations to make.'

In essence, of course, their initial response of 12 July 2019 had already made clear that the Swedish government had 'no further observations to make' – just more verbosely and with fourfold reference to the independence of the Swedish judiciary. Despite the Swedish government's demonstrative termination of any dialogue on this case, my follow-up letter seems to have had a quite substantial effect behind the scenes: a few days later, on

19 November 2019, the preliminary investigation into the case of S. was formally discontinued for the third and final time.

In her decision, Prosecutor Persson emphasized that S. 'has submitted a credible and reliable version of events. Her statements have been coherent, extensive and detailed.' However, she explained that 'support for the injured party's assertion – and therefore of the alleged criminal act is now deemed to have weakened, largely due to the long period of time that has elapsed since the events in question.' In the prosecutor's overall assessment, 'the evidential situation has been weakened to such an extent that that there is no longer any reason to continue the preliminary investigation. It cannot be assumed that further inquiries will change the evidential situation in any significant manner. The preliminary investigation is therefore discontinued.'

In reality, of course, there had never been any prosecutable evidence other than S.'s testimony. If the prosecutor still considered her testimony to be 'credible and reliable', then it was difficult to comprehend how its probative value could have so dramatically diminished over time. As a matter of logic, the only conceivable explanation for affirming the credibility and reliability of S.'s testimony while at the same time dismissing the credibility and reliability of the official rape narrative was that one had nothing to do with the other. This left two possibilities. The first was that, contrary to the police report based on her statement, S. herself had never alleged to have been raped, and that Prosecutor Persson had come to the same conclusion as her colleague Eva Finné nine years earlier, namely that S.'s testimony was credible but did not give rise to any suspicion of criminal conduct. The second possibility was that the facts alleged by S. constituted rape while the facts alleged by Assange did not, and that, all other evidentiary factors being equal, the suspect had to be given the benefit of the doubt – *in dubio pro reo*. In both cases, irrespective of what had really happened between S. and Assange, he had to be considered innocent as a matter of law.

Of course, all of this had been known to the Swedish authorities already in September 2010. But, even now, the prosecutor could not bring herself to say any of this. Not a word about the presumption of innocence. Not a word of regret for the almost ten years of judicial arbitrariness at the expense of all three persons concerned: Assange and the two women. No redress for the reputational harm and the hostility, humiliation and mistreatment they suffered. No compensation for Assange's nearly ten years of arbitrary detention solely due to untenable allegations of rape irresponsibly disseminated and perpetuated by the Swedish authorities. At the press conference, Persson was asked whether she regretted the way the investigation had been handled. Once more, the absence of a firm denial was more revealing than the evasive content of the reply. She could only take personal responsibility for the last six months, Persson said, and during this time she had tried to conduct the investigation as quickly and quality-oriented as possible. However, she could not comment on what had happened under the responsibility of another investigator. It was possible that the Prosecution Authority would have to 'look into this question once all of this is over'. To date, this appears to be the closest the Swedish authorities have ever come to a critical self-examination in this case.

Since the sudden invocation of due process and the rule of law by their British counterparts and the District Court of Uppsala, the Swedish Prosecution Authority had acted like a deer caught in the headlights. Desperately scrambling for new investigative measures that could be taken to maintain a façade of credibility, they saw the prospect and rationale of their case against Assange dwindle rapidly towards total collapse. Prosecutor Persson's internal directives issued during the summer of 2019 reveal the extent to which the Swedish investigation was in disarray and lacked even the most basic foundations of a prosecutable case. In her directive of 13 June, Persson writes: 'We need to make a preliminary assessment of the evidence.' Preliminary? Seriously? After nine years? How does the need for a 'preliminary assessment' chime with the publicly proclaimed, supposedly consolidated suspicion on probable cause? But Persson continues: 'It is not appropriate for us to request permission to interview [Assange] in England if we do not consider that we have sufficiently strong evidence.' This statement is quite revealing given that, in practice, even the flimsiest level of evidence is sufficient to justify interviewing a suspect. In another directive of 26 July, referring to various pieces of evidence, Persson writes: 'I'll have to read through them all and decide how strong the support for the alleged crime *really* is' [emphasis in original]. Really? How come it took the prosecutor nine years to ask the right question? According to Persson, by July 2019, 'the oral evidence in support of the alleged offence has deteriorated' – as if the original statements from 2010 could no longer be used as evidence. 'If the memory and/or willingness to contribute of [witness X.] has deteriorated in the same way as several other witnesses, I think that will be the nail in the coffin.'

My follow-up letter to the government is probably what became the final 'nail in the coffin' of the Swedish case. I had listed fifty perceived due process violations, some of them serious, and had asked fifty questions that the authorities quite evidently preferred to leave unanswered. After only two months, these fifty allegations and questions would be published on the website of the United Nations High Commissioner for Human Rights. This entailed a considerable risk of uncomfortable questions being asked by the press, in parliament, by an ombudsman, or by a court about the legal responsibilities arising in this case.

While it would have been more elegant to maintain the preliminary investigation in a state of undead paralysis until the case of S. became time-barred in August 2020, its immediate discontinuation was clearly the safer solution, because it put a formal end to the matter for everyone involved. This was a final nod to the fact that the Swedish Prosecution Authority had never really pursued justice and the rule of law in this case – neither for Assange nor for the two women. All three had been instrumentalized and abused by the authorities for the purpose of political persecution and deterrence. Even if, ultimately, the collapse of the Swedish case against Assange had been inevitable, it left a bitter aftertaste.

# 12

# Public Opinion Begins to Turn

## Setting the Record Straight

To the broader public around the world, the rather subdued discontinuation of the Swedish investigation came as a surprise. For more than nine years, the Prosecution Authority had been able to deflect criticism as to the paralysis of its investigation by accusing Assange of evading justice. But with his arrest by British police on 11 April 2019, the tables had turned. Suddenly Assange was at the disposal of the Swedish authorities, and they still had a comfortable window of sixteen months to interview and formally charge him with the alleged rape of S. But just six months after reopening the investigation, Prosecutor Persson threw in the towel and publicly admitted that the evidence at her disposal was not sufficient to initiate a criminal trial against Assange, nor was there any prospect of improving the evidentiary situation by interviewing him or taking any other investigative measures. After years of being fed an unbending 'rape suspect' narrative, the public was confused and divided: no arrest warrant, no extradition request, no interview and, worst of all, no prosecutable evidence?

Since presenting my preliminary findings in May 2019, I had been trying to raise awareness of the enormous implications of this case for the prohibition of torture and ill-treatment, for press freedom and freedom of information, for the extraterritorial overreach of US jurisdiction and, indeed, for democracy and the rule of law. But the official Swedish narrative of Assange as a fugitive rape suspect was so firmly entrenched in the public mind that it was very difficult to expose its instrumentalization for the purposes of political persecution without being misunderstood as relativizing the importance of prosecuting sexual offences. The fact that the Swedish authorities refused any constructive dialogue in the matter further complicated my investigation and required me to repeatedly adjust, clarify, and supplement my conclusions in order to accommodate new evidence.

Particularly in the early stages of my investigation, I was criticized by many who genuinely feared for the hard-fought gains of the women's rights movement. I was censured by long-time colleagues, lost a research assistant, and received letters of protest from women's rights organizations, lawyers, academics, and even one of the two Swedish women. I did my best to address these legitimate concerns, to clarify my position and to resolve misunderstandings. Most importantly, I made unequivocally clear that my criticism was in no way directed against the women or their rights and integrity, nor against the description of the alleged conduct as serious sexual offences, but solely against the authorities and their deliberate abuse of a legal process for the purposes of political persecution. In fact, I considered A. and S. to be victims of state instrumentalization just as much as Assange himself.

It was also from established women's rights organizations, such as the London-based 'Women Against Rape', and from hundreds of rape victims and their relatives that I received the most determined public support. They stood up for justice and truth in the case of Julian Assange. They rejected the deliberate instrumentalization of a rape narrative for the persecution of an inconvenient dissident, when sexual violence on the part of soldiers and agents of the same states was routinely hushed up and victims of domestic and sexual violence can rarely rely on effective protection but are often doubly humiliated and traumatized by inadequate attitudes, policies and practices.

In fact at that time, I was working on a report on domestic violence from the perspective of the prohibition of torture and ill-treatment (A/74/148), which I presented to the UN General Assembly in New York in October 2019. What most shocked me during my extensive consultations on the topic, besides the enormous scale of the violence and cruelty to which women and children especially are exposed in their own homes worldwide, was the nonchalance with which this enormously destructive form of torture and ill-treatment is routinely trivialized, ignored or even instrumentalized by governments – even though it has produced more death, suffering and injustice than all the wars in human history combined.

## A First Breakthrough

The collapse of the Swedish case and the prosecutor's formal acknowledgement of the lack of evidence put an abrupt end to the official narrative of the 'fugitive rape suspect', which for so long had haunted all efforts to raise awareness of the persecution of Assange. So far, with the laudable exception of the American magazine *Newsweek*, none of the established Western media organizations had covered my Assange investigation in any serious detail; none had even challenged the veracity of my findings in an in-depth interview, and none had confronted the relevant governments with the disturbing questions raised by my interventions. Now, suddenly the path was cleared to once again see Julian Assange as an individual entitled to human rights and dignity, as a publisher who had exposed evidence of war crimes, torture and corruption, and as a courageous dissident who had dared to stand up to the most powerful states in the world.

If there was no evidence for the rape allegations, perhaps the other accusations needed to be questioned as well? Could it be that Assange had been wrongly accused of being a hacker, a spy, a traitor and a narcissist? The increase of public interest opened up new opportunities to communicate the findings of my investigation to a wider audience. I spoke at the European Parliament, the German Bundestag, the Parliamentary Assembly of the Council of Europe, and the Swiss Parliament. I also appeared at public events and gave interviews. A first, decisive breakthrough came with a long and brilliantly conceived interview by journalist Daniel Ryser in the Swiss online newspaper *Republik*, published on 31 January 2020 in both German and English, which made my findings accessible to a wide audience and triggered renewed interest in the mainstream media, particularly in the German-speaking world.

Since the beginning of my investigation, I had also been in direct contact with a growing network of individual supporters. From outspoken celebrities like Roger Waters, Pamela Anderson, Vivienne Westwood and Joe Corré, to progressive politicians like Yanis Varoufakis, Sevim Dağdelen and Tulsi Gabbard; to fearless publicists like John Pilger, Stefania Maurizi and Craig Murray. My contacts further included Assange's lawyers and family members, WikiLeaks staff, and countless activists, journalists, professionals and former officials who, for various reasons, were able and willing to contribute important pieces to the puzzle of my investigation. For reasons of source protection, publishing a full list of their names here would be neither wise nor appropriate.

With the collapse of the Swedish case, my network suddenly expanded deep into the political mainstream to include personalities such as former German Vice Chancellor Sigmar Gabriel, investigative author Günter Wallraff, Council of Europe Commissioner for Human Rights Dunja Mijatović, and Swedish Bar Association Secretary General Anne Ramberg. Their public support convinced others and triggered a worldwide surge in solidarity and protest throughout 2020, including high-profile calls for Assange's release on the part of former heads of state, former ministers, as well as various associations of lawyers, medical doctors and journalists. One by one, entire organizations started to change course, protest against Assange's persecution and demand his release, including Amnesty International, Human Rights Watch, Reporters Without Borders, the Committee to Protect Journalists, the International Bar Association, and the Parliamentary Assembly of the Council of Europe.

From February 2020, among other things, I also supported an initiative by the government of the Canton of Geneva, championed by Member of Parliament Jean Rossiaud, to convince the Swiss federal government to issue a humanitarian visa to Assange. Should the British courts refuse Assange's extradition to the United States, or should the US and the UK both agree to release Assange on humanitarian grounds – a face-saving way out for all parties – this humanitarian visa would allow Assange to come to Switzerland for a rehabilitation stay at the University Hospitals of Geneva.

Until early March 2020, I literally gave several interviews every single day, had journalists and filmmakers in my office, spoke on video conferences, and travelled to London several times for public speeches and private meetings with Australian parliamentarians, American and British documentary makers, lawyers, and assorted celebrities. The escalating media interest was further fuelled by the beginning of Assange's extradition trial on 24 February 2020. But then came the COVID-19 pandemic and, shortly thereafter, global lockdown. The world now had other preoccupations besides the fate of Julian Assange and the broader implications of his case. Nevertheless, overshadowed by the destructive force of the pandemic, the benign seed of truth, too, had been planted and began to spread around the world. I was convinced that it was only a matter of time before the critical mass required for a worldwide change of public opinion would be reached.

## Rapporteur-Turned-Dissident

For me personally, 2019 and 2020 had been years of disillusion and resolve. The disillusion concerned the credibility of Western democracies as allies in the fight for human rights; the reliability of our constitutional checks and balances to oversee the exercise of governmental power; and the practical effectiveness of UN mechanisms in protecting human rights. But this loss of illusions also gave me the resolve to put myself on the line and confront the international community of states with its hypocrisy. The same international community that had appointed me as a UN special rapporteur in 2016, when as a senior security policy advisor to the Swiss government I was still very much part of the system. I had taken my mandate literally, had exposed torture and ill-treatment wherever I encountered it in my work and had refused to bend the rules for reasons of personal or political expediency. Now, with my investigation into the case of Julian Assange, I had inadvertently become a dissident within the system myself.

Nothing illustrated this transformation more emblematically than my brief public address on 27 November 2019, at the Brandenburg Gate in Berlin. On Pariser Platz stood a sculpture by the Italian artist Davide Dormino. Cast in bronze, Edward Snowden, Julian Assange and Chelsea Manning stood on three chairs, silent and upright. Unbowed. Next to them was a fourth chair, empty, inviting people to step up and take a stand. Very appropriately, Dormino had titled the sculpture '*Anything to say?*' Several politicians had already taken the floor at a lectern next to it. As I listened to them, the fourth chair of the sculpture looked glaringly abandoned. So, when it was my turn to speak and I was handed the microphone, I did not hesitate but stepped up onto the fourth chair. From up there I looked across the square, the huge US embassy to my right, and felt as if I were doing something forbidden. I was aware that I had crossed another line with this symbolic gesture that physically placed me in line with the three most persecuted dissidents of the Western world. It was not that I had overstepped my mandate. On the contrary, given the refusal of the involved governments to cooperate with my office, this really was the only way I could still exercise my mandate with independence and effectiveness. If I could no longer rely on the governments currently in place to live up to their international obligations, I had to directly address the people of the UN member states, because it was they who were the ultimate sovereign and had collectively committed to respecting and protecting fundamental human rights at all times. If my mandate was not to degenerate into a fig leaf for a dysfunctional system of self-deception, I could not be intimidated, but had to speak truth to power – not only with words, but whenever possible also with powerful symbolic gestures.

This is what I had to say:

'For decades, political dissidents have been welcomed by the West with open arms, because in their fight for human rights they were persecuted by dictatorial regimes. Today, however, Western dissidents themselves are forced to seek asylum elsewhere, such as Edward Snowden in Russia or, until recently, Julian Assange at the Ecuadorian embassy in London. For the West itself has begun to persecute its own dissidents, to subject them to draconian punishments in political show trials, and to imprison them as dangerous terrorists in high-security prisons under conditions that can only be described as inhuman and degrading.

'Our governments feel threatened by Chelsea Manning, Edward Snowden, and Julian Assange, because they are whistleblowers, journalists, and human rights activists who have provided solid evidence for the abuse, corruption, and war crimes of the powerful, for which they are now being systematically defamed and persecuted. They are the political dissidents of the West, and their persecution is today's witch-hunt, because they threaten the privileges of an unconstrained state power that has gone out of control.

'The cases of Manning, Snowden, Assange and others are the most important test of our time for the credibility of Western rule of law and democracy and our commitment to human rights. In all these cases, it is not about the person, the character or possible misconduct of these dissidents, but about how our governments deal with revelations about their own misconduct.

'How many soldiers have been held accountable for the massacre of civilians shown in the video "Collateral Murder"? How many agents for the systematic torture of terror suspects? How many politicians and CEOs for the corrupt and inhumane machinations that have been brought to light by our dissidents? That's what this is about. It is about the integrity of the rule of law, the credibility of our democracies and, ultimately, about our own human dignity and the future of our children. Let us never forget that!'

The sculpture subsequently toured Europe and, almost exactly eighteen months later, I once again stood on that bronze chair on the occasion of the 'Geneva Call to Free Assange' launched by the Swiss Press Club on 4 and 5 June 2021. Julian Assange was still isolated in Belmarsh, and his extradition trial had reached the appeal stage in the British High Court, but public opinion had evolved since that first speech in Berlin. By my side were not only Assange's partner Stella Moris and many other long-time supporters of Assange, but also Yves Daccord, a former director-general of the ICRC, Christophe Deloire, the secretary-general of Reporters without Borders, Carlo Sommaruga, member of the Swiss Federal Parliament, and even the mayor of Geneva, Frédérique Perler, who powerfully proclaimed that 'Assange has sacrificed his liberty in order to protect ours!'

Six months earlier, on 4 January 2021, a lower court in Britain had already set a legal precedent effectively criminalizing investigative journalism worldwide, and Assange's state of health was declining. So, when I stepped up on that fourth chair for the second time in June 2021, just a stone's throw away from the majestic Palais Wilson that hosts the Office of the High Commissioner for Human Rights, I spoke with an increased sense of urgency:

'Ladies and Gentlemen, we are in Geneva. It is the city of the United Nations, the city of the Red Cross, and it is the city of human rights. I am standing here next to Edward Snowden, Julian Assange and Chelsea Manning. The truth is: all of them are being persecuted, mistreated and demonized for one thing and one thing only; for having told the truth, the whole truth and nothing but the truth about the misconduct of Western democracies. They are the skeletons in the closet of the West.

Their persecution and mistreatment is what destroys the credibility of the West. When the Western governments today protest the persecution of Alexei Navalny and of Roman Protasevich, the responsible governments only laugh and ask, "Well, what about Edward Snowden who is being protected in Russia? What about Julian Assange, who is in solitary confinement without having committed a crime but telling the truth? What about Chelsea Manning, who was being persecuted to the point of almost dying in an attempted suicide?"

'Whistleblowers and journalists who publish such information are inconvenient truthtellers. They are as inconvenient as the fire alarm in your house. When a fire goes off in your house and there is smoke, you hear the alarm. We all know the drill: we have to leave the house, we have to leave our work, our daily routine. It is inconvenient, and many voices come up and say: "Just switch off the alarm." That is what these governments are trying to do when they persecute and isolate and silence these people. They are silencing the fire alarm in the building of democracy and the rule of law. And if I stand up here on this chair today, it is because I was the fire alarm in the United Nations for this case. And I rang the alarm bell, and I wrote to these governments, and I informed the public, but they wanted to ignore the alarm. No one reacted. So, we are inconvenient truth-tellers, the four of us and the millions of others out there that speak the truth. Inconvenient truths. You can switch off the fire alarm for now, and you will feel comfortable for a couple more moments. But the next time you open your eyes, and you wake up and look around, the whole building will be on fire! It is now in the hands of the public to react. Thank you, Geneva, for hosting us here, thank you for giving us this platform. I know this voice goes out to the world!'

# 13

# British Torture by Attrition

## Quo Vadis, Britannia?

On 11 April 2019, Alan Duncan, the British minister of state for Europe and the Americas responsible for overseeing Assange's expulsion and arrest, noted in his diary: 'It had taken many months of patient diplomatic negotiation, and in the end it went off without a hitch. I do millions of interviews, trying to keep the smirk off my face.' Indeed, that day, British politicians outdid each other in celebrating Assange's arrest, and Prime Minister Theresa May expressed her satisfaction in the House of Commons: 'This goes to show that in the UK, no one is above the law.' No one except the British authorities themselves, of course. The blatant failure of all three branches of government to uphold the rule of law when dealing with the case of Julian Assange seriously calls into question the stability and reliability of Britain's democratic institutions. But the persecution of Assange is not an isolated incident. For at least twenty years now, consecutive British governments have followed an increasingly alarming path of exceptionalism, arbitrariness and impunity that has severely eroded the country's international credibility.

Perhaps the most obvious example is Britain's eager involvement in the 2003 war of aggression against Iraq, which gravely violated the most fundamental principles of international law and order, triggering two decades of war, terrorism and corruption that killed, displaced, and traumatized millions of innocent people. Thousands of allegations of murder, torture, and rape involving British soldiers in Iraq have been deemed to be credible by Chief Prosecutor Fatou Bensouda of the International Criminal Court. However, only one British soldier has ever been convicted of a war crime by the United Kingdom, and that was because he made a voluntary confession. All other cases ended up being dropped or otherwise discontinued by the British judiciary, and neither Prime Minister Blair nor any other political leader has ever been held to account for their role in recklessly destroying Iraq and destabilizing the entire region.

The same impunity surrounds British involvement in the CIA's unlawful policy of torture and extraordinary rendition as part of the 'war on terror'. In the summer of 2018, an investigation by the Intelligence and Security Committee of the British Parliament formally concluded that British authorities had substantially contributed to the CIA's practice of torture and rendition and demanded a full judicial inquiry. Although the Convention against Torture requires that any perpetration or participation in torture must be prosecuted and punished, and although the treaty does not allow for any political discretion in this regard, the British government has prevented the judicial inquiry requested by Parliament and continues to impose impunity for the British officials involved in the CIA programme. By blocking the prosecution of war crimes, the political leadership of the United Kingdom – just like the US president – not only violate the Convention against Torture and the Geneva Conventions, but also incur international criminal responsibility in line with the customary principles of command and superior responsibility that have been recognized and confirmed by all international criminal courts and tribunals since the Nuremberg trials after World War II.

To make matters worse, the British government has recently taken considerable pains to codify the impunity of its officials in domestic law. Thus, in 2020, Prime Minister Boris Johnson's cabinet introduced two bills into Parliament designed to make it extremely difficult, if not impossible, to punish British soldiers, agents and authority representatives for crimes such as torture, murder and hostage-taking both abroad and in the UK, namely the Overseas Operations Bill and the Covert Human Intelligence Sources (Criminal Conduct) Bill. To complete the picture, a commission was appointed in the same year to review the British Human Rights Act for necessary 'reforms', which has put numerous human rights organizations on alert. Despite an uproar of international protest, including by my own office, the British government was bent on pushing the Overseas Operations Bill through Parliament without any substantial concessions, thus ensuring de facto impunity even for the most atrocious international crimes. It was only during the very last session in the House of Lords that amendments were made, after the former defence secretary and NATO secretary-general, George Robertson, had opposed the bill, stressing the enormous reputational damage that would ensue for the United Kingdom. The government finally excepted torture, war crimes, and crimes against humanity from its scope of application.

As a professor of international law at a British university, I observe this trend with growing concern. As the UN special rapporteur on torture, I am called to formally intervene with the British government ever more frequently on increasingly serious issues related to my mandate – a far cry from the traditional image of Britain as the reasonable and reliable country of the Magna Carta.

Unfortunately, the incapacity of the British authorities at all levels to ensure humane treatment and due process to Julian Assange is symptomatic of a broader trend of institutional erosion and social disintegration. It is also consistent with the government's almost complete indifference to any admonition by international organizations and observers. One can only hope that the British people will wake up to the enormous risks of this tendency and use their democratic powers to change course before the damage becomes irreversible.

Assange knew, of course, that Ecuador had not handed him over to a neutral and impartial judiciary, but to a powerful government that had spent ten years and millions of pounds in surveilling, persecuting and demonizing him. He knew that this government perceived him as an enemy of the state and could not wait to make a chilling example of him for the entire world to see. Assange's consciousness of this reality had triggered a dangerous downward spiral typical of victims of psychological torture. He had entered a vicious circle of permanent anxiety and stress, sleeplessness and helplessness, confusion and depression, which urgently needed to be stabilized through medication and, even more importantly, stress relief. As the doctors accompanying my visit on 9 May 2019 had correctly predicted, Assange's state of health deteriorated rapidly to the point where, just three weeks later, on 30 May 2019, he was no longer capable of participating in a court hearing even by video link.

## Arbitrary Isolation and Surveillance

After his transfer to Belmarsh's health care unit, Assange spent a short time in a group cell with three other inmates but was soon moved to a single cell where he was almost completely isolated. According to consistent reports, he was only allowed to leave his cell once a day to spend forty-five minutes outdoors in the courtyard – alone. Any exchange with other inmates was systematically prevented. Whenever Assange was escorted through the corridors by the guards, all other inmates were locked away first. Inside his cell, he was monitored around the clock. All these measures were ostensibly taken for his own safety, to protect him from himself and from his fellow inmates. Far from showing any aggression, however, it was precisely those fellow inmates who petitioned the prison director in solidarity with Assange, demanding that he be transferred back to the general prison population because of the cruelty of long-term solitary confinement.

They were right. The United Nations Standard Minimum

Rules for the Treatment of Prisoners, also known as the 'Nelson Mandela Rules', make clear that solitary confinement – that is, 'the confinement of prisoners for twenty-two hours or more a day without meaningful human contact' – is permissible only in exceptional circumstances and for short periods of time. Prolonged solitary confinement, lasting more than fifteen consecutive days, is expressly prohibited as a form of torture or other cruel, inhuman or degrading treatment or punishment.

Constant surveillance, too, seriously interferes with privacy rights and can only be justified in exceptional circumstances and for a short time, for example in order to prevent an imminent risk of suicide. Unfortunately, this 'suicide watch' regime is not always used in good faith, but increasingly to covertly erode a prisoner's resistance. Suicide prevention was also the reason given for tormenting Chelsea Manning with constant surveillance for nine months, a practice that was later condemned as arbitrary and abusive not only by my predecessor, Juan Méndez, but also by the judge presiding over the trial of Chelsea Manning.

As we have seen, however, the British authorities always had an explanation ready: when Assange was in poor health, his isolation and surveillance had to be maintained to protect him. But then, when his health stabilized, this was taken as evidence that Assange's isolation had a positive effect on his health and needed to be continued. What was deliberately ignored, of course, was that Assange had not committed any offence that could have justified his detention in a high-security prison, and that his health crisis had been caused by the very isolation, surveillance and arbitrariness that now supposedly had to be used to protect him. This resulted in an artificial vicious circle, which strongly suggests that the authorities were much less interested in protecting Assange's health than in ensuring he would remain silenced through isolation.

Significantly, his solitary confinement was not lifted even after 25 September 2019, when Assange had served half of the fifty-week sentence imposed for his bail violation, and the remainder of his sentence had to be waived for good conduct. As a matter of law, Assange was now no longer serving a sentence, but should have been a free man allowed to pursue his professional and family life without restriction, so long as he remained available for the US extradition trial. Because of Assange's previous escape to the Ecuadorian embassy, however, the judge ruled that, as a precaution, he could not be released but had to remain in custody for the entire duration of the extradition proceedings.

Quite obviously, however, for purely preventive custody, the extremely restrictive conditions at Belmarsh were neither necessary nor proportionate – two mandatory basic requirements for any lawful interference with fundamental rights. Instead, Assange should have been moved to a less securitized institution or to guarded house arrest, with unrestricted access to his professional activities, to his family, his lawyers and the outside world more generally. But that, of course, would have looked too much like a victory for Assange and would have undermined the real purpose of his continued solitary confinement: to silence him and to intimidate the free press.

## Undermining Defendant Rights

In addition to silencing, intimidating, and breaking Assange, his isolation at Belmarsh had a second, probably equally intentional effect. Belmarsh being a high-security prison, security measures are particularly strict. This is not only reflected in the extremely elaborate entrance procedures for outside visitors, which we had experienced ourselves, but it also complicates and slows down everything going on inside the prison, such as social contacts, telephone calls, mail distribution, library visits, sports and exercise, work, hygiene, and doctor's visits. Everything is minutely regulated and carried out under strict supervision. The personal items permitted to inmates inside the cell are limited, as are the number of visitors they can receive.

Even external visits that have been notified and authorized in advance are routinely affected by delays. Assange's lawyers have complained that they are not allowed to visit him with sufficient frequency and that, when such visits are granted, Assange or the visiting lawyer are either brought to the meeting room late or picked up too early, purportedly due to a shortage of available prison staff, which routinely reduces the meeting time to half of the reserved timeslot. For example, after the Swedish investigation had been reopened on 13 May 2019, Assange's Swedish lawyer, Per Samuelson, travelled to London for a two-hour meeting with his client to discuss the case documents, which were available in Swedish only. But Assange was brought to the meeting with Samuelson one hour and forty-five minutes late, shortening the meeting time to fifteen minutes. Moreover, Samuelson was not allowed to hand over any documents to Assange, and, ultimately, was required to leave without having been able to fulfil his function as defence counsel. According to the prison administration, this was just a regrettable misunderstanding – a misunderstanding, however, that kept recurring with routine predictability.

Others who complained about obstructive delays were Assange's London legal team, led by Gareth Peirce and Jennifer Robinson, as well as Dr Sondra Crosby and Assange's private visitors. During my own official visit in May 2019, I had the same experience. All of these instances, too, were presumably just 'regrettable misunderstandings'. As external visitors are not allowed to hand over anything to Assange, medical and legal documents must be sent through ordinary mail, which commonly results in delivery delays of up to two months, and, reportedly, in the unauthorized opening of confidential attorney's correspondence. No doubt all such incidents, too, are just 'regrettable misunderstandings'.

Immediately after his arrest in April 2019, Assange had requested the allocation of a laptop so that he could read the court files in electronic form and draft notes and statements for his own defence. Again, owing to further 'regrettable misunderstandings', the request was not granted until ten months later, after the extradition hearing had already begun in February 2020. Even when Assange was finally given the laptop, the keyboard had been blocked with glue to prevent him from typing. Regrettable? Certainly. A misunderstanding? Certainly not.

Much as the authorities tried to disguise their obstruction behind a smokescreen of bureaucratic, logistical and security imperatives, they could not possibly have acted in good faith. They knew, of course, that Assange was not their average convict or remand prisoner with, at the most, one pending trial or appeal process to prepare. In his case, several highly complex proceedings were simultaneously underway in different states. On the one hand, he had to prepare for the US extradition proceedings, in which he faced the most powerful state in the world with its army of lawyers and its unlimited financial, political and military resources and leverage. On the other hand, there was also the British bail violation, the reopened Swedish investigation, the Spanish case against UC Global for illegal surveillance at the embassy, and a possible case against the Ecuadorian authorities, who had illegally retained Assange's belongings after his expulsion and handed them over directly to the US government.

Even under ideal circumstances, five proceedings in three different languages involving five distinct jurisdictions would have been an arduous, almost unmanageable challenge. Under the conditions of isolation imposed on him at Belmarsh, however, Assange clearly had no chance to protect his legitimate interests in any of these proceedings, to study the extensive case files, or to adequately prepare his defence. This was particularly alarming with regard to his potential extradition to the United States, which would almost certainly result in lifelong solitary confinement under cruel, inhumane and degrading conditions. Both during my personal meetings with the responsible authorities, and in my formal letters to the British government, I had repeatedly stressed that Assange's most fundamental due process rights were being violated, and demanded immediate action. To no avail.

Despite the gravity and continuity of these procedural violations, no one wanted to take responsibility. As usual, of course, the British authorities had no bad intentions whatsoever, but insurmountable constitutional or bureaucratic obstacles prevented them from taking the slightest action on behalf of Assange. Whenever his lawyers complained, the prison administration felt unable to interfere with judicial proceedings and the judge felt unable to interfere with prison conditions – because, as is well known, the United Kingdom is a rule-of-law democracy in which the separation of powers prevails, and the judiciary and the executive must always be careful not to tread on each other's areas of responsibility. Except, of course, when it serves the interests of those in power. No one seems to have wasted a thought on the fact that any legal proceeding affected by systematic due process violations of such gravity must be regarded as irreparably arbitrary and, therefore, invalid.

## Assange and Pinochet: An Instructive Comparison

In a democracy governed by the rule of law, everyone is equal before the law. In essence, this means that comparable cases must be treated equally. Like Julian Assange today, the Chilean ex-dictator Augusto Pinochet was also held in British extradition custody, from 16 October 1998 to 2 March 2000. Spain, Switzerland, France and Belgium wanted to prosecute him for torture and crimes against humanity. Like Assange today, Pinochet then described himself as 'Britain's only political prisoner'.

Unlike Assange, however, Pinochet was not accused of having obtained and published evidence for torture, murder and corruption, but of actually having committed, ordered, and consented to such crimes. Moreover, unlike Assange, he was not considered a threat to the interests of the British government, but a friend and ally from the era of the Cold War and – crucially – the Falklands War.

Thus, when a British court dared to apply the law and lift Pinochet's diplomatic immunity, that decision was immediately overturned. The reason given was a possible bias on the part of one of the judges. Apparently, the judge in question had at some point volunteered for a local fundraiser of the human rights organization Amnesty International, which was a joint plaintiff in the case. Fast forward to the case of Assange. Here, Judge

Arbuthnot, whose husband had been repeatedly exposed by WikiLeaks, was not only allowed to decide on Assange's arrest warrant in 2018 but, despite a well-documented application for recusal, also to preside over his extradition proceedings until Judge Baraitser took over in the summer of 2019. None of her decisions were overturned.

Pinochet, accused of being directly responsible for tens of thousands of serious human rights violations, was not insulted, humiliated or ridiculed by British judges in public court hearings, nor was he held in solitary confinement at a high-security prison. When Pinochet was taken into custody, Prime Minister Blair did not express his satisfaction in Parliament that 'in the UK, no one is above the law', and there was no open letter from seventy members of Parliament fervently demanding that the government extradite the ex-dictator to the requesting countries. Instead, Pinochet spent his extradition detention in luxurious house arrest in a villa outside London, where he was allowed to receive unlimited visitors, from a private Chilean priest at Christmas to former prime minister Margaret Thatcher. The inconvenient truthteller Julian Assange, however, who is accused of journalism rather than torture and murder, is not being granted house arrest. He is being silenced in solitary confinement.

Like Assange's, Pinochet's state of health was a decisive issue. Although the general himself categorically dismissed the idea of a release on humanitarian grounds, Home Secretary Jack Straw personally intervened. Straw ordered a medical examination of Pinochet, which concluded that the former military putschist and dictator was suffering from amnesia and poor concentration. When several governments requesting his extradition demanded an independent second opinion, the British government refused. Instead, Secretary Straw himself decided that Pinochet was not fit to stand trial and ordered his immediate release and repatriation. Contrary to the United States in the extradition trial of Assange, the states requesting Pinochet's extradition were not given the opportunity to appeal.

In the case of Assange, several independent medical reports, as well as my official findings as the UN special rapporteur on torture were ignored and, even when he was barely able to state his own name in court, the trial continued without regard for his deteriorating health and unfitness to stand trial.

Just as with Pinochet, Assange's extradition was – at least initially – refused on medical grounds. But while Pinochet was immediately released and repatriated and the states requesting his extradition were deprived of all legal remedies, Assange was immediately returned to solitary confinement, his release on bail was refused, and the United States were invited to appeal to the High Court, thus ensuring the perpetuation of Assange's ordeal and silencing for the remainder of an extradition proceeding that could easily be spun out for several years.

The comparison of these two cases demonstrates the double standard applied by the British authorities and how, in the United Kingdom, not everyone is equal before the law after all. In Pinochet's case, the aim was to provide a former dictator and loyal ally with impunity for alleged crimes against humanity. In Assange's case, the aim is to silence an inconvenient dissident whose organization, WikiLeaks, challenges precisely this type of impunity. Both approaches are motivated purely by power politics and are incompatible with justice and the rule of law.

## The Torture Proves Effective

'I was deeply shaken while witnessing yesterday's events in Westminster Magistrates' Court. Every decision was railroaded through over the scarcely heard arguments and objections of Assange's legal team, by a magistrate who barely pretended to be listening.' Those are the words of Craig Murray, a former British ambassador and a personal friend of Assange's, describing his impressions after witnessing a case management hearing on 21 October 2019. This type of hearing exists to give all parties the opportunity to clarify procedural issues in advance of the substantive extradition hearing.

It is the first time Assange participates in such a hearing in person, after he has previously been medically unfit to attend or has participated only via video link. Murray is shocked at the sight of his friend being led into the courtroom. Assange is limping, he has lost at least fifteen kilos in weight, his hair has become thin, and he looks prematurely aged. Even more frightening is the deterioration of his mental state. Assange struggles visibly to follow the hearing, to speak and even to recall his own name and date of birth.

The hearing is presided over by Vanessa Baraitser, a district judge subordinate to Senior Judge Arbuthnot who has been tasked with Assange's extradition trial – presumably in order to pre-empt further recusal applications against Arbuthnot. Despite strong objections on the part of Assange's lawyers, who demand more preparation time, Judge Baraitser confirms that the extradition hearing will begin on 24 February 2020 as requested by Prosecutor Lewis on behalf of the United States. The venue will then not be Westminster Magistrates' Court, but Woolwich Crown Court, a highly securitized courtroom in the immediate vicinity of Belmarsh prison, which normally hosts trials against suspected terrorists.

At the end of the hearing, the judge finally turns to Assange, orders him to stand, and asks him whether he has understood the proceedings. He replies in the negative, says that he cannot think, and appears disoriented. Then, Murray recounts, Assange seems to find an inner reserve of strength. And says: 'I do not understand how this process is equitable. This superpower had ten years to prepare for this case and I can't even access my writings. It is very difficult, where I am, to do anything. These people have unlimited resources.' After that the effort seems to become too much, his voice drops, and he becomes increasingly confused and incoherent. Judge Baraitser is as unmoved by Assange's evidently precarious state of health as she is by his express objections regarding the fairness of the proceedings. If he could not understand what had happened during the hearing, his lawyers can explain it to him, she says, dismisses the parties and closes the hearing.

## Assange's Life Is in Danger!

In the autumn of 2019, the signs that Assange's health had deteriorated further became more pronounced. It was not easy to obtain an objective assessment, but the alarming information I received from several reliable sources confirmed the prediction we had made after my visit in the event that no measures were taken to alleviate the pressure on Assange.

As Murray had vividly described, the damaging effects of such relentless exposure to isolation, surveillance, and arbitrariness were now becoming plainly visible to the outside world, even to medical laypersons. While Assange had still seemed relatively resilient during my visit in May 2019, I now began to seriously fear for his life. With increasing duration, the destabilization of the personality caused by psychological torture tends to accelerate in a regressive downward spiral towards total psychological and physical collapse. Either the victim abandons all physical and mental resistance and sinks into total confusion, neglect and apathy, or the process culminates in an often-life-threatening crisis event, such as a cardiovascular breakdown, a stroke, or a suicide attempt. In the autumn of 2019, the unmistakable evidence was that Julian Assange was fast approaching a point where his life was in acute danger. So it was clear to me that I needed to intervene, and I needed to do it now.

On 29 October 2019, I sent an urgent appeal to the British government, listing perceived due process violations, denouncing Assange's reported conditions of detention and calling for his immediate release or, at least, his transfer to an environment that would enable the protection of his health and human rights. The official letter was accompanied by a press statement, which I sent to the British ambassador in Geneva forty-eight hours in advance of its release on 1 November 2019, as required by our standard procedures. The purpose of this 'advance warning' is to give the concerned government time to point out errors and request amendments, and to prepare their own public response to any press requests they may receive.

However, the British ambassador did not reach out to my

office. Instead he went to see the high commissioner for human rights, Michelle Bachelet. I was told that, during their meeting, the ambassador expressed concern about the wording of my planned press release. In particular, he took issue with the title – 'UN expert on torture sounds alarm again that Julian Assange's life may be at risk' – and with my accusation of 'blatant and sustained arbitrariness shown by both the judiciary and the Government in this case'. In the view of the ambassador, these statements lacked the necessary impartiality. The ambassador also advised that Mr Assange was indeed receiving proper medical care and that he had access to his lawyers. In addition, I was informed that the 'issue of the Code of Conduct was also raised' – a thinly veiled warning making it clear that Britain's patience with me would not be endless.

The ambassador knew, of course, that he would not achieve anything by complaining to the high commissioner. Although her office provides my secretariat, she is not my superior and has no authority to direct my work. What counted was the gesture – not talking to me in my presence, but about me in my absence. And, as I would soon learn, not only with the high commissioner, but also with ambassadors of other UN member states. In this way, the question of British compliance with the prohibition of torture and ill-treatment suddenly morphed into a question of my personal compliance with the Code of Conduct for Special Procedures Mandate Holders.

The British strategy was blatant but not harmless. The same formula had already been used very effectively against countless other inconvenient messengers worldwide – including, of course, Assange himself. It was not by accident that the world no longer discussed the war crimes revealed by WikiLeaks, but only the person of Assange. But the ambassador's ominous invocation of the Code of Conduct would not intimidate me. Like any other independent expert or arbiter, I conduct my investigations observing the strictest standards of objectivity and impartiality. Once I have come to the conclusion that an act of torture has been committed, however, my task is not to be impartial between torturers and victims. Instead, I must cry foul and insist on justice, reparation and the rule of law. If the state in question cooperates, all of this can be done discreetly and diplomatically. But if a government refuses to engage in constructive dialogue and repeatedly violates its obligations in a serious way, then there is a point when I must make myself unpopular and mobilize the public. Anything else would make me a traitor to my mandate. Which is precisely why I am writing this book.

## The World's Doctors Take Action

My press release of 1 November 2019 did not miss its mark. Especially after the collapse of the Swedish rape narrative, the way was now clear to allow the demonized monster to become a human being again, an individual whose fate should be of concern to any responsible citizen. It was as if a curse had been lifted. Media interest increased steadily, and more and more people in different circles began to see through the contradictions of the official narrative. An important breakthrough came as early as 22 November 2019, a mere three days after the end of the Swedish investigation, when a group of sixty medical doctors – 'Doctors for Assange' – wrote an open letter to the British Home Office appealing to have Assange transferred from Belmarsh prison to a university hospital, where he could receive the care he needed. British Home Secretary Priti Patel did not respond directly but, three days later, her spokesperson made the following statement to the press: 'The allegations Mr Assange was subjected to torture are unfounded and wholly false. The UK is committed to upholding the rule of law, and ensuring that no one is ever above it.'

But public perceptions of British credibility had changed, and the doctors could no longer be appeased with such platitudes. They followed up with a second letter on 4 December 2019 which likewise remained unanswered. The group, which had grown to 117 medical doctors from eighteen countries, now decided to publish a public appeal in *The Lancet*, one of the world's most prestigious medical journals, in February 2020: 'Should Assange die in a UK prison, as the UN Special Rapporteur on Torture has warned, he will effectively have been tortured to death. Much of that torture will have taken place in a prison medical ward, on doctors' watch. The medical profession cannot afford to stand silently by, on the wrong side of torture and the wrong side of history, while such a travesty unfolds.'

In parallel, in an open correspondence with the Australian government between December and March 2020, the doctors exposed the formalistic prevarications of the Australian authorities with hard facts and unequivocally demanded that Australia finally use its considerable political clout to protect its citizen. The doctors also raised the particular danger to prison inmates posed by the Corona pandemic, which was just beginning to break out on a global scale. But as soon as it became clear that the doctors would not be satisfied with the usual half-hearted bromides coming from Canberra, the Australian government ceased to respond.

Nevertheless, the doctors had already achieved a great deal. They had rocked the boat in the medical community and ensured that the case of Julian Assange was perceived not just as a question of individual fate, but as a failure of systemic proportions in which the principles of medical ethics were disregarded with the same contempt as the rule of law. A second appeal in *The Lancet*, on the occasion of International Torture Victims Day on 26 June 2020, displayed over 250 signatures of medical professionals from thirty-five countries. It was clear that a critical mass had now been reached, the tide had turned and the momentum – however small – had started picking up. Assange's supporters would no longer be muzzled and were increasingly able to influence perceptions and opinions in politics, the media and, through this, the general public.

# 14

# Anglo-American
# Show Trial

## The Show Trial Begins

The trial for Assange's extradition to the United States began on
24 February 2020. The public gallery at Woolwich Crown Court,
next to Belmarsh prison, only has space for sixteen observers.
To get one of these coveted seats, people started queuing outside
the courthouse in the cold and wet February weather before
dawn. However, even those lucky, determined and organized
enough to end up first in line when the doors finally opened
could be arbitrarily denied access without explanation. Thus, on
the second day of the trial, WikiLeaks editor-in-chief Kristinn
Hrafnsson was about to enter the public gallery when a court
official called out his name and function and informed him that
the judge had decided to exclude him from the hearing. It was
only when Assange's family members threatened to leave the
courtroom in protest that Hrafnsson was allowed to enter.

Representatives of the press had to observe the trial by video
link from an adjoining room. The quality of the transmission
was appalling. Throughout the morning of the first day, the legal
counsel for the prosecution, James Lewis, was barely audible,
and Judge Baraitser could not be heard at all. In the course of the

trial, it would become increasingly difficult to escape the impression that the eyes and ears of the public were not welcome in Baraitser's courtroom. Given the excessively obstructive restrictions imposed on Assange, it almost looked like she would have preferred to exclude the defendant himself from his own court hearing. Like a violent criminal, Assange was locked inside a box made of bulletproof glass that was placed in the back of the courtroom, away from his lawyers. During the hearing, he was not allowed to receive any documents from his lawyers, to pass notes to them, or even to shake their hands through the narrow slit in the glass front.

From inside the glass box, Assange had difficulties hearing what was being said in the courtroom. When he repeatedly signalled the problem to Judge Baraitser, she blamed it on the background noise made by demonstrators outside the building, even though this could be heard only faintly inside the courtroom. When Assange tried to speak, Baraitser cut him off and insisted he could only be heard through his defence counsel. But when his defence counsel asked the judge to allow that Assange sit with his lawyers during the hearing, which would have enabled him to give proper instructions, she refused the request, claiming with a straight face that this would be tantamount to a release from custody, which could only be considered in the framework of a formal bail application. In order to appear in court, Assange was reportedly strip-searched twice, handcuffed a total of eleven times and locked up in five different holding cells – all in a single day. Moreover, the prison management seized all his court documents, including confidential material from his lawyers, thus depriving him of his last means of defence.

When Assange's defence counsel protested in court that these obstructive conditions severely jeopardized due process, the arbitrariness had become so blatant that even the prosecution counsel, James Lewis, stood up to assert that he wanted Assange to have a fair trial, that he was not convinced a bail application was required to allow Assange to sit with his legal counsel, and that it would be standard practice for the judge to intervene with the prison authorities in order to ensure due process. But

Baraitser was not swayed. She insisted that she had no jurisdiction over the prison authorities and refused to allow Assange to leave his glass box. After all, she said in all earnest, he might pose a danger to the public – it was a question of health and safety. Overall, it appeared that, to Judge Baraitser, Assange's presence was a nuisance at best, and a welcome opportunity to intimidate and humiliate him at worst. Either way, given the political importance of this case, it seems inconceivable that she would have so openly disregarded due process without instruction, consent, or acquiescence from above.

The unfolding travesty of justice later prompted the International Bar Association's Human Rights Institute (IBAHRI) to issue an unusually harsh press release: '[IBAHRI] condemns the reported mistreatment of Julian Assange during his United States extradition trial in February 2020, and urges the government of the United Kingdom to take action to protect him. ... It is deeply shocking that as a mature democracy in which the rule of law and the rights of individuals are preserved, the UK Government has been silent and has taken no action to terminate such gross and disproportionate conduct by Crown officials. As well, we are surprised that the presiding judge has reportedly said and done nothing to rebuke the officials and their superiors for such conduct in the case of an accused whose offence is not one of personal violence. Many countries in the world look to Britain as an example in such matters. On this occasion, the example is shocking and excessive.' The press release concluded with a reference to my official statement to the UN Human Rights Council in Geneva of 28 February 2020, when I had presented my annual report explicitly citing Assange's years of cruel, inhuman, and degrading treatment by the United Kingdom, Sweden, Ecuador and the United States as a concrete example of psychological torture.

During the next four days, the prosecution and the defence delivered their opening arguments. Assange's barristers submitted various bundles of evidence aiming to disprove the facts alleged by the prosecution and delivered legal arguments both orally and in writing. In essence, their reasoning against

Assange's extradition to the United States can be summarized in four principal arguments.

First, counsel argued that the decision to prosecute Assange was politically motivated, and that seventeen of the eighteen counts of the US indictment concerned espionage, which is the classic textbook example of a political offence. Given that the Anglo-American extradition treaty expressly prohibits extraditions for political offences, Assange could not lawfully be surrendered to the United States. Second, during his asylum at the Ecuadorian embassy, Assange had been systematically surveilled, and notably his confidential conversations with his lawyers were recorded by agents cooperating with US intelligence services. This constituted such a serious abuse of process, that it rendered the entire extradition proceeding irreparably arbitrary. Third, no person could be lawfully extradited to a state when such extradition would have to be regarded as oppressive. If extradited to the United States, there was a real risk that Assange would be exposed to a flagrant denial of justice both at trial and at the sentencing stage, that he could receive a grossly excessive sentence of up to 175 years in prison, and that he would be subjected to cruel, inhuman and degrading detention conditions, all of which set an insurmountable bar against his extradition. Fourth, based on the requirement of dual criminality, Assange's extradition to the United States can be permissible only if the offence for which his extradition is sought is punishable in both the US and the UK. This raised the question of whether the activity Assange is accused of – namely, 'unauthorized obtaining, receiving and disclosure of National Defense Information' – can constitute a criminal offence at all, particularly in view of the public interest in having that information disclosed, and of the protection of the freedom of expression under both international and domestic law.

For the prosecution, James Lewis began by focusing strongly on distinguishing Assange's alleged offences from journalistic work protected by the freedom of expression and stressing that Assange's prosecution did not create any precedent for the criminalization of mainstream journalism. Lewis emphasized that

Assange was not being prosecuted for responsible journalism but for endangering the lives of informants by publishing their unredacted names, for conspiring with Chelsea Manning to attempt computer intrusion and for causing her to unlawfully provide him with national defence information.

According to observers, during this initial segment of his argument, Lewis did not address the judge, but primarily spoke to the media representatives. At one point, he even repeated a sentence, explaining that it was important to make sure the journalists had understood his point. The prosecution had even prepared handouts for the journalists in printed and electronic form, which facilitated cut-and-paste reporting in line with US positions. As Lewis was doubtlessly aware, journalists, too, are human and therefore tend to choose the path of least resistance. Apart from that, the fact that Lewis did not appear to find it necessary to convince the judge of his arguments suggests that the United States was not worried about the position of the British judiciary but was primarily concerned with avoiding negative headlines by reassuring and appeasing the mainstream press. By and large, the established media seemed to take the bait and obediently reported on the superficial 'he said, she said' played out in court, rather than decrying the disembowelment of justice and the rule of law occurring right there in front of their eyes. None of WikiLeaks' former media partners involved in publishing the sensational leaks of 2010 and 2011 had the courage to protest the blatant arbitrariness with which Assange was being hounded and abused for the sins they had committed together with him. Even the venerable BBC, once the mouthpiece of the free world, took the easy way out and made sure to miss the forest for the trees.

Lewis subsequently went to great lengths to demonstrate that, in line with the requirement of 'dual criminality', each of the actions taken by Assange would be punishable not only under the US Espionage Act, but also under the British Official Secrets Acts, an equally archaic piece of legislation criminalizing the possession and disclosure of official secrets without giving the accused the right to raise a public interest defence.

The prosecution also tried to deny that, if punishable at all, Assange's publications could constitute a political offence barred from being grounds for extradition. Lewis offered two rather far-fetched reasons for this conclusion. First, WikiLeaks lacked a political motivation, because the organization did not seek to overthrow the US government or to persuade it to change its policies. Second, Assange was not physically present in the United States when he published the Afghan War Diary, the Iraq War Logs and CableGate.

Both arguments were unconvincing, to say the least. Leaving aside the plainly absurd issue of government overthrow, any interview with Julian Assange would have provided ample evidence for his political motivation as an activist promoting policy change towards achieving peace, truth and transparency. Moreover, from a legal perspective, there is absolutely no reason why the extraterritoriality of Assange's activities should prevent their characterization as 'political', particularly given that the United States claims extraterritorial criminal jurisdiction over the exact same activities. Apparently growing concerned over the weakness of the prosecution's reasoning, Judge Baraitser at the end of the second day hastened to equip Lewis with an alternative argument, which he gratefully adopted.

According to the judge, while the Anglo-American extradition treaty ratified in 2007 indeed prohibited extraditions for political offences, the British Extradition Act of 2003, based on which the Anglo-American treaty had been concluded, did not. In a fit of judicial acrobatics reminiscent of the British Supreme Court's decision on the Swedish extradition request in 2012, albeit inverting its contortionist logic, Baraitser then argued that the British courts could not apply the Anglo-American treaty, because it was an international agreement and not part of English domestic law. In deciding on the US extradition request for Assange, the British judiciary could therefore only rely on the British Extradition Act, which did not contain a political offence exclusion.

It was almost surreal: whereas the Supreme Court ruled in 2012 that the British Extradition Act must necessarily be interpreted in line with the United Kingdom's international obligations under the EU Framework Decision, and then freely invented an interpretation that was neither required nor proposed by that instrument, Judge Baraitser now found that the same Extradition Act could under no circumstances be interpreted in line with the United Kingdom's international obligations under the Anglo-American extradition treaty, which expressly prohibits extraditions for political offences. As a matter of juridical logic, both decisions are equally unsustainable and seem to unscrupulously instrumentalize judicial power for the achievement of a desired political outcome.

Accurately understood, the British Extradition Act is simply an 'enabling' act, which authorizes the British government to conclude extradition treaties with other states, but – in accordance with the longstanding principle 'no treaty, no extradition' – cannot serve as a direct basis for individual extradition requests. While bilateral or multilateral treaties may not be more permissive than the enabling act on which they are based, for example by interpreting the term 'judicial authority' more expansively, they can be more restrictive and, for example, contain a 'political offences' exclusion.

Therefore, the British Extradition Act clearly restricted the interpretation of the term 'judicial authority' in the EU Framework Decision, on which the Swedish request of 2010 was based, while the implementation of the Extradition Act is just as clearly restricted by the 'political offence' exclusion in Art. 4 of the Anglo-American treaty, on which the US extradition request is based. In fact, if the Anglo-American treaty could not be applied by the British courts, as asserted by Judge Baraitser, then the US extradition request itself would lack a valid legal basis and would have to be dismissed without further consideration. No treaty, no extradition!

After four days of opening arguments, the evidential hearing was initially adjourned until 18 May 2020. Shortly thereafter, the COVID-19 pandemic hit Europe and required a second adjournment until 7 September 2020.

## Pandemic and Second Superseding Indictment

In May 2020, only the United States registers more deaths from COVID-19 than the United Kingdom. After many years of government-enforced austerity, the resulting depletion of the British public health care system comes back to bite. Clinics and institutions lack everything: protective gowns, masks, gloves, corona tests. Thousands of patients lose their lives and even healthcare workers are paying the ultimate price. Among the most vulnerable groups, along with the elderly, are those with pre-existing respiratory health conditions. The risk of contracting COVID-19 also increases wherever social distancing rules cannot be observed and adequate medical care is not guaranteed. Thus, shelters, migrant reception centres, and prisons become places of high risk.

On 26 June 2020 – International Torture Victims Day – the 'Doctors for Assange' group launch their second public appeal in the medical journal *The Lancet*: 'Mr Assange is at grave risk from contracting COVID-19. As he is non-violent, being held on remand, and arbitrarily detained according to the UN Working Group on Arbitrary Detention, he meets internationally recommended criteria for prisoner release during COVID-19. A bail application with a plan for monitored home detention was refused, however, and Mr Assange is held in solitary confinement for 23 h each day.' Stella Moris, Assange's partner and mother of their two young sons, later confirms that, in case of a temporary release, Assange would have been accommodated with her and their children. But her hopes are dashed. With the onset of the pandemic, the prison goes into lockdown and prohibits all external visits, reducing Assange's contact with the outside world to short, strictly regulated and monitored phone calls.

The lockdown restrictions also pose a major problem for Assange's legal team, as the ban on personal visits severely jeopardizes their ability to prepare for the extensive evidential hearing scheduled to begin on 7 September 2020. To make matters worse, without prior notice, the US Department of Justice publishes a second superseding indictment on 24 June

2020. This supersedes the previous superseding indictment of 23 May 2019 which, in turn, had superseded the original indictment of 6 March 2018. While the eighteen counts of May 2019 remain unchanged, the underlying description of facts has once more significantly expanded: from a mere six pages in 2018, to thirty-seven pages in 2019, and now to a total of forty-eight pages. The factual allegations of the 2020 indictment no longer focus primarily on the reception and publication of leaked material and, thus, on genuinely journalistic activities. Instead, they describe in detail Assange's alleged contacts with certain hacker groups, which he is accused to have incited to steal and deliver classified information.

Strikingly, most of these contacts are alleged to have taken place after 2010 and, therefore, cannot possibly be related to the Manning leaks upon which all eighteen counts of the indictment are based. From a prosecutorial perspective, the inclusion of these allegations only makes sense if the United States intends, at a convenient time in the future, to further expand the charges against Assange. The likely aim would be to add a greater number of computer crimes and related conspiracy and incitement charges that are not protected by press freedom. After a US federal judge dismissed the Democratic Party's lawsuit against Assange and others over the DNC leaks in July 2019 based on press freedom, it would not be surprising if the government sought to expand its own indictment against Assange to activities lying outside the protective scope of the First Amendment of the US constitution. Moreover, the new hacking allegations probably also aim to appease the press and influence public opinion by portraying Assange as a sleazy 'hacktivist' who has nothing in common with a 'real' journalist.

One year later, in an interview given to the Icelandic newspaper *Stundin* in June 2021, a key source for these new allegations will retract their veracity. Named 'Teenager' in the 2020 indictment, the witness is a diagnosed sociopath with criminal convictions for numerous instances of fraud, forgery, theft and sexual abuse of minors. He admits to having fabricated false allegations against Assange for the 2020 indictment in return for a generalized non-prosecution agreement for himself with the FBI and the US Department of Justice. Revealingly, although the story has been meticulously researched and consolidated with reliable evidence, it is not picked up by any of the mainstream media in the United States, the United Kingdom or Australia.

But for the time being we are still in late June 2020, one year before the 'Teenager's' admission of false testimony. The timing of the submission of the second superseding indictment can only be described as deliberately obstructive. Initially, it is published exclusively on the official website of the US Department of Justice. Although it is an absolutely fundamental legal document for the extradition proceeding, the new indictment is transmitted to the British authorities only a full month later, on 29 July 2020. By then, the evidential hearing is a mere five weeks away and the deadline set for Assange's defence team to submit evidence for these hearings has passed one week earlier. The United States' new extradition request that must be drafted based on the new indictment arrives another two weeks later, on 12 August. Finally, on 21 August, the United States transmits an addendum clarifying that, in considering the extradition request, the British court should also take into account the facts newly asserted in the second superseding indictment.

As expected, Assange's lawyers object and point out that this new and untimely submission deprives them of any fair possibility to adequately prepare for the evidential hearing. When the judge offers to adjourn the case for several months, Assange's lawyers initially decline, because it would be unfair to keep him in prison for several additional months while his health continues to deteriorate due to the extremely restrictive detention conditions. Instead, they request that new factual allegations submitted by the US government should be excluded from the Court's deliberations, because the deadline for the completion of the US extradition request had passed more than a year prior to the submission of the new indictment.

But Judge Baraitser seems to have found a more convenient solution. She does not exclude the new factual allegations of the United States as a late submission related to the original extradition request but appears to treat them as the basis for a separate, entirely new extradition request. Accordingly, when the evidential hearing begins on 7 September 2020, she writes off the 2019 extradition warrant, releases Assange and immediately re-arrests him based on the new 2020 extradition warrant. Inexplicably, however, Baraitser nevertheless insists on the procedural deadlines set in relation to the previous extradition request and, therefore, does not allow Assange's defence lawyers to submit any evidence whatsoever in response to the new factual allegations made in the new US indictment. Faced with the absurd situation of being prevented by the judge herself from fulfilling their function as defence attorneys, Assange's lawyers now have no other choice but to request the adjournment of the case until January 2021 that had been previously proposed by the judge. To their surprise, however, Baraitser has now changed her mind: no adjournment!

## The Show Trial Continues

And so the show trial pursues its course. This time, the hearings take place in central London, in the Central Criminal Court known as the Old Bailey, near St Paul's. Even here, however, Judge Baraitser succeeds in almost completely excluding the public from her courtroom. The social distancing rules of the COVID-19 pandemic now serve as a welcome excuse to admit only five persons into the public gallery. Once admitted, however, social distancing rules no longer apply. All five observers are seated perilously close together in one row of seats, whereas two additional rows of seats remain empty. Three additional seats are reserved for representatives of the Australian diplomatic representation in London – the Australian High Commission. They remain vacant throughout the entire hearing. It seems the Australian diplomats have more important things to do than to follow the fate of their national.

Just as in February in Belmarsh, journalists, NGOs and other observers are asked to follow the proceedings in an adjoining room via video transmission. Just as in February in Belmarsh, the quality of sound and image is appalling. And just as in February in Belmarsh, this is not happening in a technologically backward province of a developing country, but in the heart of the British capital. By now, Judge Baraitser no longer even pretends that she is interested in public scrutiny. On the very first day of the hearing, she unceremoniously revokes the video link access granted to some forty officially registered trial observers from the European Parliament and human rights organizations such as Amnesty International and Reporters Without Borders. According to Baraitser, in this case, such remote access is not 'in the interest of justice'. Both the European parliamentarians and Amnesty International repeatedly intervene with the judge in the following days, reminding her that independent trial observation is an essential prerequisite of the rule of law. However, Baraitser declines to reconsider. The fact that, in terms of procedural transparency, the British judiciary now officially falls behind Guantánamo, Bahrain and Turkey, where Amnesty International has been admitted to observe trials, does not seem to bother the judge at all.

During the hearing, several dozen defence witnesses are set to testify, both in court and remotely. Unsurprisingly, the video and audio connection of those testifying remotely is disastrous: the video image fails repeatedly; audio files are not played back properly; and the timeline increasingly veers out of control. Despite strong objections from the defence team, Baraitser decides that witness statements that have already been submitted to the court in writing are not to be repeated in the oral hearing. This requires journalists and other observers wishing to understand and publicly report on the relevant evidence to separately research the written submissions beforehand – for most of them, predictably, this is a bridge too far.

Having thus reduced the risk of effective public scrutiny to almost zero, Judge Baraitser now starts moving the goalposts regarding the evidence itself. First, she rules that defence witnesses may be cross-examined by the prosecution at length, while prosecution witnesses who are employed by the US government may not be cross-examined by the defence attorneys at all. Second, in response to a US government request, she obediently declares the famous 'Collateral Murder' video and any other evidence detailing US war crimes and torture as inadmissible. Third, while the judge cannot reasonably disallow the testimony of the German-Lebanese torture victim Khaled El-Masri, which the US government has vehemently tried to prevent, his statement is made technically impossible, supposedly by an unfortunate breakdown of the video connection. However, unlike other witnesses who had experienced comparable technical difficulties, El-Masri is not given the opportunity to testify on a later date. Even though it is true that this proceeding is not about prosecuting war crimes, the reality of these crimes and the total impunity granted to the perpetrators and their superiors are important factual circumstances explaining not only Assange's motivation for their publication, but also the reasons for his relentless persecution by the United States.

Next, Baraitser decides to prevent any personal participation of Assange in the hearing, presumably because his voice and statements might have reminded the few souls left in the courtroom of his humanity and desperation. So, the judge once again keeps him locked away behind bulletproof glass, far from his lawyers. She also reiterates her gag order for Assange, insisting that he may not speak in person, but may only participate in the proceedings through his lawyers. When on one occasion Assange cannot help but exclaim 'nonsense' in response to a statement made by the prosecutor, Baraitser immediately threatens to have him removed from the courtroom if he should dare to open his mouth again.

Just as in a dictatorial show trial, the choreography of this proceeding seems predetermined and must be strictly observed. Any human emotion, inconvenient truth, or other unforeseen factor that could alter the outcome must be immediately suppressed. Nevertheless, to those who know him, Assange's agony and exhaustion are perceptible even through the bulletproof walls of his cage. Each day of the hearing, early in the morning, he is strip-searched, X-rayed, handcuffed and moved to a holding cell before being shipped to court, standing upright in a claustrophobically narrow prison transport van for ninety minutes in each direction.

As a professor of law at a British university, I have been profoundly shocked, in a politically prominent case like this, to see the British judiciary dehumanize the defendant; refuse to admit evidence of central importance to the defence; disregard fundamental principles of due process; and almost completely exclude the public from the courtroom. The fact that this travesty of justice did not prompt the entire defence team to leave the courtroom in protest, that it did not trigger a public outcry in the established media, and that the political leadership seemed to be content with Assange undergoing a show trial more redolent of an authoritarian regime than a mature democracy, shows how far British society has already become desensitized to the formal requirements and practical importance of the rule of law.

## The Evidential Hearing

In the course of the evidential hearing, which lasted from 7 September to 1 October 2020, it became devastatingly clear why Judge Baraitser had done everything to exclude the public from her courtroom and suppress any form of effective scrutiny by the media, civil society and international observers. Every day, one by one, witness testimonies and expert reports systematically dismantled the legal and factual building blocks of the entire US case against Assange, leaving nothing but the plain proof of a ruthless political persecution.

Much of the factual and legal evidence brought during the hearing has already been discussed elsewhere in this book and will not be repeated here. Nevertheless, to enable full appreciation of the flagrancy with which the rule of law is being violated in this case, it is nevertheless important to provide an overview of the most important topics and how they were addressed in context.

The most decisive issue discussed during the evidential hearing was without doubt Assange's physical and mental health. Numerous witnesses commented on this question, including Dr Sondra Crosby, who had examined Assange five times, both at the Ecuadorian embassy and at Belmarsh, and whose medical report to the Office of the High Commissioner for Human Rights had contributed decisively to triggering my own involvement in the case. Another important witness was Professor Michael Kopelman, an experienced psychiatrist who had visited Assange a total of nineteen times at Belmarsh and had traced his medical history back to his youth in Australia. Kopelman warned of severe depression; post-traumatic stress disorder (PTSD); anxiety disorder and traits of autism spectrum disorder (ASD); resulting in acute suicidal tendencies: 'I am as certain as a psychiatrist ever can be that, in the event of imminent extradition, Mr Assange would indeed find a way to commit suicide.' Other experts also diagnosed him with depression and Asperger's. The overall picture was that of a person who, despite remarkable resilience, had suffered massively from years of persecution and isolation, and who was determined to avoid extradition through suicide. In responding for the prosecution, James Lewis tried to downplay concerns over Assange's state of health and to undermine the credibility of witnesses and evidence. He also repeatedly insinuated that Assange was malingering or exaggerating his symptoms in order to induce a diagnosis that would help him avoid extradition, but was unable to provide any evidence supporting these claims.

Lewis then turned his attention to my own official letter to the British government of 27 May 2019, which he knew could not reasonably be omitted from the record of the hearing. He did so conveniently while cross-examining medical doctors as witnesses for the defence, who were not human rights experts competent to examine the accuracy of my legal findings. Without any explanation as to my mandate and function, Lewis read out several pages of my letter in court, predominantly non-medical passages relating to due process violations and persecutorial collusion between the involved states. In doing so, he made sure to impress on the mind of the witnesses his unreserved indignation at my unflattering observations. Lewis then tried to manipulate the medical experts into agreeing that my legal and factual findings were 'neither balanced nor accurate' and not 'worthy of reliance in any part'. The witnesses realized, of course, that as medical doctors they could not be expected to judge the accuracy of my legal conclusions and prudently limited themselves to concurring with the medical findings of the two doctors who had accompanied my visit to Belmarsh.

When he did not succeed in getting the medical experts to discredit my legal findings, Lewis skilfully tricked them into referring to the non-medical passages of my letter as 'political' (rather than 'legal'), simply by putting the desired word into their mouths. Sensing the danger but missing the fine print, the doctors wisely declined to give a substantive opinion on the 'political passages'. In reality, of course, official communications transmitted by UN human rights experts are of an exclusively legal, never political, nature, and therefore are directly relevant for the legal determinations to be made in court. By characterizing my findings as 'political', the prosecution sought to dismiss their relevance for the legal questions put before the court, and Judge Baraitser gratefully played along. Lewis concluded the matter by summarily dismissing my observations as 'obvious, palpable nonsense' – conveniently in my absence, without risking that I might substantiate my unwelcome findings under cross-examination. Judge Baraitser apparently found no fault in Lewis's manipulative and plainly offensive dismissal of the official findings submitted by a UN Special Rapporteur based on a prison visit and medical examination conducted upon invitation of the British government.

Moving on to a different topic, several experts confirmed that Assange's fear of disappearing into a US Supermax prison for the rest of his life was by no means irrational. Even the prosecution witnesses acknowledged the real risk that, if extradited to the United States, Assange would be held under Special Administrative Measures (SAMs) both during pre-trial detention and while serving his sentence. In effect, that meant total isolation from any interpersonal contact. Strikingly, the discussion in court on SAMs focused primarily on whether, in view of Assange's state of health, these conditions of detention should necessarily – or only possibly – have to be considered as 'oppressive' and, thus, as violating the prohibition of torture and ill-treatment. The prosecution argued that it could not be predicted with certainty whether Assange would indeed be subjected to SAMs. Moreover, even if SAMs were imposed, they would be periodically reviewed by the attorney general with a view to their possible mitigation or termination. Therefore, should Assange's extradition be granted, neither the risk of inhuman treatment nor the likelihood of suicide could be reliably predicted. It was a feeble attempt to undermine overwhelming evidence that the detention regime awaiting Assange in the United States was utterly incompatible with the absolute and universal prohibition of torture and other cruel, inhuman or degrading treatment or punishment.

A particularly shocking revelation was the extreme intrusiveness of Assange's surveillance inside the Ecuadorian embassy, as well as the fact that the Spanish security company UC Global, which had been contracted to guard the embassy, had worked for a US intelligence agency behind the back of its primary client, the Ecuadorian government. As became apparent, UC Global's cooperation with US intelligence included not only the systematic audio and video surveillance of Assange's confidential meetings with lawyers, doctors and private visitors, but went much further. Written witness statements by former UC Global employees confirmed, among other things, that plans had been drawn up to leave the embassy doors open so that agents from the outside could enter and kidnap or poison Assange.

While Lewis dismissed these testimonies, too, as 'completely irrelevant', their legal significance for the extradition proceeding cannot be overstated. Apart from the obvious criminality of any plan to kidnap or murder Assange, his secret surveillance at the behest of the US government constitutes such a grave violation of due process principles, attorney–client confidentiality, doctor–patient confidentiality, and personal privacy that the entire case affected by it, including both the US prosecution and the related extradition request, can only be dismissed as irreparably arbitrary.

A central argument of Assange's defence team against his extradition and prosecution for his publishing activities remained his right to freedom of expression and freedom of the press. Trevor Timm, defence witness and executive director of the Freedom of the Press Foundation, pointed to the Watergate scandal. At the time, in the early 1970s, the corruption within the Nixon administration was only exposed because investigative journalists Bob Woodward and Carl Bernstein of the *Washington Post* could pursue their work without fearing that their revelations would be prosecuted as espionage. Another witness, the attorney and activist Carey Shenkman, emphasized the frequency with which classified material is being deliberately leaked by US government agencies themselves in order to influence public opinion. Needless to say, none of these leaks have ever resulted in criminal prosecution.

Even Daniel Ellsberg, by now almost ninety years old, gave testimony. Famously charged with espionage for blowing the whistle in the 1971 Pentagon Papers case, Ellsberg insisted that the WikiLeaks publications were protected under the First Amendment of the US Constitution. This followed from the US Supreme Court's landmark ruling in the Pentagon Papers case, which had reaffirmed and strengthened press freedom and the public's right to know. As a matter of logic, if Assange could be charged with espionage for publishing classified documents, then the same had to apply to WikiLeaks' media partners, first and foremost the *New York Times*, the *Guardian*, *Der Spiegel*, *El País* and *Le Monde*. But this would be a frontal attack on press freedom and the precedent set by the Supreme Court in 1971. This dilemma, the so-called '*New York Times* problem', was what had persuaded the Obama administration not to prosecute Assange.

Addressing the related allegations that Assange had 'conspired' with Chelsea Manning to violate her duty of non-disclosure, numerous defence witnesses confirmed that it is part and parcel of any investigative journalist's daily routine to solicit sources and encourage them to share evidence, even if the information is classified as secret. Journalists also have a duty to take active source protection measures that make the identification of whistleblowers more difficult or even impossible. Adopting the same position as US federal judge Koeltl in his 2019 dismissal of the DNC lawsuit against Assange and others, they argue that the line towards criminality is only crossed once journalists themselves participate in the act of data theft, for example by illegally penetrating a protected computer system in order to obtain secret information. But that is not what Assange is accused of. His source, Chelsea Manning, already had full access to all the leaked information. Instead, Assange was alleged to have tried – unsuccessfully – to help Manning crack a password hash that would have allowed her to log into the same system under a different identity and, thus, to cover her tracks within that system. This was a typical source protection measure and could not be regarded as aiding and abetting, or incitement, of a computer crime. There was therefore no legal or factual basis for the US conspiracy charges brought against Assange.

Importantly, it was made clear that the right to freedom of opinion and expression is not restricted to journalists, but applies to anyone, so that the eternal discussion as to whether or not Assange can be regarded as a 'proper' journalist has never had any real legal relevance. Juridically unsustainable, too, is the argument made by the Trump administration that Assange, having acted as a foreigner abroad, is not entitled to constitutional freedom of expression protections, but that he can nevertheless be prosecuted under the US Espionage Act for the same conduct. If nothing else, this demonstrates that, in the event of his extradition to the United States, Assange would not be guaranteed effective human rights protection.

Numerous witnesses also refuted allegations that Assange had knowingly endangered human lives by publishing the unredacted names of local informants and collaborators of the United States, thereby exposing them to acts of revenge. Although, to this day, the US government has not succeeded in producing any reliable evidence to that effect, the 'put-lives-at-risk' narrative is one of the oldest, most die-hard myths surrounding the WikiLeaks publications. Already at the trial of Chelsea Manning in 2013, the

US Department of Defense explicitly acknowledged that it had 'no concrete example' of any individual having suffered harm or being exposed to a serious threat as a consequence of the WikiLeaks publications. Seven years on, at the evidential hearing in London in September 2020, nothing had changed.

On the other hand, numerous journalists and other witnesses expressly confirmed that Assange had handled sensitive data responsibly. For example, John Sloboda of the Iraq Body Count project and former *Der Spiegel* journalist John Goetz had both been involved in the publication of the Iraq War Logs in 2010. Now they recalled the irritation of WikiLeaks' established media partners when Assange insisted that Iraqi names be filtered out of the documents and redacted before publication. Australian journalist Nicky Hager then formally made the point that it was not Assange, but two *Guardian* journalists, who had first made the unredacted CableGate documents accessible to the public.

The story is well known. In their book, *WikiLeaks: Inside Julian Assange's War on Secrecy*, published in February 2011, Luke Harding and David Leigh of the *Guardian* revealed the password that Assange had confidentially shared with his media partners enabling them to access and work on the unredacted material which had been stored in a single backup file at various locations on the internet. Another journalist, at the German weekly *Der Freitag*, had detected the location of the file and, with the password published by Leigh and Harding, was able to access and download a full copy of the original unredacted material. Instead of keeping this information confidential, *Der Freitag* published the scoop in late August 2011, providing sufficient information to make the unredacted CableGate file accessible to any interested party. *Der Freitag*'s editor-in-chief Jakob Augstein, also a defence witness, confirmed that Assange had personally urged them not to go public with this information and had expressed concern that individuals named in the unredacted documents might be exposed to harm. A full audio recording of a phone conversation between Assange and his contacts at the US State Department, which circulates on the internet, proves that Assange immediately informed the US government of the security leak and recommended urgent harm reduction measures for the protection of individuals that might be put at risk – a far cry from the image of the reckless narcissist 'with blood on his hands' that has been fed to the public.

The objective chronology of the unredacted CableGate publication was scientifically reconstructed by expert witness Christian Grothoff, professor of computer science in Switzerland. His meticulous report provides irrefutable technical evidence that Assange had published the original unredacted material only after it had already been made publicly available, against his will, by Leigh and Harding, in conjunction with *Der Freitag*. This demonstrated that WikiLeaks was not the original publisher, but only the re-publisher of the unredacted CableGate file, and that the responsibility for any harm or threat resulting from its unredacted publication could not be attributed to Assange. The fact that neither the two *Guardian* journalists nor *Der Freitag* were ever held accountable for their conduct is a clear indication that the 'put-lives-at-risk' narrative was deliberately misused as just another tool to demonize Assange, and to divert attention from the inconvenient content of the leaked documents.

## The Screaming Silence of the Press

The strong support and solidarity that Assange has received from journalists testifying in court stands in stark contrast to the pervasive media silence outside the courtroom. By media silence I do not mean to say that nothing has been reported about Assange and his case, but that what has been reported has been largely irrelevant or missing the point.

Interestingly, the German language press became the first mainstream media to have a change of heart. Starting in 2019, papers such as the *Süddeutsche Zeitung* as well as the Swiss *Wochenzeitung* and *Sonntagsblick* prepared the ground. On 31 January 2020 my interview with the Swiss online paper *Republik* appeared – a first important breakthrough. Just in time for the beginning of Assange's extradition hearing three weeks later, it shocked with a concise summary of my investigative conclusions and with a few pieces of leaked correspondence illustrating the deliberate abuse of process against Assange. Supported by the relentless advocacy of countless activists, personalities, and organizations, a slow but steady change in public opinion was set in motion and kept gaining momentum.

German public broadcasters now reported not only on the latest developments in the extradition hearings, but increasingly also featured critical interviews, investigative documentaries, and in-depth analysis. In contrast to the gleeful malice which permeated media commentary following Assange's arrest in April 2019, journalists now started to express genuine concern about the implications of this case for press freedom and the rule of law. Thus, in September 2020, the *Süddeutsche Zeitung* wrote: 'In London, the United States' war on whistleblowers and their supporters is about to reach its climax so far. A war which will re-examine the limits of press freedom. This case will determine, among other things, what journalists will still be able to publish in the future – without fear of being prosecuted in the United States.' Slowly but surely, journalists began to understand that the trial of Julian Assange was not as much about Assange as it is about them. At Number 10 Downing Street, the organization Reporters Without Borders attempted to hand over a petition with 80,000 signatures, calling on the British government not to extradite Assange – but the authorities refused to receive the petition.

The established press in the US, UK and Australia, on the other hand, still does not seem to have understood the existential danger posed by the trial of Julian Assange to press freedom, due process, democracy and the rule of law. The painful truth is that, if only the main media organizations of the Anglosphere so decided, Assange's persecution could be ended tomorrow. The case of Ivan Golunov, a Russian investigative journalist specialized in exposing official corruption, may serve as a textbook example. When Golunov was suddenly arrested for alleged drug offences in the summer of 2019, the Russian mainstream press immediately saw through the game. 'We are Ivan Golunov' read the identical front pages of Russia's three leading dailies, *Vedomosti*, *RBC* and *Kommersant*. All three papers openly questioned the legality of Golunov's arrest, suspected that he was being persecuted for his journalistic activities, and demanded a thorough investigation. Caught in the act and exposed by the spotlight of their own mass media, the Russian authorities back-pedalled a few days later. President Putin made a point of personally ordering Golunov's release and dismissing two high-ranking Interior Ministry officials. If nothing else, this proved that Golunov's arrest had not been the result of misconduct on the part of a few incompetent police officers but had been orchestrated at the highest level.

Without a doubt, a comparable joint action of solidarity by the *Guardian*, the BBC, the *New York Times* and the *Washington Post* would put an immediate end to the persecution of Julian Assange. For if there is one thing governments fear, it is the unforgiving spotlight of the mass media and their critical scrutiny. But what is happening in the British, American and Australian mainstream media is simply too little, too late. As ever, their reporting continues to oscillate between tame and lame, obediently journaling the daily events in court without even grasping that what they are witnessing are the side effects of a monumental societal regression from the achievements of democracy and the rule of law back into the dark ages of absolutism and the 'arcana imperii' – a governance system based on secrecy and authoritarianism. A handful of half-hearted opinion pieces in the *Guardian* and the *New York Times* rejecting Assange's extradition are not bold enough, and so fail to convince. While both papers have timidly declared that convicting Assange of espionage would endanger press freedom, not a single mainstream media outlet protests the blatant violations of due process, human dignity and the rule of law that pervade the entire trial. None holds the involved governments to account for their crimes and corruption; none has the courage to confront political leaders with uncomfortable questions; none feels dutybound to inform and empower the people – a mere shadow of what was once the 'fourth estate'.

## My Last Appeals

In the weeks that followed until the end of November 2020, the prosecution and defence submitted their written closing statements. Assange remained isolated in Belmarsh prison. The seventh of December 2020 marked the tenth anniversary of Assange's first arrest by British police. On that day, I sent an urgent appeal to the British government, which was published the next morning: 'UN expert calls for immediate release of Assange after 10 years of arbitrary detention'. In the meantime, the COVID-19 pandemic had broken out at Belmarsh. For Assange, this posed an acute threat, as he suffered from a chronic respiratory disease and his resistance had been weakened for years. 'Mr Assange is not a criminal convict and poses no threat to anyone, so his prolonged solitary confinement in a high security prison is neither necessary nor proportionate and clearly lacks any legal basis', I wrote, clarifying that this detention regime, in view of its long duration, also violates the prohibition of torture and ill-treatment. I therefore called on the British government to immediately release Assange or place him under guarded house arrest, where he could lead a normal family, social, and professional life, recover his health, and prepare his defence in the US extradition proceedings. I concluded with an urgent appeal to the British authorities not to extradite Assange to the US under any circumstances, due to serious human rights concerns. Once more, the British government did not find it necessary or appropriate to respond.

By contrast, a group of fifteen members of the British Parliament, led by Richard Burgon and Jeremy Corbyn, granted me an online hearing on the Assange case on the evening of 8 December 2020. Based on my conclusions that Assange's human rights were being violated by the British authorities, the lawmakers sent a concerned letter to Secretary of State for Justice Robert Buckland on 16 December, requesting 'that provision be made to hold an online video discussion between Julian Assange and a cross-party group of UK parliamentarians' before the judicial decision on his extradition was made. The declared purpose of the meeting was to discuss with him his treatment and the wider implications of his case. But, once again, the executive branch demonstrated its disdain for Parliament. Six months later, in June 2021, Burgon wrote another letter to the governor of Belmarsh and Secretary Buckland, expressing strong frustration at 'the ongoing refusal of you and the Justice Secretary to allow an online video meeting between Julian Assange and a cross-party group of British parliamentarians … It is simply unacceptable that six months on this simple request continues to be met with such intransigence. You have the authority to grant such a meeting and we call on you to facilitate an online meeting without further delay.'

But, for now, we are still in December 2020, and Judge Baraitser has announced her decision on Assange's extradition to the United States for 4 January 2021. I assume that the date was set so late in order to allow British authorities to wait for the outcome of the US presidential election on 3 November 2020, and then tailor the extradition decision to the wishes of the winner. I was under no illusions about the prevailing power-political context. After all, following the completion of Brexit – the British exit from the European Union – by the end of the year, the United Kingdom would become completely dependent on its 'special relationship' with the United States and could not afford any disagreements on any issue of foreign policy. As noted by Alan Duncan, then British minister of state for Europe and the Americas, on 8 April 2019, three days before Assange's arrest: 'Everything we believe in is ultimately subordinated to our not wanting to clash with the US.' Accordingly, with the victory of Joe Biden over Donald Trump, the British government needed time to find out what Biden's position would be on the extradition of Assange after his inauguration on 20 January 2021.

But first, with the impending departure of Donald Trump, another possibility came into play: the presidential pardon. The US Constitution gives the president the power to grant a federal 'pardon' to defendants or convicts, or to shorten or commute a sentence, whether threatened or imposed. This prerogative can be exercised throughout the term of office, but pardons are traditionally concentrated in the last weeks of the presidency. Beginning in late November 2020, many celebrities began to speak out publicly, urging President Trump to pardon Assange, and I decided to make my own appeal as well. I thought it was worth a try, and at the same time it would allow me to reach out to the broader American public with a message that challenged the prevailing narrative about Assange. I wrote my open letter to President Trump on 21 December 2020, two years to the day after my own subconscious bias had led me to decline co-signing an appeal for the release of Assange together with my UN colleagues. Ironically, this time it was the other mandate holders who declined to co-sign. All of them. And so I was the only one to sign the following appeal to President Trump:

Mr. President,

Today, I respectfully request that you pardon Mr. Julian Assange. Mr. Assange has been arbitrarily deprived of his liberty for the past ten years. This is a high price to pay for the courage to publish true information about government misconduct throughout the world. I visited Mr. Assange in Belmarsh High Security Prison in London, with two independent medical doctors, and I can attest to the fact that his health has seriously deteriorated, to the point where his life is now in danger. Critically, Mr. Assange suffers from a documented respiratory condition which renders him extremely vulnerable to the COVID-19 pandemic that has recently broken out in the prison where he is being held.

I ask you to pardon Mr. Assange, because he is not, and has never been, an enemy of the American people. His organization, WikiLeaks, fights secrecy and corruption throughout the world, and, therefore, acts in the public interest both of the American people and of humanity as a whole. I ask because Mr. Assange has never published false information. The cause for any reputational harm that may have resulted from his publications is not to be found in any misconduct on his part, but in the very misconduct which he exposed. I ask because Mr. Assange has not hacked or

stolen any of the information he published. He has obtained it
from authentic documents and sources in the same way as any
other serious and independent investigative journalists conduct
their work. While we may personally agree or disagree with their
publications, they clearly cannot be regarded as crimes. I ask
because prosecuting Mr. Assange for publishing true information
about serious official misconduct, whether in America or
elsewhere, would amount to 'shooting the messenger' rather than
correcting the problem he exposed. This would be incompatible
with the core values of justice, rule of law and press freedom, as
reflected in the American Constitution and international human
rights instruments ratified by the United States. I ask because
you have vowed, Mr. President, to pursue an agenda of fighting
government corruption and misconduct; and because allowing
the prosecution of Mr. Assange to continue would mean that,
under your legacy, telling the truth about such corruption and
misconduct has become a crime.

In pardoning Mr. Assange, Mr. President, you would send a
clear message of justice, truth and humanity to the American
people and to the world. You would rehabilitate a courageous
man who has suffered injustice, persecution and humiliation for
more than a decade, simply for telling the truth. Last but not
least, you would give back to Mr. Assange's two young sons the
loving father they need and look up to. You would also reassure
these children, and through them all children of the world, that
there is nothing wrong with telling the truth, but that it is the
right thing to do; that it is honourable to fight for justice and,
indeed, that these are the values America and the world stand for.

For these reasons, I respectfully appeal to you to pardon Julian
Assange. Whatever our personal views and sympathies may be,
I believe that, after a decade of persecution, this man's unjust
suffering must end now. Please, use your power of pardon to
right the wrongs inflicted on Julian Assange, to end his unjust
ordeal and reunite him with his family! I respectfully thank
you for considering this appeal with foresight, generosity and
compassion.

And finally, on Sunday, 3 January 2021, the eve of the first instance verdict in the Anglo-American extradition trial, I published a short personal appeal to Judge Vanessa Baraitser, this time on Twitter for lack of official channels:

> Tomorrow you will render verdict on the extradition of Julian Assange. Today, from lawyer to lawyer, I would like to share with you a quote by the late Thomas Franck, which has inspired and guided me throughout my career as a legal professional. May Lady Justice be with you!
>
> 'What, then, is the proper role for the lawyer? Surely, it is to stand tall for the rule of law. What this entails is self-evident. When the policy makers believe it to society's immediate benefit to skirt the law, the lawyer must speak of the longer-term costs. When the politicians seek to bend the law, the lawyers must insist that they have broken it. When a faction tries to use power to subvert the rule of law, the lawyer must defend it even at some risk to personal advancement and safety. When the powerful are tempted to discard the law, the lawyer must ask whether someday, if our omnipotence wanes, we may not need the law. Lawyers who do that may even be called traitors. But those who do not are traitors to their calling.'

## Setting the Precedent: The Verdict of 4 January 2021

Finally, the day had come. It was 4 January, the first Monday of 2021. In Britain, the new year had started with alarming statistics on the COVID-19 pandemic: record numbers of new infections and unprecedented numbers of deaths. Nevertheless, once again outside the Old Bailey Assange's supporters had gathered long before sunrise to await the verdict in his extradition trial. Once again, the public was de facto excluded from the courtroom. Only a few observers had been granted access to an adjoining room from where they could follow the hearing through video link and keep the outside world informed through social media. Once again, they complained about poor audio quality. The problem was well known by now, and the authorities clearly had no intention to have it resolved.

Despite these difficulties, fragmentary messages kept trickling through, a new element every few minutes, and over the course of an hour coalesced into the usual picture of unconditional British compliance with US government interests. Step by step, even the most aberrant arguments advanced by the prosecution were unreservedly upheld. At the same time, almost as if in passing, Judge Baraitser dismissed even the most legitimate legal objections and even the strongest exculpatory evidence raised by the defence team.

The indictment and extradition request initiated by the United States: not politically motivated. The prohibition of extradition for political offences in Article 4 of the Anglo-American extradition treaty: not applicable. The surveillance of Assange in the Ecuadorian embassy and the wiretapping of his confidential conversations with medical doctors and lawyers: not objectionable. The impact of the threat of extradition on Assange's partner and their two children: nothing unusual. The trial awaiting him at the Espionage Court in Virginia: fair. The jury that would decide on his guilt or innocence: unbiased. Assange himself: a threat to US national security. Assange's publication of evidence for war crimes, torture and corruption: not protected by press freedom. Instead, according to Baraitser, Assange had actively assisted Chelsea Manning in obtaining classified documents, thereby well overstepping the bounds of investigative journalism. Moreover, he had endangered people because their names had not been redacted prior to publication. Therefore, Assange should not be considered a journalist, but simply a data thief and hacker. Finally, Assange's conduct was punishable not only under the US Espionage Act, but also under the British Official Secrets Act, thus meeting the extradition requirement of dual criminality. The judge completely ignored the fact that, in the course of the evidential hearing, every single allegation on which she based her argument had been proved unsustainable.

The Twitter posts from the observers were sounding increasingly fatalistic. A text message sent to me by one of Assange's lawyers summed things up: 'It's bad.' I had already given up hope and begun to focus on other things when suddenly a sentence leaped out at me from my computer screen, as if written all in caps: 'OH MY GOD.' Over the next few minutes, media posts and messages rushed by, snippets of words complemented and contradicted each other, nothing seemed to make any sense. I hastily clicked from one Twitter feed to another, eventually running five separate feeds across my screen at once, until finally there was clarity: 'Extradition denied!'

I couldn't believe my eyes. What had happened? For a few moments, there was complete silence. It was as if a meteorite had struck. Then cheers broke out outside the courthouse, the first explanations started to circulate, and soon the written verdict was published. Judge Baraitser had rejected the US extradition request on medical grounds. Based on the evidence provided by psychiatric experts on Assange's mental health, and by other expert witnesses on the reality of US detention conditions under Special Administrative Measures, Baraitser found that it would be oppressive to extradite Assange to the United States. 'It is my judgment that there is a real risk that he will be kept in the near isolated conditions imposed by the harshest SAMs regime, both pre-trial and post-trial. ... Mr Assange undoubtedly has the determination, planning and intelligence to circumvent ... suicide preventative measures. ... I am satisfied that, in these harsh conditions, Mr Assange's mental health would deteriorate causing him to commit suicide with the "single-minded determination" of his autism spectrum disorder. I find that the mental condition of Mr Assange is such that it would be oppressive to extradite him to the United States of America.'

I immediately had a flashback to a moment during my conversation with Assange, when he told me about the razor blade that had been found in his cell two days earlier, and made it unequivocally clear that he would not be extradited to the United States alive. This determination gave a very real and immediate meaning to Assange's departing appeal to me – 'Please, save my life!' However, I had never spoken about this publicly until Assange's lawyers decided to openly address his suicide risk during the evidential hearing in September 2020. In a way, the possibility of ending his own life was Assange's last resort to retain a modicum of control over his own destiny and to escape his utter dehumanization in US Supermax detention. I respected his human dignity too much to undermine this last refuge of his by exposing his plans.

With her verdict, the judge had confirmed my own findings in two respects. First, she acknowledged Assange's deplorable state of health, which we had diagnosed already during our visit to Belmarsh eighteen months earlier, and which had further deteriorated due to the constant exposure to arbitrariness and isolation. What Baraitser did not say, however, was that Assange's frailty was by no means his natural constitution, but a direct consequence of ten years of relentless persecution and mistreatment by Sweden, the United Kingdom, Ecuador and the United States. Second, the judge also confirmed the inherent inhumanity of the detention conditions likely to be imposed on Assange in a Supermax prison. In this context, Baraitser explicitly spoke of 'near total isolation', 'cages', and 'extreme conditions'. In doing so, the judge also acknowledged, at least implicitly, that Assange's permanent fear of extradition to the United States, his asylum at the Ecuadorian embassy, and his refusal to travel to Sweden without a non-refoulement guarantee, had been legally justified, and that he had been wrongly convicted and sentenced for bail violation.

From the perspective of my UN mandate, this was, of course, an accurate and welcome assessment. Nevertheless, I was under no illusions: the US, Britain, Sweden and Ecuador had not spent a decade and millions of dollars persecuting, defaming and spying on Assange, only to now set him free on humanitarian grounds. I therefore feared that, in truth, Baraitser's denial of extradition was not a victory of the rule of law, humanity, or even justice, but rather a brilliantly conceived trap.

The primary purpose of persecuting Assange is not – and never has been – to punish him personally, but to establish a generic precedent with a global deterrent effect on other journalists, publicists and activists. This purpose Judge Baraitser had achieved with terrifying effectiveness. Her ruling not only confirmed the entire legal rationale of the United States, which ultimately amounts to criminalizing investigative national security journalism as espionage; but it also expressly extended the scope of this rationale to the British Official Secrets Act, a piece of legislation which has served as a model for secrecy laws in many countries of the British Commonwealth. Thus, Judge Baraitser laid the legal foundation for the prosecution of anyone, anywhere in the world, who dared to expose the dirty secrets of the governments concerned, and for depriving defendants of the right to justify their action based on public interest. In effect, she had set a legal precedent introducing an absolute duty of silence on classified evidence for state-sponsored crimes – a global *lex omertà*.

In doing so, Judge Baraitser had fulfilled the entire wish list of the US government. Had she also allowed the extradition to go ahead, this certainly would have triggered an appeal by Assange, challenging the permissibility of her legal precedent before the British High Court. At the High Court, the case would be examined by a more experienced and authoritative panel of judges, whose decision would be difficult to predict. In order to avoid a full legal review of her judgment by the High Court, Judge Baraitser had to forestall an appeal by Assange's legal team. If the main rationale of the first instance ruling remained unchallenged, the desired legal precedent would be created 'under the radar' of the higher levels of the judiciary, of the public and of the independent press – a precedent whereby troublesome journalists could be prosecuted and silenced worldwide and press freedom would be de facto abolished.

By refusing to extradite Assange, Judge Baraitser conveniently put the ball into the court of the United States. This means that it would be up to the US government, and not Assange, to lodge an appeal and, therefore, to select the legal questions that would be reviewed by the High Court. Predictably, the US appeal would challenge only those aspects of Baraitser's ruling with which the US government disagreed, in particular the finding that, if extradited to the United States, Assange was at real risk of exposure to inhumane detention conditions and would almost certainly find a way to commit suicide. These were factors which the United States could easily address without endangering the desired legal precedent of criminalizing investigative national security journalism. In fact, all the US needed to do was to provide the High Court with diplomatic assurances that Assange would not be subjected to SAMs or other forms of inhumane treatment and that his suicide could be effectively prevented in US custody. Based on such assurances, the appeal judges could potentially conclude that Assange's extradition would no longer be oppressive and permit his surrender to the United States.

In this scenario, the British High Court would not have to examine any of Assange's legal objections regarding the political nature of the prosecution, the prohibition of extraditions for political offences, freedom of speech, or the systematic abuse of process throughout this case. All these objections had been rejected in Baraitser's ruling and would not be revisited by the High Court as long as her judgment remained unchallenged in this respect. Thus, the only way to prevent Assange's fast-track extradition based on US diplomatic assurances was for Assange's lawyers to lodge a cross-appeal against Baraitser's ruling as far as those issues were concerned. But that would require frequent and extensive preparatory meetings with Assange, rendered practically impossible by his arbitrary isolation at Belmarsh.

Not surprisingly, Baraitser's verdict did not cause undue distress on the other side of the Atlantic. Without missing a beat, and perhaps rather too smoothly, the US Department of Justice declared that 'While we are extremely disappointed in the court's ultimate decision, we are gratified that the United States prevailed on every point of law raised. In particular, the court rejected all of Mr. Assange's arguments regarding political motivation, political offence, fair trial, and freedom of speech. We will continue to seek Mr. Assange's extradition to the United States.' Indeed, on that day the US government had come a big step closer to criminalizing inconvenient journalism. At the same time, ideal conditions had been created for Assange's non-extradition to be overturned on appeal.

Baraitser's ruling of 4 January concluded with the words: 'I order the discharge of Julian Paul Assange'. The judge was fully aware, of course, that her order would not be executed but would be appealed by the US government. Two days later, she rejected Assange's release on bail on grounds of flight risk during the appeals proceedings. The fact that the very same purpose – flight prevention – could have been achieved through guarded house arrest demonstrates that Assange's continued incarceration in Belmarsh has nothing to do with flight risk, but everything with wanting to keep him silenced and under pressure.

As long as Assange remains isolated in prison, neither the United States nor the United Kingdom will be in a hurry to bring the extradition proceeding to a conclusion. The longer every procedural step can be spun out, the more Assange's health and stability will deteriorate, and the stronger the deterrent effect on other journalists and whistleblowers will be. As the authorities know very well, it is only a matter of time before Assange's resilience breaks. If he should die in prison, or if his mental health should deteriorate to the point where he can be stripped of his legal capacity and locked away in a closed psychiatric institution for the rest of his life, then the case could be closed without fear of the judicial precedent of 4 January 2021 being overturned by a panel of conscientious judges at the higher British courts, the European Court of Human Rights or, ultimately, the US Supreme Court. Should Assange have the strength to withstand the pressure of his isolation until the end of the extradition proceedings, on the other hand, his resilience will no doubt be used against him as purported evidence disproving his medical frailty and suicide risk. Once the judiciary has been instrumentalized for political purposes, there is no escape.

## Playing Out the Plot: US Appeal to the High Court of Justice

Tellingly, although the US government had transmitted its provisional grounds for appeal to the British High Court of Justice as early as 15 January 2021, followed by a perfected version on 11 February, it would take a full six months after Baraitser's ruling just for the High Court to decide on the next procedural step. This was extremely slow, particularly given that, during that whole period, Assange remained incarcerated under needlessly restrictive conditions for purely preventative purposes.

By an order signed on 5 July 2021, High Court Justice Jonathan Swift finally granted the United States permission to appeal the ruling on three out of five grounds. Most importantly, Justice Swift rejected any effort of the US government to second-guess District Judge Baraitser's conclusions on the validity and weight of medical and expert evidence brought by the parties during the extradition hearing, in particular concerning the assessment of Assange's mental health and the resulting risk of suicide. On these points of fact, Judge Baraitser's evidential findings were found to fall within the bounds of reasonableness, which makes them difficult for the US to challenge.

Crucially, however, Justice Swift decided that the High Court would hear the appeal on the three remaining grounds. First, in the view of the United States, Judge Baraitser had not correctly applied the legal criteria set out in the 2003 Extradition Act for determining whether it would be oppressive to extradite Assange on grounds of his mental condition. Most notably, according to the US government, Baraitser had not sufficiently evaluated the measures in place in US prisons for the prevention of suicide, but had simply jumped to the conclusion that Assange was sufficiently determined and intelligent to circumvent any such measures regardless. Second, Judge Baraitser should have afforded the United States the opportunity to provide 'undertakings' – that is, diplomatic assurances – that would have alleviated her concerns about Assange being subjected to excessively harsh detention conditions and, in particular, to SAMs.

Thirdly, and accordingly, the United States provided the United Kingdom with what it described as 'a package of assurances which are specifically responsive to the findings made by the District Judge' and which 'deal comprehensively with the conditions of detention which the District Judge found would precipitate Mr

Assange becoming suicidal'. In particular, the United States guaranteed that Assange would not be subject to SAMs or imprisoned at the infamous ADX Supermax facility in Florence, Colorado, unless he were to do something subsequent to the offering of these assurances that would justify such measures or designation. Moreover, the United States guaranteed that Assange would 'receive any such clinical and psychological treatment as is recommended by a qualified treating clinician employed or retained by the prison where he is held in custody'. Last but not least, the United States also assured that Assange would be allowed to serve any US-imposed prison sentence in his native Australia.

None of this came as a surprise to me, and none of it came as a relief. As always when governments give diplomatic assurances, these undertakings look decent on paper but play out completely differently in practice. While the US government may have excluded the application of SAMs to Assange, as well as his imprisonment in a particular institution, that assurance remains extremely narrow and can easily be circumvented. In reality, on any given day, approximately 80,000 prisoners are being held in solitary confinement across the United States. Only a few hundred of them are imprisoned at ADX Florence, and only about fifty are under SAMs. In fact, most federal and state prisons in the United States have a solitary confinement unit, where inmates are isolated for a range of punitive, disciplinary or administrative reasons. Instead of 'Special Administrative Measures', these detention regimes may be called 'Administrative Segregation', 'Restrictive Housing', 'Communication Management Units' or 'Involuntary Protective Custody', and may be imposed by an authority other than the US attorney-general. But in essence it all amounts to the same torturous practice of keeping inmates locked up in tiny concrete cells with no meaningful activity or human interaction for more than twenty-two hours per day, often for prolonged periods ranging from several weeks to several decades, and without any effective legal remedy. In result, the assurances given would do nothing to protect Assange from being held in prolonged solitary confinement and other cruel, inhuman or degrading detention conditions.

As for the assured medical and psychological treatment, this would depend entirely on the assessment and recommendations made by a doctor or nurse employed at the prison where Assange is incarcerated, which in reality is of the same value as making no assurance at all. Finally, Assange's assured eligibility for serving his US custodial sentence in Australia only becomes relevant 'following conviction, sentencing and the conclusion of any appeals'. Assange would therefore have to remain in the United States for the entire duration of his legal proceedings and until the exhaustion of all legal remedies. Given the complexities of his case, this entire process could well last a decade or more. In other words, as a matter of law, none of the assurances made by the United States would provide Assange with any legal protection from being subjected to prolonged solitary confinement, excessive shackling, sensory deprivation, medical negligence, and various other forms of cruel, inhuman or degrading treatment routinely employed in the US prison system.

Just as importantly, of course, these assurances do not even begin to address any of the legal issues of paramount importance that were simply swept under the carpet by Judge Baraitser. This includes, most notably, the massive due process violations Assange has been exposed to through unlawful surveillance and irregular confiscation of his belongings by the United States, the notoriously unfair trial awaiting him at the Espionage Court in Alexandria, and the fundamentally flawed nature of the US indictment in view of press freedom protections, the prohibition of extradition for political offences, the fabrication of false witness testimonies and the reported discussions at the highest levels of the US government of kidnapping, irregularly rendering or even assassinating Assange. In order for any of these issues to receive a proper judicial review, along with the systematic violation of Assange's rights during the British proceedings, his legal team must be allowed to cross-appeal.

On 11 August 2021, High Court Justices Timothy Holroyde and Judith Farbey upheld an appeal by the US government against Justice Swift's decision of 5 July and granted the United States permission to appeal Baraitser's ruling on all five grounds, including challenging the evidence on Assange's mental health and suicide risk. The main appeals hearing was held on 27 and 28 October 2021 before Chief Justice Ian Duncan Burnett, the most senior judge in England and Wales, and, again, Justice Holroyde. The hearing did not bring any surprises. The US presented its case, attacked the credibility of the medical experts and evidence relied upon by Judge Baraitser, downplayed Assange's health issues and suicide risk and emphasized the beneficial effects of the assurances offered. The defence team in turn insisted on the reliability of the relevant medical evidence and demonstrated how easily the US diplomatic assurances could be circumvented in practice. By and large, the judges asked questions of clarification and, at the end of the second day, concluded the hearing without announcing a date for the rendering of their judgment.

So, where do we go from here? Which one of the many conceivable scenarios will materialize? Will the British High Court of Justice live up to its honourable name, function and reputation? Will the judges have the personal courage and professional integrity to call the bluff of the US government's assurances and reject their appeal? Will they call out the British authorities for their corrupt persecution of Assange, and overturn Baraitser's unsustainable judicial precedent? Or will they choose the path of least resistance, and allow themselves to be instrumentalized? Will they engage in wilful blindness, self-deception and judicial contortion, and either allow the extradition to go forward or perpetuate Assange's arbitrary detention in Belmarsh by sending the case back to the Magistrates' Court for retrial?

While it is difficult to predict the exact evolution of these proceedings in the coming months and potentially even years, from a legal perspective they have long become a travesty of justice whose sole purpose is to silence Assange and to intimidate journalists and the broader public worldwide.

From a strictly procedural point of view, after the British High Court, both parties could appeal to the highest court in the United Kingdom, the Supreme Court. After that, if extradition is confirmed, Assange could still appeal to the European Court of Human Rights in Strasbourg. At the snail's pace currently imposed by the British judiciary, all of these procedural steps and remedies could take several years – and this is discounting the duration of subsequent proceedings at the 'Espionage Court' and related legal remedies in the United States. After more than a decade of judicial persecution in four jurisdictions, one cannot help but hear the chilling echoes of Stratfor's 2010 recommendation: 'Pile on. Move him from country to country to face various charges for the next twenty-five years.'

In my assessment, in terms of legal process and the enormous socio-political risks associated with it, the trial of Julian Assange may well prove to be the biggest judicial scandal of our times. The merciless persecution that this man has been exposed to, and the shameless betrayal of justice and human rights demonstrated by all the governments involved are beyond disgraceful – they profoundly undermine the credibility, integrity and sustainability of Western democracy and the rule of law.

By now, it is clear that the United States will never succeed in building a legally sustainable case against Assange, whether under the Espionage Act or under the Computer Fraud and Abuse Act or any other legislation, and that his publishing activities related to WikiLeaks are fully protected under international human rights law and the First Amendment of the US Constitution. It is therefore high time for this hopeless case to be abandoned and for Assange's freedom and human dignity to be restored, along with the credibility and integrity of the United States and its allies in terms of press freedom, justice and rule of law.

But let us also remember that, so far, the letter of the law has been all but irrelevant in this case and that the only decisive factors throughout all involved jurisdictions have been political interests. Ultimately, therefore, the fate of Julian Assange depends on President Joe Biden and his administration. For eight years, Biden was vice president in the Obama administration, which declined to prosecute Assange but never explicitly guaranteed him immunity from prosecution. Even when President Obama finally commuted Manning's sentence, he opted not to let Assange off the hook but to perpetuate the deterrent effect of his confinement at the Ecuadorian embassy.

It is to be hoped that Biden has more to offer than repeating Obama's mistakes. In December 2010 Vice President Biden described Assange as a 'high-tech terrorist', but he did so on the basis of assumptions that have since been disproved. In the same month, Biden also publicly acknowledged that WikiLeaks' releases had caused 'no substantive damage' other than to be 'embarrassing' for the US government. May he now be inspired by another predecessor of his, former president Jimmy Carter, who once said, 'I did not deplore the WikiLeaks revelations. They just made public what was actually the truth. Most often, the revelation of the truth, even if it's unpleasant, is beneficial … I think that, almost invariably, the secrecy is designed to conceal improper activities and not designed for the well-being of the general public.'

Indeed, today it is palpably obvious that Assange is not an enemy of the United States or of any other country in the world. Rather, he is an inconvenient truthteller and messenger, who holds up a mirror to all of us and shines a spotlight on our systemic and societal failures. Sure, we can angrily smash this mirror and make the unwanted reflection go away, but the harmful effects of our collective shortcomings will still be there. The only honest response to this challenge is to leave the mirror intact and even polish it, so that we may better see and correct our own failures. Anything else is a denial of reality comparable to ignoring the fire alarm in the house of our civilization, and comes at a price which we, as a species, soon will no longer be able to afford.

Whether President Biden will have the wisdom, integrity, and courage to end the persecution of Assange remains to be seen. For these three – wisdom, integrity, and courage – are the qualities that make a great statesman, those which only few have the strength to honour when it matters most, and without which not one of the great global challenges of our time can be resolved.

# Epilogue

This book has shown that, first and foremost, the trial of Assange is a story of persecution – the persecution of an inconvenient dissident who has exposed the dirty secrets of the powerful. In doing so, this book points far beyond the individual case of Assange. It exposes a systemic failure of our democratic institutions under the rule of law – institutions that ordinary citizens tend to rely on without ever seriously questioning their fundamental integrity. This systemic failure, in turn, raises questions about truth, deception and self-deception, about our own lethargy and passive co-responsibility. It is not by chance that this book begins with my own difficulties in recognizing and overcoming personal prejudice.

Ultimately, this is a book that concerns every single one of us, that confronts us with our own blind spots in our perception of reality, and that challenges us to look honestly into the mirror and take both personal and political responsibility. Today, humanity faces profound problems that, within a few decades, will seriously threaten our collective survival and that cannot be overcome or eliminated through smooth talk, self-deception and denial. Self-awareness, honesty, and responsibility have therefore ceased to be simply a matter of personal morality, belief, or lifestyle, and instead have become a question of collective survival.

While investigating the case of Assange, I repeatedly had the impression of being plunged into a real-world version of

'The Emperor's New Clothes'. The folk tale is well known: an emperor is offered a new outfit by swindlers, clothes that are supposedly visible to everyone except the 'stupid' and 'incompetent'. In reality, of course, the clothes so dearly sold to the emperor are not only invisible, but inexistent. However, since neither the emperor nor his subordinates wish to be considered stupid or incompetent, they all pretend to see the new clothes, and at a public parade the entire nation applauds the ruler's imaginary costume. But then, suddenly, a child breaks the spell by exclaiming: 'Look, the emperor is naked!'

So it is with the trial of Assange. Although the crimes and arbitrariness on the part of the various authorities have become increasingly blatant and obvious over the past decade, this dimension of the case has been almost completely ignored by other governments, the established media, and the general public. Instead, the official narrative has been obediently assimilated, repeated and perpetuated: Assange the rapist, hacker, spy, and cowardly narcissist, who has the blood of innocents on his hands and must finally be brought to justice. Here, too, someone had to come along, take a fresh and objective look at everything, and break the spell exclaiming, 'Look, the emperor is naked!' This, dear reader, is the purpose of this book.

We must not allow Assange's persecutors to dictate his story, for those who suppress their own crimes and misconduct are unlikely to tell us the truth about a man who lifted the veil and exposed their corruption. We must not allow ourselves to be side-tracked or confused but must always insist that the spotlight be directed where our attention belongs: not on Assange, the man, but on Assange's persecutors, the states. For Assange is not persecuted for his own crimes, but for the crimes of the powerful. Their impunity is what the trial of Assange is really about. It is the powerful – whether governments, corporations, or organizations – who undermine our democratic institutions and the rule of law; who refuse to prosecute torture, war crimes, and corruption; who betray our legal systems and shared values for self-serving purposes. The persecution of Assange establishes a precedent that will not only allow the powerful to keep their crimes secret but will even make the revelation of such crimes punishable by law. Let us not fool ourselves: once telling the truth has become a crime, we will all be living in a tyranny.

If the governments persecuting Assange had acted in good faith, they would have prosecuted the crimes revealed by WikiLeaks as required under the rule of law. After all, we are talking about wars of aggression, torture, murder and corruption. The fact that not a single military commander, political leader, soldier or other official has been held accountable gravely sabotages the credibility, legitimacy and authority of our democratic institutions, and should send a cold chill down our spines.

The problem really is not that we do not know the truth, but that we do not want to know it. The problem is that we allow the powerful, against our better judgment, to disregard justice and the rule of law, and that we do not hold them accountable, either legally or politically, but celebrate them as great leaders and possibly even honour them with Nobel Peace Prizes. The problem is that we allow corporate bosses to ruthlessly destroy our livelihoods and shamelessly exploit the vast majority of the world's population, and still admire them as benefactors and philanthropists when they donate a few billion dollars from their looted wealth for the mitigation of humanitarian disasters they helped to create. We do not want to see that the corporate media that feed us our understanding of world politics, and our personal circumstances, are owned by the very same people who also finance the election campaigns and careers of our politicians. Nor that those politicians, in turn, pass the laws and make the billion-dollar investments that keep allowing an increasingly narrow segment of society to enrich themselves at the expense of the general public and of future generations.

This inherently exploitative, destructive and inhumane system is promoted in the name of the rule of law, democracy, national security and the free market economy. And anyone who does not believe in the official narrative is branded 'stupid' or 'incompetent,' just like in the old story of the emperor's new clothes. And since none of us wish to be considered 'stupid' or 'incompetent', we usually do not dare to question and expose the nonsense before us. Most of us are also too busy taking care of daily life to ask fundamental systemic questions and demand a public debate on them. And so, both the sweet lies of the powerful and the conspiracy theories of the sceptics become increasingly absurd, and produce a public opinion marked by uncertainty, confusion and a lack of verifiable fact – we have arrived in the era of 'post-truth'.

After more than twenty years of experience in the international system, I know too much to be either an idealist or a conspiracy theorist. I know the political mills of the United Nations just as well as the purported constraints of national economic, foreign and security policies; I know the law, treaties and jurisprudence just as well as the world of diplomatic negotiations and the brutal realities of war, crisis and disaster. Governments around the world are increasing their efforts to divert public attention from war crimes, abuse, and corruption. Secrecy, impunity, and arbitrariness are poisoning our democratic institutions and robbing them of their integrity. Interventions by mandated UN mechanisms are ignored or even condemned as interference with internal affairs. Press freedom, transparency and accountability – indispensable prerequisites for the democratic oversight of any public authority – are now more threatened than ever.

When the truth is suppressed by rampant secrecy and censorship; when war criminals and exploiters enjoy impunity; when investigation reports on state-sanctioned torture are classified as secret; when documents released by authorities under freedom of information laws are almost entirely redacted; when the established press no longer exercises its role as the 'fourth estate', but meekly censors itself – then we really live in a virtual world, deprived of any possibility to find out what exactly our governments are doing with the power and tax money we have entrusted to them. Then we need leaks in the system, cracks through which the light can penetrate and provide us with information.

As soon as those in power see their essential interests threatened, they tend to disregard the rule of law as a boundary for their conduct. While this may be crudely evident in authoritarian states, the same tendencies are at play in mature democracies, albeit generally disguised in a cloak of legality or, if all else fails, secrecy. This is not because those in power have maliciously conspired against us, but simply because that is how we, as human beings, are wired and have always behaved. In the absence of social control, we all tend to pursue short-term self-interest, and to overlook the long-term societal harmfulness of our behaviour. The problem is not the good or bad character of those at the top, but that we have created and maintain a political and economic system that allows for unmitigated power, secrecy and impunity. With such a lopsided system, we will not be able to effectively respond to the enormous challenges we face as a global community. Whether for climate protection, economic justice or human rights, we need a system that is transparent, fair and sustainable. To achieve this, we must start by opening our eyes and, without condemnation or idealization, acknowledge who we really are and how we really function. Only on the basis of a sober sense of self-awareness will we be able to take political responsibility, expose harmful power structures, make the necessary systemic adjustments, and hold decision-makers accountable.

Even in the darkest room, the light of a single candle is enough to enable everyone to see. Julian Assange has lit such a candle with his work. He has exposed crimes, abuse and corruption that had been concealed behind a curtain of secrecy. It was only a brief glimpse behind the curtain, but sometimes one glimpse is enough to change our entire worldview. We now know that this curtain of secrecy exists and that a parallel universe of dirty secrets hides behind it. Secrets that many of us might prefer not to know, because that knowledge forces us to wake up, grow up and step up. Beyond the discomfort of disillusion, however, that same knowledge also empowers us to carry out the systemic governance reforms required to save us from certain self-destruction. Each and every one of us can change the world through courageous action. To make the darkness disappear, we need not look elsewhere for the light. It is sufficient to let our own light shine, right where we are in our everyday life. To do this, all we need is the courage to be honest with ourselves and with the world.

# Selected Documents

## Press Releases

05.04.2019: 'UN expert on torture alarmed at reports Assange may soon be expelled from Ecuador embassy' (ohchr.org)

31.05.2019: 'UN expert says "collective persecution" of Julian Assange must end now' (ohchr.org)

01.11.2019: 'UN expert on torture sounds alarm again that Julian Assange's life may be at risk' (ohchr.org)

08.12.2020: 'UN expert calls for immediate release of Assange after 10 years of arbitrary detention' (ohchr.org)

22.12.2020: 'UN expert asks US President Donald Trump to pardon Julian Assange' (ohchr.org)

05.01.2021: 'UN expert cautiously welcomes refusal to extradite Assange' (ohchr.org)

## Official Interventions

*Ecuador*

18.04.2019: Allegation Letter sent by the Special Rapporteur to His Excellency Mr José Valencia, Minister of Foreign Affairs and Human Mobility, Ecuador (AL ECU 5/2019) (spcommreports.ohchr.org)

28.05.2019: Urgent Appeal sent by the Special Rapporteur to His Excellency Mr José Valencia, Minister of Foreign Affairs and Human Mobility, Ecuador (UA ECU 10/2019) (spcommreports.ohchr.org)

17.06.2019: Response from the Permanent Mission of Ecuador to the United Nations Office in Geneva (spcommreports.ohchr.org).

26.07.2019: Response from the Permanent Mission of Ecuador to the United Nations Office in Geneva (spcommreports.ohchr.org).

02.10.2019: Allegation Letter sent by the Special Rapporteur to His Excellency Mr José Valencia, Minister of Foreign Affairs and Human Mobility, Ecuador (AL ECU 15/2019) (spcommreports.ohchr.org)

02.12. 2019: Response from the Permanent Mission of Ecuador to the United Nations Office in Geneva (spcommreports.ohchr.org)

### Sweden

28.05.2019: Urgent Appeal sent by the Special Rapporteur to Her Excellency Ms Margot Wallström, Minister for Foreign Affairs, Sweden (UA SWE 2/2019) (spcommreports.ohchr.org)

12.07.2019: Corrigendum sent by the Special Rapporteur to Her Excellency Ms Margot Wallström, Minister for Foreign Affairs, Sweden (OL SWE 3/2019) (spcommreports.ohchr.org)

12.07.2019: Response from Ambassador Elinor Hammarskjöld, Director-General for Legal Affairs, Ministry for Foreign Affairs, Sweden (spcommreports.ohchr.org)

12.09.2019: Allegation Letter sent by the Special Rapporteur to Her Excellency Ms. Margot Wallström, Minister for Foreign Affairs, Sweden (AL SWE 4/2019) (spcommreports.ohchr.org)

11.11.2019: Response from Ambassador Carl Magnus Nesser, Director-General for Legal Affairs, Ministry for Foreign Affairs, Sweden (spcommreports.ohchr.org)

## United Kingdom

27.05.2019: Urgent Appeal sent by the Special Rapporteur to His Excellency Mr Jeremy Hunt, Secretary of State for Foreign and Commonwealth Affairs, United Kingdom (UA GBR 3/2019) (spcommreports.ohchr.org)

07.10.2019: Response from Ambassador Julian Braithwaite, Permanent Mission of the United Kingdom of Great Britain and Northern Ireland to the United Nations Office in Geneva (spcommreports.ohchr.org)

29.10.2019: Urgent Appeal sent by the Special Rapporteur to His Excellency Mr Dominic Raab, Secretary of State for Foreign and Commonwealth Affairs, United Kingdom (UA GBR 6/2019) (spcommreports.ohchr.org)

## United States of America:

28.05.2019: Urgent Appeal sent by the Special Rapporteur to His Excellency Mr Michael Richard Pompeo, Secretary of State, United States of America (UA USA 14/2019) (spcommreports.ohchr.org)

16.07.2019: Response from Mr Sean M. Garcia, Acting Human Rights Counselor, Permanent Mission of the United States of America to the United Nations Office in Geneva (spcommreports.ohchr.org)

12.09.2019: Allegation Letter sent by the Special Rapporteur to His Excellency Mr Michael Richard Pompeo, Secretary of State, United States of America (AL USA 17/2019) (spcommreports.ohchr.org)

## Thematic reports

Report of the Special Rapporteur on torture and other cruel, inhuman or degrading treatment or punishment to the General Assembly, 'Extra-custodial use of force and the prohibition of torture and other cruel, inhuman or degrading treatment or punishment', 20 July 2017 (A/72/178) (documents-dds-ny.un.org/doc)

Report of the Special Rapporteur on torture and other cruel, inhuman or degrading treatment or punishment to the Human Rights Council, 'Migration-related torture and ill-treatment', 23 November 2018 (A/HRC/37/50) (documents-dds-ny.un.org/doc)

Report of the Special Rapporteur on torture and other cruel, inhuman or degrading treatment or punishment to the Human Rights Council, 'Corruption-related torture and ill-treatment', 16 January 2019 (A/HRC/40/59) (documents-dds-ny.un.org/doc)

Report of the Special Rapporteur on torture and other cruel, inhuman or degrading treatment or punishment to the General Assembly, 'Relevance of the prohibition of torture and other cruel, inhuman or degrading treatment or punishment to the context of domestic violence', 12 July 2019 (A/74/148) (documents-dds-ny.un.org/doc)

Report of the Special Rapporteur on torture and other cruel, inhuman or degrading treatment or punishment to the Human Rights Council, 'Psychological torture', 20 March 2020 (A/HRC/43/49) (documents-dds-ny.un.org/doc)

Report of the Special Rapporteur on torture and other cruel, inhuman or degrading treatment or punishment to the Human Rights Council, 'Effectiveness of the cooperation of States with the mandate holder on official communications and requests for country visits', 22 January 2021 (A/HRC/46/26) (documents-dds-ny.un.org/doc)

Report of the Special Rapporteur on torture and other cruel, inhuman or degrading treatment or punishment to the General Assembly, 'Accountability for torture and other cruel, inhuman or degrading treatment or punishment', 16 July 2021 (A/76/168) (documents-dds-ny.un.org/doc)

# Index

# Index